Islam in Europe

Events over recent years have increased the global interest in Islam. This volume seeks to combat generalisations about the Muslim presence in Europe by illuminating its diversity across Europe and offering a more realistic, highly differentiated picture. It contends with the monist concept of identity that suggests Islam is the shared and main definition of Muslims living in Europe. The contributors also explore the influence of the European Union on the Muslim communities within its borders, and examine how the EU is in turn affected by the Muslim presence in Europe. This book comes at a critical moment in the evolution of the place of Islam within Europe and will appeal to scholars, students and practitioners in the fields of European studies, politics and policies of the European Union, sociology, sociology of religion, and international relations. It also addresses the wider framework of uncertainties and unease about religion in Europe.

Aziz Al-Azmeh is Professor in the School of History at the Central European University, Budapest.

Effie Fokas is a Research Fellow at the Hellenic Foundation for European and Foreign Policy (ELIAMEP) and teaches in the Government Department of the London School of Economics.

Islam in Europe

Diversity, Identity and Influence

Edited by

Aziz Al-Azmeh and Effie Fokas

CAMBRIDGE
UNIVERSITY PRESS

BP
65
. A1
I 86
2007

CAMBRIDGE UNIVERSITY PRESS
Cambridge, New York, Melbourne, Madrid, Cape Town, Singapore, São Paulo

Cambridge University Press
The Edinburgh Building, Cambridge CB2 8RU, UK

Published in the United States of America by Cambridge University Press,
New York

www.cambridge.org
Information on this title: www.cambridge.org/9780521860116

First published 2007

Printed in the United Kingdom at the University Press, Cambridge

A catalogue record for this publication is available from the British Library

ISBN 978-0-521-86011-6 hardback
ISBN 978-0-521-67751-6 paperback

Contents

Figures

Contributors

VALÉRIE AMIRAUX Centre National de la Recherche Scientifique (CNRS), Paris

DIA ANAGNOSTOU Department of Political Science and Public Administration, University of Athens

AZIZ AL-AZMEH School of History, Central European University, Budapest

XAVIER BOUGAREL Turkish and Ottoman Studies Research Unit, Centre National de la Recherche Scientifique (CNRS), Paris

JOCELYNE CESARI Centre National de la Recherche Scientifique (CNRS), Paris, and Visiting Professor in the Anthropology Department, Harvard University

EFFIE FOKAS Government Department, London School of Economics, and Hellenic Foundation for European and Foreign Policy, Athens

BÉRENGÈRE MASSIGNON Ecole Pratique des Hautes Etudes (EPHE), Paris, and Groupe de Sociologie des Religions et de la Laïcite (GSRL), CNRS

TAREK MITRI World Council of Churches, Geneva

JORGEN NIELSEN Centre for the Study of Islam and Christian–Muslim Relations, University of Birmingham, UK

WERNER SCHIFFAUER Professor of Social and Cultural Anthropology, Europa University Viadrina Frankfurt/Oder

Abbreviations

ACC	Association of Candidate Countries
AIEF	Association of Islamic Students in France
AKP	Justice and Development Party (*Adalet ve Kalkinma Partisi*)
BSP	Bulgarian Socialist Party
CCEE	Council of European Bishops' Conferences (Catholic)
CEC	Conference of European Churches
CESE	Central-East and Southeast Europe
CMCE	Muslim Council of Cooperation in Europe
CO.RE.IS	*Comunità Religiosa Islamica* (Italy)
COMECE	Commission of the National Bishops' Conferences of the European Union
CSF	Community Support Framework
DITIB	Turkish Islamic Union for Religious Affairs (*Diyanet Isleri Türk Islam Birligi*)
DIYANET	Presidency of Religious Affairs (*Diyanet İşleri Başkanlii*)
EC	European Community
ECHR	European Court of Human Rights
EEC	European Economic Community
EECCS	European Ecumenical Commission for Church and Society
EKD	Evangelical Church of Germany
ELIAMEP	Hellenic Foundation for European and Foreign Policy
EMP	Euro-Mediterranean Partnership
EPP	European People's Party
EU	European Union
EUMC	European Monitoring Centre on Racism and Xenophobia
FAST	Forecasting and Assessment in Science and Technology
FEMYSO	Forum of European Muslim Youth and Student Organisations
FIOE	Federation of Islamic Organisations in Europe

FSU	Forward Studies Unit
GDP	gross domestic product
GOPA	Group of Policy Advisers
HRWF	Human Rights Without Frontiers
INED	the French National Demographics Institute
IRN	Islamic Council of the Netherlands
ISPA	Instrument for Structural Policies for pre-Accession
ISSR	International Society for the Sociology of Religion
JMF	*Jeunes Musulmans de France*
MEP	Member of the European Parliament
MRF	Movement for Rights and Freedom
NGO	non-governmental organisation
NMSV	National Movement of Simeon II
NOCRIME	Network of Comparative Research on Islam and Muslims in Europe
OCIPE	Catholic European Study and Information Centre
PHARE	*Pologne-Hongrie: aide à la reconstruction économique*
PKK	Kurdistan Workers Party (*Partiya Karkerên Kurdistan*)
ROP	Regional Operational Programme
SAPARD	Special Accession Programme for Agricultural and Rural Development
SBiH	*Stranka za Bosnu i Herzegovinu*
SDA	Party of Democratic Action – *Stranka Demokratske Akcije*
SP	*Saadet Partisi*
TESEV	Turkish Economic and Social Studies Foundation
UCOII	*Unione delle Comunità ed Organizzazioni Islamische in Italia*
UDF	Union of Democratic Forces
UIOE	Union of Islamic Organisations in Europe
UNESCO	United Nations Educational, Scientific and Cultural Organization
US	United States
WP	Welfare Party (*Refah Partisi*)
ZMD	Central Council for Muslims in Germany (*Zentralrat der Muslim in Deutschland*)

Preface

This text emanates from a research project based at the Hellenic Foundation for European and Foreign Policy (ELIAMEP), entitled 'Forum for the Interdisciplinary Study of Christian–Muslim Relations in twenty-first Century Europe'. The project entailed a series of seminars, conferences and workshops which brought together scholars from all parts of Europe for rich discussion on the development of Christian–Muslim relations as we know them and on prospects for the future of Islam in Europe. The breadth of discussions in these gatherings is far too great to capture in a single text, but the contributions of all participants helped to shape the present volume: we would like to express our gratitude for this, as well as our thanks to Elizabeth Phocas for initiating this project, to Thanos Dokos and Christianna Karageorgopoulou for their involvement throughout, and to the devoted and hospitable ELIAMEP staff.

The chapters in this volume reflect a consensus amongst all the contributors in terms of their shared aim for the literature on Islam in Europe. Beyond this, though, each author presents a very distinct voice on his or her particular theme and also uses Muslim terminology, and spelling, in his or her preferred manner, explaining the use of certain terms as needed. Accordingly, we have not provided a glossary for the text as a whole and allow rather this element of diversity in the writing on Islam.

Budapest   AZIZ AL-AZMEH
                                                                    and
London   EFFIE FOKAS

1 Introduction

Effie Fokas

It is a daunting task to introduce a text on this subject today, given the rapid pace of change surrounding Islam in Europe. The vast dimensions of this change defy simple summary and necessitate new, continuous and multifaceted research. By contrast, it is all too easy to list developments that have saturated print and electronic media coverage of Islam and of Muslims – even if only superficially related to the latter. The list ranges from examples of extremism such as the killing of Theo van Gogh and the Madrid and London bombings, to controversies pivoting on Islam, such as the eruptions following the printing of the cartoons of Mohammed in the Danish *Jyllands-Posten* and the reprinting elsewhere (aftershocks continue to be felt in the form of intense debates on free speech versus blasphemy, or versus religion, or versus Islam, depending on the inter-locutor's perspective), and following Pope Benedict XVI's denigrating words on Islam in his Regensburg University speech. Meanwhile, also contentious have been plans for the subjection of immigrants to 'citi-zenship tests' aimed at assessing whether their values are compatible with those of the majority community. The Dutch example is the most poignant, suggesting little tolerance for immigrants who do not embrace Dutch values of tolerance, and raising further debate on whether 'some values are better than others'.[1] International press reports also bring to light national-level debates, such as controversy over the 'identity soup' served in soup kitchens in France to the exclusion of Muslims (and Jews), renewed disputes regarding the wearing of headscarves in public schools, and tensions concerning the building of mosques (most acute in France, Italy and of course Greece).[2] This current mediatic attention honing

---

[1] And in this, echoing the words of the leader of another liberal European country – Denmark's Anders Fogh Rasmussen – that 'Danes for too many years have been foolishly kind. They have not dared to say that some values are better than others. But this must happen now.' See European Monitoring Centre on Racism and Xenophobia (EUMC) European Roundtables Meetings report of 2003, accessible via the EUMC website: www.eumc.europa.eu/eumc/index.php

[2] See special issue of *Journal of Ethnic and Migration Studies*, vol. 31, no. 6, 2005, devoted to the issue of conflicts over the building of mosques in European cities. Much like the

1

especially on Islamist extremism or, at best, on points of tension between Muslims and non-Muslims, serves either to produce or reinforce popular perceptions of Islam as a (violent) monolith and as the shared and main definition of Muslims living within Europe.

Against this background, the present volume derives from the contention that, beyond new research, what is critically needed is methodological rigour in the study of Islam in Europe, aimed to counter two trends in particular. The first is cultural differentialism, and the second is monist conceptions of identity. Hackneyed dichotomous representations of 'liberal' versus 'traditional', moderate versus radical, and 'authentic' versus 'reactionary' Islam are clearly insufficient. A more nuanced approach is necessary, taking into account a number of key factors (as well as *combinations* of them, where applicable), including whether Muslim groupings are autochthonous or immigrant; the origins of immigrant communities (e.g. Arab, African or Asian Muslims, Bengali or Pakistani) and particularities of the host communities; differences according to generation and gender; objective versus subjective conceptions of identity; and cultural, ethnic, political and/or theological references and motivations. Such an approach goes a long way towards reflecting the intricate realities of Islam in Europe which tend to be so far from public purview: it also reveals the tremendous diversity of Muslim collectivities across Europe, including such contexts as Germany, France, the United Kingdom and Greece, with proportionately large numbers of Muslims; the differences between the experiences of Muslims living in Thrace and of those in other parts of Greece; and the clashes in perspective amongst Muslim intellectuals of the autochthonous Muslim communities in Bosnia – all of which relate to a number of factors well beyond culture and religion. This nuanced approach thus serves to counter tendencies towards cultural differentialism. Even deeper examination is needed to comprehend the diversity of individual identities, including the many shades of relation to Islam, and to different interpretations of the faith. Such examination renders evident the fact that, as Aziz al-Azmeh has articulated, 'there are as many Islams as there are situations that sustain it',[3] and that these situations are national, local, familial *and* interpersonal.

This careful attention to diversity and identity is important not least for the fundamental objectives of accuracy and academic integrity of the researchers, but also as a sound basis upon which to think in policy terms. Here a dialectical approach is instructive in highlighting

---

headscarf issue, the mosque conflicts play an important role in bringing Islam from the private to the public sphere.

[3] See Aziz al-Azmeh, *Islams and modernities*, London: Verso, 1993. Citation from p. 1.

the inter-influence between Islam and Europe. Islam in Europe is in a state of flux, but so is religion in general in Europe, and it is useful to recognise how these two dimensions affect one another: understanding, in other words, how European policies impact upon Muslim communities and individuals, but also how activities and discourse of Muslim individuals and groups influence changing conceptions and policy considerations on the place of religion in the European public sphere. Discussions of religion's proper place in the European public sphere have not found much of a formal discursive space within the EU thus far, but one may wonder how long these conversations will be delayed, given their increasing salience in so many EU member states. A case in point is the present state of somewhat muddled questioning of the assimilationist model of integration in France following the Paris riots of 2005, and of the multiculturalist model in Denmark and Britain following especially the murder of Theo van Gogh and the London 2005 bombings, respectively and – in most cases – separately. In general, the EU finds itself at what seems to be a critical juncture in its relationship to religion; currently we experience an unhealthy situation in which definitions of this relationship are being drawn on a *reactive* basis, in a climate of frequent, attention-grabbing 'events'.

Why Europe?

Much of the above is applicable, of course, well beyond the case of Europe. The rationale for the European focus here is threefold. First, the historical interchange between Islam and Europe specifically is marked by clichéd notions of tensions which permeate both European (in general terms) and national narratives and which are often used by Muslims and non-Muslims seeking to perpetuate such tension. The process of weakening of the Ottoman Empire in the eighteenth century and increasing exposure to secular European influence, together with the waves of secularising reforms in the nineteenth century, comprise a triad providing the cornerstones of an account of friction between Islam and 'the rest' worldwide. Meanwhile, the history of European colonialism lends increased fervour to such accounts, whether by dint of collective memory or as the result of selective politicisation of the past by certain Muslim leaders – or, at least, as a highly charged point of reference for comparisons between this period and certain current US, and European, policies related to Islam. For their part, non-Muslims in the business of perpetuating tension refer to such aspects of history as the 1453 fall of Constantinople, and the 1683 siege of Vienna. However distant and essentialised they may be, these are specifically European images which operate quite powerfully in the imaginations of many Muslims and non-Muslims in Europe (and beyond).

A second particularly significant dynamic of the European context is the sheer size of the Muslim presence. This, together with the rise in numbers through immigration and relatively high birth rates, and the increasingly visible religiosity amongst Muslims, has led to both real and perceived transformations in the social fabric of European societies. When we add to this list of developments the facts of the continent's declining and aging population and its declining (visibility of) traditional Christian religiosity, we find the underpinnings of a great deal of right-wing anti-immigration rhetoric, reflected in the striking wave of right-wing electoral victories across the continent in the early part of this decade.

Third, and related to the above, Europe offers a kaleidoscope of policies and approaches to religious pluralism in general, and to Muslim communities in particular. The diverse approaches to the 'headscarf issue', and the even more diverse motivations for these approaches, are paradigmatic of this situation. Whilst our purpose here is not to explore and appraise the broad range of policies related to Islam, this volume does touch on the question of cause and effect, and on the extent to which the host community and its policies influence the trajectory taken by Muslim groups living therein.

To propose to offer a solution for the tensions surrounding Islam in Europe today would certainly be unwise. There is a marked lack in consensus amongst scholars and practitioners concerning the roots of particular problem points – including references to prejudice, 'clash of civilisations', 'clash of interpretations', varying degrees of assimilation, socio-economic underdevelopment and/or exclusion, etc. Discussions comparing the assimilationist policies of the secular French republic against the multiculturalist policies of the United Kingdom, for example, lead to cyclical debates regarding 'the root of the problem' – socio-economic underdevelopment in the former being pegged as a clear cause of the riots which swept across France in October–November 2005, whilst educated and financially secure British Muslims perpetrated the London bombings of July 2005. Clearly, generalised prescriptions are futile.

Nor, of course, is there consensus on these matters amongst Muslims in Europe. How are we to reach sound conclusions when division and controversy mark different 'strands' of radical, fundamentalist, reformist, and moderate Islam? And this when, meanwhile, the lines of communication and influence between immigrant communities and their countries of origin are so variable? Policies and attitudes towards women entail one of the areas of most acute divergence within various groups, revealing such discrepancies as women marching in Morocco to free Islam of the secularising influence of the West and to maintain family codes which significantly limit their freedoms and equality, and Moroccan women in Paris working hard to free Islam of 'imported' elements, i.e. the national and ethnic, usually traditional and conservative. Likewise, there is a significant rift amongst Muslim thinkers (as amongst many non-Muslims) regarding multiculturalism and cultural relativism, with calls for multiculturalist policies being countered by condemnations of these as cultural relativism which betrays reformist trends in Islam and which protects 'culture' at the cost of continued segregation in society.

Contextualising our study

Many scholars have sought to understand the potency behind particular aspects of Islam which serve as mobilising forces. Though they may disagree on the cause, they have no illusions as to the powerful *effect* of uses of the conceptual 'substratum' of Islam.[4] As Fred Halliday notes with reference to invocations of the *umma* in a variety of time periods and contexts,

> the terms and images used were . . . an eclectic mixture, with no theological or conceptual coherence to them; the cupboard of Islamic and Arab themes was ransacked for whatever was there, from the Prophet to heroes on horses, dreams and *munafiqin* and much else besides.[5]

Our subject of study is not the substratum, per se, but we are interested in the preconditions for such forms of mobilisations to take place. More specifically, we are concerned with the preconditions insofar as they point to misconceptions of ourselves and of others – hence our specific focus on *identity*. The authors who have contributed to this volume make a concerted effort to shed light on the multifaceted nature of individual and collective identities, including elements of continuity and of contingency, and objective and subjective dimensions. On the whole, they point to a multiplicity of factors which shape different stances, within Muslim communities, on areas of potential tension between Muslim and non-Muslim groups. The message which

---

[4] Of course, the best of these are equally attuned to exceptions and failed attempts to manipulate religion for non-religious purposes. See, for example, Fred Halliday, 'The politics of the *umma*', in B.A. Roberson (ed.), *Shaping the current Islamic reformation*, London: Frank Cass, 2003, pp. 20–41.

[5] Ibid., p. 29.

emanates from this text is that neither culture nor Islam can alone be used to explain tension where it does arise.

A degree of intellectual honesty suffices to remind us that the political uses of religion are old, and they are widespread across cultures and faiths. One illustration of this is the fact that news reports in the immediate aftermath of the 7 July 2005 bombings in London included reports of the Srebrenica massacre tenth anniversary (11 July 1995), as well as the ninth anniversary of the Manchester IRA bombing (15 July 1996), with little to no attention to any similarities between these events: 'Islamic terrorism' is treated as entirely in a class of violence of its own (and with this, Islam is presented as in a religious class of its own, and Muslims as unified in it). But such mobilisations to violence are of course limited neither to Islam nor to religion; rather, political movements use whatever aspects of the 'substratum' are available and functional in a given context.[6] As Maxime Rodison writes, in graceful understatement: 'For their faith and/or their homeland, people are commonly induced to perform splendid deeds as well as hideous crimes', even if 'they do not always have a good understanding of either that faith or of the plans of the leaders of that homeland'.[7] In this context, misunderstandings of ourselves and others are conspicuous in such developments as the fact of sexual assaults by 'coalition of the willing' troops in the Iraqi Abu Ghraib prison; the tension between the US Senate and White House over a possible ban on 'cruel, inhuman or degrading treatment or punishment' of anyone in US custody, which, the latter feared, might 'unduly constrict Americans who are leading the difficult fight against terrorism'; and the statement of one US senator, during discussions of the anti-torture bill, that 'every one of us . . . knew and took great strength from the belief that we were different from our enemies'.[8] Seen in the light of such developments, when an example of Islamist terrorism is described as 'a return to a primitiveness that we in the West had assumed a progressive history had left behind';[9] the irony is all the more acute, as should be our awareness of a pattern of misconceptions.

The bit of conventional wisdom on religion which is so often overlooked in relation to Islam is worthwhile mentioning here: religion does

---

[6] See Halliday, 'The politics of the *umma*', p. 38.

[7] Maxime Rodinson, in *Europe and the mystique of Islam*, Seattle: University of Washington Press, 1987, p. xv.

[8] See Brian Knowlton, 'Bush repeats threat to veto torture curb', in *International Herald Tribune*, 7 October 2005, p. 4.

[9] Quotation taken from Charles Krauthammer, 'Europe's native-born enemy', *The Washington Post*, 15 July 2005, p. A23.

not operate in a vacuum, and its influence is mediated by that of a series of other factors.[10] In fact, if we seek to locate the role of Islam, or of culture, in 'Islamic militancy', perhaps we should contemplate what proportion of the foreign relations of Muslim states – e.g. Iran's movements on nuclear weapons, the conflict in Somalia, Syrian claims on Lebanon – is to do with religion or culture. Clearly, very little. This is not to say that all Islamic militancy is devoid of religious meaning, but here it is absolutely critical to distinguish between fundamentalist movements and activities, and those of Muslims in general. This we do with relative ease when we think of Christianity in its relation to examples of Christian fundamentalist activities, such as the bombing of abortion clinics.[11]

As noted above, a red thread which runs throughout this book is a statement against culturalist differentialism. In this vein, the present study should be located within the broader framework of uncertainties and unease about religion in Europe *in general*. The debates emanating from many European countries on references to religion in the Preamble to the Constitutional Treaty of the EU and on Turkey's potential membership within the EU signal an ambiguity concerning the role of religion in contemporary Europe which goes beyond the EU as such and, indeed, beyond the question of Islam. These issues have challenged Europeans to clarify their notions of European identity: how can a Christian element be found there where Christianity's presence is ever-disappearing – except, that is, where it has to do with culture? The prejudiced manner with which this term is sometimes used is evident in the German case of debate and court cases on the crucifix and the headscarf in schools – in the case of the crucifix, decisions allowing it because of its supposed historic and cultural meaning, and in the case of the headscarf disallowing it on the same basis.[12]

Indeed, Christianity maintains a distinctly strong presence in Europe through culture and tradition (e.g. church weddings, baptisms and

---

[10] Bhikhu Parekh makes this point well in an article entitled 'Is Islam a threat to Europe's multicultural democracies?', in Krzysztof Michalski (ed.), *Religion in the new Europe*, Budapest: Central European University Press, 2006, pp. 111–21 (esp. p. 117).

[11] On this subject, see Malise Ruthven, *Fundamentalism: the search for meaning*, Oxford: Oxford University Press, 2004. See also Olivier Roy, 'Islam in Europe: clash of religions or convergence of religiosities?', in K. Michalski (ed.), pp. 131–44.

[12] Astrid Reuter has presented an astute analysis of this situation in her unpublished paper, 'Headscarf and crucifix: on the politics of interpreting religious symbols', presented at the International Society for the Sociology of Religion (ISSR) Conference in Zagreb, July 2005. For a further comparison between German and French handlings of religious symbols in general, see Leonora Auslander, 'Bavarian crucifixes and French headscarves', *Cultural Dynamics*, vol. 12, no. 3, pp. 283–309.

funerals) and through architecture and town planning.[13] The latter fact is particularly clear in Greece and Spain, where plans for the building of mosques have led to public backlash and demonstrations, respectively. Christianity also maintains a presence for many through a 'chain of memory', linking individuals to a community through memory of a shared past, with religion deeply rooted in tradition which persists in the (increasingly secular) present and, it must be noted, through a range of church–state relations privileging majority Christian churches across Europe, under 'a chimera of neutrality'.[14] Meanwhile, studies have shown the large extent to which Europeans 'believe without belonging' (to traditional Christian churches), or 'belong without believing', as well as various expressions of public religion within Christian contexts.[15] The latter illustrates clearly that ambiguity regarding the role of religion in politics and public life goes well beyond the case of Islam.

There is a budding discussion, with many and diverse intellectual centres of gravity, regarding the place of religion in the European public sphere. From vastly different perspectives, the concept of the EU's 'secular neutrality' has been questioned most recently by José Casanova, Jürgen Habermas and Francis Fukuyama.[16] Brief attention to their perspectives gives a sense of the depth and breadth of the discussion which is hitting at the core of deep-rooted conceptions regarding religion's proper place in European society. According to Casanova, secularist assumptions 'turn religion into a problem', thus precluding the resolution of religion-related challenges in a pragmatic manner. He argues that 'to guarantee equal access to the European public sphere and undistorted communication, the European Union would need to become not only post-Christian but also post-secular'.[17] Habermas also

---

[13] See chapters 4 and 5 of David Martin's *On secularization: towards a revised general theory*, Aldershot: Ashgate, 2005.

[14] See Hervieu-Léger, *La religion pour mémoire*, Paris: Éditions du Cerf, 1993, and J. Madeley and Z. Enyedi (eds.), *Church and state in contemporary Europe: the chimera of neutrality*, London: Frank Cass, 2003.

[15] See Grace Davie *Religion in Britain since 1945. Believing without belonging*, Oxford: Blackwell, 1994; and José Casanova, *Public religions in the modern world*, Chicago: University of Chicago Press, 1994.

[16] For Casanova, see 'Religion, European secular identities, and European integration', in Timothy Byrnes and Peter Katzenstein (eds.), *Religion in an expanding Europe*, Cambridge: Cambridge University Press, 2006, pp. 65–92; for Habermas, see 'Religion in the European public sphere', in *European Journal of Philosophy*, vol. 14, no. 1, 2006, as well as a lecture delivered upon receipt of the Holberg Prize, on 'Religion in the public sphere', 28 November 2005 (available online at: www.holberg.uib.no/downloads/Habermas_religion_in_the_public_sphere.pdf); in terms of Fukuyama's work, of special interest here is his 'Identity, immigration and liberal democracy', in *Journal of Democracy*, vol. 17, no. 2, April 2006.

[17] Casanova 2006, p. 82.

speaks of the necessity for secular citizens to learn to live in a post-secular society, rather than the current 'asymmetric distribution of cognitive burdens' which prevails: 'Religious citizens, in order to come to terms with the ethical expectations of democratic citizenship, have to learn to adopt new epistemic attitudes toward their secular environment, whereas secular citizens are not exposed to similar cognitive dissonances in the first place'.[18] This he sees as an imbalance which needs to be rectified. For his part, Fukuyama concerns himself with the 'valuelessness of postmodernity', and the rise of relativism which bars 'postmodern peoples' from asserting their positive values and shared beliefs. He locates this problem specifically within the domain of Muslim immigration in Europe, and he finds that Europeans have not suitably addressed the problem of Muslim integration due to a pervasive political correctness stemming from the limitations set by the rise of relativism. He suggests that Europe may have much to learn from the US in terms of how to integrate its Muslim minorities.

As a whole, these proposals may come across as fairly radical, normative, and/or highly un-European. They certainly seem radical against the backdrop of the debates on reference to religion in the Constitutional Treaty, which suggested that Europeans are generally not ready to agree, at least, on any formal changes to the stable notion of European secularity. This secularity is conceived as a fundamental aspect of European *collective* political identity and is, for many Europeans, a prized point of difference between Europe and the United States.

Yet, in spite of the above, it is the Muslim presence in Europe which is perceived, more than any other factor, as a challenge to conceptions of a secular Europe. In general, increasing religious diversity within and across Europe related to Islam has led to examination and re-examination of models of church–state relations, as new methods for protecting religious pluralism have had to develop – both at the national level and within the context of the European Union. Meanwhile, Islamist terrorism, and backlashes against Muslims in the wake of terrorist attacks, have served to bring the state, including the police, deeper into religion-related matters at a time when, across Europe, states have operated comfortably in a practical separation from religion. Thus, to a certain extent, contemporary developments in Islam in Europe can be viewed from within the wider lens of the struggle between the secular and the religious. This is but one of many new forms of Islam's influence on Europe.

---

[18] Habermas, 2005.

Introduction to the chapters

Our exploration of Islam in Europe begins with an historical overview of the relations between Muslims and Christians in Europe, highlighting the role of collective memory in relations between Muslim communities in Europe and their host communities. Along these lines, Tarek Mitri addresses the historical interchange between Islam and Europe and offers important insight into the malleability of collective memory, variously leading to amity and to enmities but of course, most visibly to enmities. Mitri explores reactivations of enmity-prone collective memory for the sake of political mobilisation and shows how the success of such mobilisation depends on the mediation of contemporary education and communication. In keeping with the text's general theme, this chapter focuses on the inter-influence between Christians and Muslims, illustrating how constructed conceptions of collective *differences*, and not religiosities, have underlain enmities between Christians and Muslims in Europe. This chapter places our focus on Europe in its proper historical context, exploring the particular relationship between Islam and Europe.

In Chapter 3, Jorgen Nielsen parallels Mitri's survey in contemporary context by considering the developing notion of a particular Islam in Europe: 'Euro-Islam'. Nielsen examines divergent uses of the term 'Euro-Islam' and how these are indicative of two trends emanating from within Muslim communities in Europe. In some contexts, the term is being used to imply the development across Europe of forms of expression and thinking which allow Muslims' constructive participation in their various countries and localities. In other contexts, use of the term 'Euro-Islam' shows signs of acquiring an ideological content infiltrated from outside the communities (or, at best, from the margins), a process which in the view of some is aimed at controlling and setting limits to European Muslim expression. Nielsen's chapter explores these two trends and evaluates their impact on the place of Muslims in European society.

Together, Nielsen's text and that of Jocelyne Cesari (Chapter 4) serve to make the point that Muslim identity in Europe should be understood in terms of a process, rather than a static structure: Muslim *identification*, instead of identity, is their subject matter. In Chapter 4, Cesari discusses the fact that the forms of identifying oneself as Muslim are profoundly influenced by a narrative (active from the local to the international level) that puts into circulation a whole series of images and stereotypes which make Islam seem religiously, culturally and politically foreign and backward. This does not necessarily mean, however, that Muslim responses to this narrative are predetermined. Cesari's aim is to explain the gaps between the 'racialisation' of national discourses, the meta-discourse on Islam as an enemy, and the diversity and fluid nature of Muslims' attitudes. Through the latter especially, Cesari seeks to redress the 'snare of exceptionalism' which seems to prevail in research on Islam in Europe – that is, the tendency to reduce all explanations of Muslim actions to their presence as an exceptional case within Europe. In fact, her description of how daily concrete practices amongst some Muslim groups are revealing an acculturation to the secularised context and a kind of 'homemade' version of Islam is very similar to Hervieu-Léger's concept of 'bricolage', describing that religion in Europe in general (i.e. including Christianity) as no longer embedded in the culture in a taken-for-granted manner, but rather becoming an object of individual choice. Cesari's chapter frames the volume's more general approach to identity, its aim being no longer to grasp, as certain culturalist-based approaches have sought to do, the traditional attributes that define an individual or group essence. Rather, she emphasises the fact that the ways an individual defines him-/herself are both multidimensional and likely to evolve over time.

Again, in the contemporary context awareness of the diversity of Muslim communities in Europe is increasingly important – beyond, though, the typical dichotomous views of 'liberal' versus 'traditional', and 'authentic' versus 'reactionary' Islam. In other words, what is needed is greater specificity, and insight into the intricacies of developments within Muslim communities in Europe. Accordingly, we have sought scholars' expertise for analyses of current *divergent* trends in Islamic expression within Europe, emphasising the multiplicity of variables that must be taken into account when studying contemporary Muslim communities. Such focus on diversity precludes prediction of the form Islamic self-expression will take in a given community. Here, contributors take us beyond examples of ethnic or national specificities and, rather, indicate axes of difference even within groups normally lumped together. This particular endeavour begins with the chapter by Werner Schiffauer (Chapter 5) on the development of transnational Islam in Europe amongst diasporic communities. Here he explores how the efforts of Muslim communities in Europe to 'locate themselves' with respect to their country of immigration, their country of origin, and global Islam lead to the development of several competing positions. Referring to the example of Turkish Sunnites in Europe, the chapter discusses this development over two generations. A general shift from an exilic Islam of the first generation to a diasporic Islam among second generation immigrants can be observed. Yet Schiffauer demonstrates that even within 'exilic' and 'diasporic' Islam, a multiplicity of expressions has been on the rise. Based on close examination of two generations of Turkish Sunnites in Germany, cross-referenced with research elsewhere in Europe, Schiffauer argues that neither country of residence, nor country of origin or generational situation, will fully determine whether liberal, orthodox, or ultra-orthodox positions will emerge in a given context.

Xavier Bougarel continues the theme on diversity in Chapter 6, focusing on Bosnian Islam. Here he addresses the 'rediscovery' of an ancient and autochthonous Muslim presence in the Balkans following the Yugoslav wars and the efforts of Bosnian Muslims, within this context, to present Bosnian Islam as an archetypical 'European Islam'. Yet even this joint 'cause' has faced significant challenges. Through an in-depth analysis of the perspectives of three contemporary Bosnian Muslim intellectuals, Bougarel reveals the roots of competing definitions of the Islamic presence in contemporary Bosnia-Herzegovina (Islam defined as an individual faith, as a common culture or as a discriminatory political ideology). Although these competing definitions are vividly illustrated through the thinking of particular individuals, they apply well beyond the Bosnian case. Together, they demonstrate that there are many Islams in Europe but, Bougarel argues, there is not (yet) a 'European Islam', in the sense of a shared religious and intellectual space for debate on issues common to all European Muslims.

Bougarel's text thus offers a fitting introduction to the theme of Muslim influence in Europe, addressed by the following three chapters. These chapters focus in particular on Islam in relation to the European Union, seeing the latter as a significant domain through which Islam both influences and is influenced by European policy. In spite of self-proclaimed religious neutrality and the secular nature of the supranational state structure, the EU is inevitably drawn into the mire of religious issues and, in this context, Islam represents a special challenge to the European Union. This much is evident in the Muslim contributions to what was an already contentious debate on reference to Christianity in the Preamble to the Constitutional Treaty. Meanwhile, uncertainty regarding Islam's place in the EU continues to plague discussions of Turkey's long-standing application for membership. Of special relevance here is the extent to which EU policies affect particular Muslim communities in particular contexts and, furthermore, whether EU policy may affect the Muslim experience in Europe in general. Through in-depth attention to specific policy areas, the contributors illustrate both the strengths and weaknesses of the Union's approach to Muslim communities and to Islam.

Bérengère Massignon launches this exploration in Chapter 7 by examining the formal processes of influence between the EU and religious groups, focusing on the very complex relationship between the European Commission and Muslim groups. Massignon takes as her starting point the Delors presidency of the European Commission (1985–95), during which the Commission began establishing a framework for communication with religious and humanist groups. The chapter traces the gradual emergence of European-Muslim organisations and their representation in Brussels, and emphasises the challenges to such forms of organisation compared with their Christian and humanist counterparts. Massignon makes clear that what is at stake in the context of Muslim groups' efforts to establish a voice in Brussels is the desired degree of pluralism in the emerging European model for the regulation of religion – a matter which remains ambiguous, especially in the aftermath of 11 September 2001 and subsequent Islamist-related violence throughout Europe.

The Commission's efforts to maintain lines of communication with various religious groups entail one of the few areas of influence directly related to religion and, as such, to Islam. The following two chapters explore *indirect* influences of and on Islam. For her part, Dia Anagnostou elucidates, in Chapter 8, the vast potential effects of EU integration on minority communities in Southeast Europe, by focusing on two specific contexts of domestic, regional economic and institutional changes which have taken place though EU regulations. Concentrating mainly on Muslim minority communities in Greece and Bulgaria, the chapter seeks to understand the consequences of such changes for the interests and identities of Turkish Muslim minorities in border regions. Anagnostou shows here how even the historically close relationship between ethnic–national identity, religion and territory among Muslim minorities in the Balkans can be altered ('albeit in diverging ways in different parts of the region') through EU-related economic and institutional changes. The chapter describes two distinct modes of political incorporation of minorities promoted by economic development policies, in conjunction with minority protection policies, of European institutions before and after the disintegration of communism, respectively. As Anagnostou explains, the two trends have potentially distinct implications for the nature and politics of minority rights within the European Union.

The second area of the indirect – ever-taboo – influence of Islam is in Turkey's tumultuous relations with the European Union. The Turkish case is, in many ways, pivotal to any discussion of Islam in relation to both Europe in general and the European Union in particular. First, the obvious point that 'European identity' and conceptions of Europe as

Christian were largely shaped in relation to the Ottoman Muslim 'other'. Meanwhile, Turkey has a marked presence within the EU in the form of sizeable immigrant communities, and a marked *absence* from the EU, in terms of its long-standing application for membership and multiple 'rejections'. In Chapter 9, Valérie Amiraux addresses the debates on the secular European Union's 'reluctance to admit a *secular* Muslim country'. Against this backdrop, she considers the 'pro-Islamist' Justice and Development Party's experience in government, and Turkey's prospects for EU membership in the light of this experience. Amiraux highlights the discrepancy between what Turkey represents in the EU member state public opinions and the process of secularisation that marks Turkish society. Indeed, the case of Turkey–EU relations is perhaps the example *par excellence* of the intense relationship between Islam and Europe: each bearing great potential to influence the other, and each characterised by misconceptions of self and other.

The book is drawn to a close by Aziz al-Azmeh with a consideration of the state of current discourse, and research, on Islam in Europe. In particular, he draws attention to the pitfalls of culturalist differentialism. Taking as pivotal points recent events such as the July 2005 bombings in London and the October/November 2005 social upheavals in Paris (with riots spreading throughout France), al-Azmeh demonstrates how the bulk of the current approaches to the study of Islam in Europe not only ill-equip us for understanding the subject at hand, but also dangerously further the potential for conflict and mutual misconceptions between Muslim and non-Muslim Europeans. In so doing, al-Azmeh draws from the chapters in this volume critical suggestions concerning the direction that future research on Islam in Europe must take if it is to serve the purpose of increasing the potential for a happier future for Islam in Europe. We hope that knowledge communicated through this book serves as a useful stepping stone in this process.

Bibliography

al-Azmeh, Aziz, *Islams and modernities*, London: Verso, 1993.

Auslander, Leonora, 'Bavarian crucifixes and French headscarves', *Cultural Dynamics*, vol. 12, no. 3, 2000, pp. 283–309.

Berger, Peter, *The desecularization of the world*, Washington, DC: Ethics and Public Policy Center, 1999.

Casanova, José, *Public religions in the modern world*, Chicago: University of Chicago Press, 1994.

'Religion, European secular identities, and European integration', in Timothy Byrnes and Peter Katzenstein (eds.), *Religion in an expanding Europe*, Cambridge: Cambridge University Press, 2006, pp. 65–92.

Davie, Grace, *Religion in Britain since 1945. Believing without belonging*, Oxford: Blackwell, 1994.

EUMC (European Monitoring Centre on Racism and Xenophobia) European Roundtables Meetings report of 2003, accessible via the EUMC website: www.eumc.europa.eu/eumc/index.php

Habermas, Jürgen, lecture delivered upon receipt of the Holberg Prize, on 'Religion in the Public Sphere', 28 November 2005 (available online at: www.holberg. uib.no/downloads/Habermas_religion_in_the_public_sphere.pdf).

'Religion in the European public sphere', in *European Journal of Philosophy*, vol. 14, no. 1, 2006, pp. 1–25.

Halliday, Fred, 'The politics of the *umma*', in B.A. Roberson (ed.), *Shaping the current Islamic reformation*. London: Frank Cass, 2003, pp. 20–41.

Hervieu-Léger, Danièle, *La religion pour mémoire*, Paris: Éditions du Cerf, 1993.

Knowlton, Brian, 'Bush repeats threat to veto torture curb', in *International Herald Tribune*, 7 October 2005, p. 4.

Krauthammer, Charles, 'Europe's native-born enemy', *The Washington Post*, 15 July 2005, p. A23.

Madeley, J. and Z. Enyedi, eds., *Church and state in contemporary Europe: the chimera of neutrality*, London: Frank Cass, 2003.

Martin, David, *On secularization: towards a revised general theory*, Aldershot: Ashgate, 2005.

Parekh, Bhikhu, 'Is Islam a threat to Europe's multicultural democracies?', in Krzysztof Michalski (ed.), *Religion in the new Europe*, Budapest: Central European University, 2006, pp. 111–21.

Reuter, Astrid, 'Headscarf and crucifix: on the politics of interpreting religious symbols', unpublished paper, presented at the International Society for the Sociology of Religion (ISSR) Conference in Zagreb, July 2005.

Rodinson, Maxime, *Europe and the mystique of Islam*, Seattle: University of Washington Press, 1987.

Roy, Olivier, 'Islam in Europe: clash of religions or convergence of religiosities?' in Krzysztof Michalski (ed.), *Religion in the new Europe*, Budapest: Central European University, 2006, pp. 131–44.

Ruthven, Malise, *Fundamentalism: the search for meaning*, Oxford: Oxford University Press, 2004.

2 Christians and Muslims: memory, amity and enmities

Tarek Mitri

In today's world, the waves of economic, technological and ecological forces at work favour integration and uniformity. Increasingly, we are all tied together by communications, information systems, commerce and entertainment. Images and perceptions gain an unprecedented role in shaping realities: 'he who screens history can make history'.[1]

Many structures of governance have become much less able to address major problems and take major decisions. Within this context, the exercise of power within the limits of a national territory is weakened substantially. But national governments have become, at the same time, too complex to deal with small problems. One need not give examples of the many existing nations that are considered unsuitable for accommodating all those who would have liked to live together, or unstable as they impose an undesired coexistence on religious communities and ethnic groups.

The awakening of nationalism and the rift in nations are concomitant. In many situations, we see the logic of economy favouring interdependence and regional integration while that of politics seems to follow the path of national fragmentation. An interpretation widespread in the West, based on a primordialist understanding of the nation, considers nationalism to be an archaism, something like a return of history. At best, it is a late and disordered construction that is still thought to be the way of access, in many societies, to modernity. Politicians evoke a world to be ruled by the universal principles of market economy, democracy and human rights, but which is threatened by 'ancestral hatred'. It is true that most of the protagonists in conflicts arouse passions as they invoke history. Collective memories are reactivated for the sake of political mobilisation. However, the success of such mobilisation is not determined by ancestral atavisms but by political strategies of power conquest or preservation.

---

[1] Gore Vidal, *Screening history*, Harvard University Press: Cambridge, 1992, p. 81.

History, as it is present in the public arena, is neither an ancestral memory nor a collective tradition. It is mediated by contemporary education and communication. Hatred is inculcated as much, or even more, by a modern discourse than by memory. It is often stirred up by radio broadcasts, articles in the press and television programmes, rather than inherited from parents. If the past does not meet the needs of the present, another one can always be invented.[2]

In our religiously pluralist contexts, whether rooted in history or recent, a secularist option continues to be widespread. Religions are seen as divisive and their manifestations, beyond the private sphere, are not considered conducive to peaceful and harmonious living together. Such an assumption is, more than ever before, questionable. Concomitant to the secularist approach, we find an essentialist one which, aggravated by the reductionist sensationalism of the media, amplifies the differences between religious communities.

This duality of perceptions accounts, to some extent, for the difficulty faced everywhere in dealing with the reality of religious pluralism. While the idea of an integrated society based on a secularist assumption minimises religious differences, its alternative model, the multiculturalist one, maximises differences and tends to drive minority communities into a ghetto-like existence. In the first case the right of being a full member of a religious community is not sufficiently taken into account. In the other, persons are viewed as parts of a collectivity and embodiment of a community essence.

In short, Christians and Muslims find themselves caught between the forces of homogenisation and those of self-affirmation. The former favour relativism, syncretism and religious consumerism. The latter, as they overstate the religious markers of nationalism or ethnicism, breed fanaticism and intolerance.

Actualities of amity

It is true that the complex history of relations between Christians and people of other religions, especially Muslims, has known rivalry and war. But it is often forgotten that there were some rich and fertile encounters, in the realms of life and ideas alike. One of the features of our historical memories, as deplorable as it may be, has been the way in which conflicts overshadow peaceful experiences and reproaches drown the voices of comprehension. This is paralleled at the level of religious views, though it

[2] Eric Hobsbawm, 'A new threat to history', in *The New York review of books*, New York, vol. 40, no. 21 (December 16) 1993, p. 62.

is often admitted that changes in one's theology and perceptions of the other do, on the whole, linger behind the dynamics of life.

It remains true, however, that traditional universes were self-contained. Exclusivist and reductionist attitudes towards the religious have prevailed in history. John of Damascus and many of his followers saw in Islam a Judeo-Christian heresy. Muslim religious scholars affirm that the Council of Nicea falsified the Gospel and associated Jesus with divinity; the Quranic revelation alone restores, therefore, the truth of Christianity. Be that as it may, Islamic history bears witness, especially during the formative phase of Arab-Islamic civilisation, to a capability of inviting and consequently integrating the multiform contribution that Christians were able, and eager, to offer. Active in transmission and beyond, in the various fields of sciences and philosophy, Christians could engage in dialogue, not only in the apologetic mode, on matters of revelation and reason.

Notwithstanding the many limitations imposed by the political and juridical systems on social interaction and equitable civil relationships, collaboration and exchange were possible. Genuine encounters occurred between persons in a climate of theological discretion, if not silence. Theology could not always make sense of the spiritual and intellectual experience in the encounters between people of different faiths. At the popular level, ways of life and sentiments were shared with an almost identical sense of transcendance, confidence in Divine Providence and humble submission to the will of God. Among intellectuals, a genuine dialogue was, parallel to apologetics, mediated through philosophy. Many spiritual figures were not immune to one another: we cannot turn away from what has been said about Jesus (the 'Seal of Holiness' as Ibn Arabi calls him) among Muslim mystics, nor from the similarities between Christian hesychasm and the *dhikr* – the invocation of the name of God.

In modern times and in many countries, national identities – rooted in cultural bonds and in the awareness of a common destiny – drew Christians and Muslims closer to one another. An unprecedented relationship transcending traditional barriers, distinct from the one derived from religious affiliation without necessarily opposing it, found its way into mentalities and models of society. These relationships gave, in a sense, primacy to collaboration over dialogue. This is still often the case in many countries, although ethnic and communal self-assertions, in other countries, have put national unity in jeopardy or have torn apart modern national constructs.

It is needless to say that the exclusive use of one hermeneutical key does not enable us to embrace the complexity of broader Christian–Muslim relations through history. At the global level, they have known rivalry and war. Feelings of contempt and superiority were strong on both sides but they were tampered, even in times of military confrontation as in the Crusades, with feelings of doubt, curiosity and even admiration. Yet collective memory emphasises the former. In times of tensions and conflicts, a significant number of Christians demonstrate that they have passively inherited certain prejudices, mostly in the religious realm.

Before the rise of Islam, Christianity had established categories for the religious other: Jew, pagan and heretic. When Christians encountered Muslims they perceived their religious otherness in terms of these categories. They did not use the words 'Muslims' and 'Islam'. Instead, they used ethnic terms such as Arabs or biblical terms such as Ishmaelite, Hagarean and Saracen: did not Sarah send Hagar away empty? The Muslim invaders were scourges sent by God to punish Christians for their sins. But this was no small gain to be rescued from Roman imperial oppression, writes the ninth-century Syrian Christian chronicler Dionysus Tel Mahre. Sebeos the Armenian had written as early as 661 that God had granted to Arabs the lands he had promised to Abraham and gave them victory over the impious Byzantines. Also in the seventh century, we know of at least one mirror image of the views of Sebeos: Anastasios, a monk of Saint Catherine's monastery in Sinai, portrays the Arab invasions as a punishment for the monophysicism of Heraclius.

The Muslim strength and unity coincided with Byzantine weakness. The swift early conquests of Muslims confirmed their belief that God was on their side. This self-assured sense of divine mission was certainly a key factor in the success and rapidity of subsequent conquests. They did not fight against Christians or force them to convert, but granted them freedom to practise their religion and offered protection under tutelage. The various *dhimma* pacts reflected this notion, with varying degrees and forms of Christian subordination. The guiding principle of the *dhimma* pact stated: 'to them belongs whatever belongs to us, and incumbent upon them whatever is incumbent upon us'. A political allegiance, involving a certain form of submission, materialised in the paying of a poll tax (the *jizya*).

However Christians had an opportunity to influence the self-definition of the dominant community. They were instrumental, through transmission – but also creation – in the various fields of human knowledge, in the construction of a religiously rationalised non-Christian order. They posed many of the critical questions and provided much of the material and method with which Muslims could frame their own answers. But they were pushed toward the margin when the task was done.

Though still a numerical majority in many parts of the Muslim Empire, Christians turned inwards and closed upon themselves. Their creative urge and the cultural achievements became confined largely to preservation. In addition, there were times when suspicion of and pressure on Christians accelerated the process of marginalisation. Christian communities (or fractions of them) either identified or were *perceived* to identify with external enemies of the Muslim *Ummah*. Distrust led to the elaboration and enforcement of a more rigid code of *dhimmi* rights and obligations.

It is true that legal inferiority and occasional changes in political loyalties brought about an erosion of Christians' energies, but tolerance ensured their survival. Be that as it may, the concern for self-preservation and survival defined a circumscribed entity. The *dhimma* pact reached its most elaborate form of codification in the *millet* system under the Ottoman Empire. *Millets* were not nations, as is often suggested, and nor was the Empire a sort of multinational association. *Millets* were multicultural and multilingual religious communities. The world *millet* comes from the quranic Arabic word *milla*, which means creed or religious way. The *millet* system followed the *dhimma* principle of a contractual relationship. Religious communities had their own administrative and juridical institutions under the authority of the Church's hierarchies. The Islamic central power exercised an overall control but did not interfere in the internal functioning of *millets*.

But the non-territorial *millets* were not immune to foreign intervention, and European support to different Christian communities gradually modified the balance of power within the Ottoman Empire. Projects of national revival and emancipation were at work among Christians. At the same time, their interests served as excuses for outsiders' interference. The cultural component of religious plurality was greatly affected. The diffusion of Western education through missionary schools accentuated differences between communities. Christians were opened to a new type of culture to which Muslims had a limited access. This acculturation provided the hitherto weaker Christians with a new means of self-affirmation. For them, Western influence was also frequently a source of economic prosperity and of subtle forms of political power. Majority–minority relations were thus modified. New political opportunities permitted some Christian communities (or fractions of communities) to move rapidly, some would say abruptly, from passive acceptance of the *millet* system into a rather militant nationalist and separatist strategy. This sheds some light on the subsequent tragic massacres and deportations of Armenians, Assyrians, Greeks and others.

But here were Christians who were opposed, sometimes passionately, to the separatist tendencies of their coreligionists. Some opted for modern and universalist ideologies that enabled them to shake loose their minority identity which they thought to be retrogressive and artificially divisive. They emphasised their common ethno-cultural identity with Muslims as the basis of independence and modern nation building. The patriotic bond cemented opposition to the Ottoman central and oppressive power and later to dominating European powers. Thus in the struggle for and achievement of independence, the pact of citizenship was established, superseding the former *dhimma* pact. In the case of Palestine, the pact of citizenship was affirmed as Christians and Muslims suffered dispossession and expulsion together.

In the Arab world and beyond, it remains true that the *milletist* attitudes did not fade away. In the search for independence and liberation, Islamic self-awareness was intensified. A sometimes violent self-assertion gained visibility and appeal against the failure of modern, more or less secular independent and authoritarian governments. In some instances, this has led to anti-Christian feelings. It was said (and believed) that the colonial powers, and national governments later, gave a preferential treatment to Christians and used them to benefit their domination. No matter how questionable these perceptions, there will always be people, today like yesterday, who cannot, or do not dare, oppose those who make them angry. They look unconsciously for substitutes and often find them.

Overstating religion in enmity

Today, it has become difficult to discard the resonating effects, in many parts of the world, of a discourse on the global confrontation between Christianity – or the West – and Islam. In short, misinterpretions or exaggerations of the role of religions in the relations among and within nations mark attitudes and perceptions of various local tensions or conflicts, thus leading to their aggravation. Local relations between Muslims and Christians are significantly affected by the propagation of a globalist discourse.

Historically specific or culturally, politically and religiously diverse, the situations of Muslims in relation to non-Muslims remain, in the eyes of many, essentially the same. Many do not seem to be willing or able to recognise plurality, avoid precipitated comparisons and refrain from amalgamation. At best, the search for intellectual rectitude is dismissed as luxury.

For their part, a mix of advocates of secular or Christian cultural supremacy and liberal proponents for respect for other cultures emphasise the distinctiveness of what is labelled Islamic culture. However, their exaggeration of the status of this culture and its role in explaining personal and collective behaviour is less perceptible when they reflect on their own situations. Culturalists do not see the world except in terms of never-ending difference. In previous times, Western secularist scholars, not only historians and sociologists of religion, searched for an essence of things religious common to all. In emphasising similarities between religions, they sought to undermine the Christian claim to uniqueness. Today, the emphasis of many anthropologists and other scholars is on difference.

Redressing media images and rectifying perceptions are, to be sure, the fruits of dialogue. At the same time, they make possible an authentic dialogue. In the present context, those who seek to hold in balance religious otherness and common humanity tread a narrow path. The globalised and consumer culture works at reducing differences. Nationalist and communalist self-assertion tend to magnify them.

Millions of uncritical consumers of information are made to see the world in the form of clear images, short stories and quotes. But undecoded images and texts little informed by context may conceal or blur, rather than unfold, the complexities of diverse and ever-changing situations.

For its part, the culturalist perception combines religious relativism and the superiority of the secular humanist culture. Medieval Christians defined their superiority over Muslims in religious terms. At present, many of their counterparts take pride in their precedence and outdistance over Muslims, on the course of religious scepticism and secularist inclination. A few decades ago, as noted above, many people searched for an essence common to all religions. Without much embarrassment, they discredited the Christian claim to uniqueness. There was a widespread interest in similarities among religions. Today, the balance is in favour of those who see not similarities but differences. It is not uncommon to see people rushing to explain terrorist violence in the light of what they perceive to be distinctive about Islam. Thus, they fail to see that such violence is not grounded in traditional Islamic values, but, quite the contrary, it is provoked by the loss of such values without a genuine compensation offered by modernity, often unaccomplished or imposed.

The emphasis on distinctiveness and discontinuity draws heavily on essentialism. In many cases sociological realities of Muslims, the diversity of their cultural and political conditions, are seen to be essentially the same. For those unable or unwilling to recognise their plurality, comparisons of national realities in the Muslim world turn into *analogies,* and specific situations that do not conform to the preconceived model are singled out as *exceptions* which confirm the rule. Essentialism does not go unnoticed. It is likely to be challenged, even in times of war. Once identified and confronted with critical knowledge or life experience, its rudimentary expressions lose much of their credibility. But in its subtle and learned forms, essentialism remains influential. It confirms crude prejudices and stereotypes. At best, it softens them.

The orientalist academic Bernard Lewis attempts to identify the root causes behind the tragic fall of Islam from the intellectual and cultural grandeur it commanded in the Middle Ages. In proposing to answer the question 'What went wrong', he looks incisively into the various facets of Western impact, from law to music, and into the Ottoman response. Understandably, as an historian of Turkey, he privileges what he knows best. But he ends his perceptive historical inquiry with a gross generalisation. In his conclusive chapter he deals with Islam as if it were one giant entity. Muslims of an undifferentiated Middle East have the feeling, he asserts, that history somehow betrayed them. To the question 'What went wrong' he suggests they substituted the question 'who did this to us?' leading only to 'neurotic fantasies and conspiracy theories'. If the peoples of the Middle East continue on the present path, he adds as he hardly dissimulates the passion of an ideologue, the suicide bomber might become a metaphor for the entire region, which would be marked by a spiral of hate, spite, rage and self-pity.[3]

Another recurring ideological approach is exemplified by those who argue that the inferiority of Christians under Islamic rule is an embodiment of a transhistorical *dhimma*, or covenant. Bat Ye'or, a widely quoted Israeli author, bestows an immutable character on the subdued Christian, or Jew, under Islam. In her view, recent changes are of little relevance, as Islam is resurgent in the form of Islamism. No modern cultural or political movement achieved an irreversible improvement on their status as inferior minorities. In fact she rebukes Christians from the Arab world for having believed that they could modernise Islam and reconcile it with their idea of a nation. In a reprehensive tone, she argues that the patriotic discourse adopted by these Christians is the expression of an internalised *dhimmitude*.

Unsurprisingly she looks for historical sources that seem to corroborate the unchanging model of majority–minority relations in the Islamic world. Consequently, she suggests that Christians pursue the 'Israeli option'. Blaming them for not having dared to imitate the Jews, her

---

[3] Bernard Lewis, *What went wrong?: the clash between Islam and modernity in the Middle East*, Oxford: Oxford University Press, 2002.

concern for their fate is meant to argue for an essential intolerance of Islam. To be sure, her comparison between Christians and Jews 'under Islam' is an additional, but not so common, apologetic tool for portraying Zionism as a liberation project for oppressed Jews, not only in Europe, but also in the Islamic world. The anachronistic twist does not seem to embarrass her.

The pitfalls of culturalism, and of the secularisation thesis

Increasingly, many secular people, as well as Christians and Muslims, depict a number of conflicts in our world as religious wars and manifestations of ancestral hatred. Religious intolerance, more particularly associated with Islam and indiscriminately attributed to Muslims, is likely invoked as a determinant in such conflicts. With more or less religious and historical overtones, reference is frequently made to *Jihad* and Crusade. Expressions of what is said to be an Islamic 'threat' continue to capture, with more intensity, the instaneity of the media's attention.

Both religious and secular people who are directly involved in, or affected by, conflicts can overstate their religious dimension. The religious dispute over Holy Places in Jerusalem overshadows, in the eyes of many, the dispossession and humiliation of Palestinians. The various calls to *Jihad* in Indonesia blurred the perception of many other causes of inter-communal tensions. In fact, the more that a religious factor, though one among many, is singled out as decisive in provoking and sustaining conflicts, the stronger becomes religion's impact on the course of these conflicts.

Meanwhile, interpretions of local tensions and disputes as manifestations of a global confrontation feed into a 'transnational discourse' on 'bloody borders' between Christianity and Islam, or between the Muslim World and the Western World. This tendency is carried sometimes by the 'diaspora' of communities and nations concerned, espoused by a number of religious organisations and, in certain cases, by policymakers.

In its turn, this discourse is often a factor of aggravation in local conflicts, for it is known that myths once propounded gain a force of their own. The vulnerability of those who are seen to be on the wrong side of such presumed borders, namely religious minorities, is accentuated.

In short, misinterpreting or exaggerating the role of religions in international and even intra-national relations marks perceptions of local conflicts, leading to their aggravation and subsequent failure in addressing them. Conflicts are also affected by the propagation of a

globalist discourse and its corollaries. Both factors are closely associated
with the rift in many nations, the legitimacy crisis of a significant
number of national projects, and the inadequacies of systems or practices of political participation in most religiously and ethnically plural
societies.

Until the late seventies, secularisation was seen, almost universally, to
be irreversible. For many years, there was a tendency to propose a
chronological scheme for the erosion of religion. Secularisation was
supposed to be its ultimate phase. Conceived as a social–historical
process of achieving an ever-greater autonomy of society and human
thought in relation to religious institutions, symbols and approaches of
reality, secularisation was equated with modernisation and progress. It
was considered inevitable. While it was recognised that many societies
did not seem to follow the universal path, their specificity was perceived
as an expression of delay, reflecting inadequate modernisation, or as a
form of provisional retrogression illustrating a last attempt of cultural
resistance before the inescapable surrender.

In communist countries, eradication of religion was thought to be
underway, despite some hurdles that caused delay. Problems of
nationalities where religious identity could not be ignored were presumably solved by deportations and population transfers in a few cases
and the granting of a limited cultural and political autonomy in others.

Throughout the world, most conflicts were perceived to be determined largely by economic interests, social contradictions and political
rivalries. Religion had little or no visible role in international relations.
Its role in national politics was seen to be declining. Theological and
political polarisations within one religious community, Christian or
Muslim, overshadowed the historical divisions between religions.
Majorities and minorities, whenever mentioned, were perceived in terms
of power relations and not numerical importance or cultural specificities. National integration was a prevailing model. Privatisation of
religion, through the combined effects of modernisation and urbanisation on one hand and state-led nation building on a non-religious or
secular basis on the other hand, seemed to limit the impact of religious
plurality on political structures. With a few exceptions, power-sharing
was hardly an inter-communal and inter-religious issue.

Traditional religious identities were said to be waning. A significant
faction of religious people and organisations made great efforts to
conform to a modernity tied to an irreversible secularisation. Religious
institutions seemed to have lost much of their influence. In this context,
a radical change in the way of transmitting a religious message, and a
transformation of its content and emphasis, occurred within Christianity

but also within Islam. When sociologists extrapolated the waning of religion, a number of Western Christian theologians pronounced the death of the traditional discourse about God. This was their way of drawing the theological consequences of the process of secularisation. One of the aspects of a certain 'liberation theology', presented itself as, and was understood to be, an attempt to rescue the revolutionary core values of faith against the eroding credibility of traditional religion.[4]

Today, a number of authors, mostly agnostic, are repeatedly predicting a 'religious' century-to-come. Some are puzzled at the prevailing expectation of a world of more mysticism and others are preoccupied with 'the return of history', fearing wars under the banner of religion. Be that as it may, it has now become clear that the predictions of technological and modernising pace expelling religion to the margins were wrong. These had allowed that faith might well survive as a valued heritage in some ethnic enclaves or family customs, but insisted that religion's days as a shaper of culture and history were over. This was not the case. Instead, religions that some theologians and other intellectuals thought had been stunted by consumerist materialism or suppressed by despotic regimes, have regained a whole new vigour.

It is true that religious beliefs and practices were, wherever they noticeably survived, clearly privatised in many societies. Collective identities associated with faith traditions seemed to find their expressions in the national–cultural self-understanding that, at best, integrated elements of religious memory. But the 'return of religion' or 'the return to religion' showed that the driving force of things metaphysical has not been consummated; nor was the power of sentiments that bind people together in one faith extinguished. This movement took many people by surprise. It was not characterised in a clear manner nor even given a precise and widely accepted name. The re-emergence of fundamentalism, the resurgence of religion, its awakening or its revival, were indiscriminately and interchangeably invoked. Manifestations of religious self-assertion, in the particularity of their context or the distinctiveness of their faith tradition, are increasingly seen as variations of a universal phenomenon.

It is needless to say that the regained interest in religion reflects two opposing, and in many instances ambivalent, attitudes. The first one reveals a satisfaction to see religion refilling a spiritual vacuum and offering meaning and hope to a world threatened by meaninglessness,

---

[4] Quite elaborate and vociferous among Christians, and less so among Muslims, liberation theology was meant to draw nearer to each other the progressive forces within all religions and among people of no religion.

nihilism and despair. But the second mirrors a fear from the eruption of dreams and other things irrational, and an anxiety facing the dangers of bigotry and fanaticism.

Today the assumption that we live in a secularised, and secularising, world does not meet with universal approval. A leading sociologist of religion does not hesitate to affirm that in present times the world, with some exceptions, is as furiously religious as it ever was and in some places more so than ever.[5] To be sure, modernisation has had some secularising effects, more in some places than others. But it has also provoked powerful movements of counter-secularisation. Certain religious institutions have lost power in many societies but old and new religious beliefs and practices find their expressions, sometimes in an explosive manner. Conversely, religiously identified institutions play social and political roles even when fewer people believe or practise the religion that such institutions represent. In some extreme cases, people fight in the name of religions in which they ceased to believe. There are conflicts between communities that have a religious past, but their religious content is of no relevance. Religions in which people have little faith continue to define communities in which they have much faith. It is therefore essential, when assessing the role of religion in politics, international or national, to distinguish between political movements that may be genuinely inspired by religion and those that use religion as a convenient legitimation for political agendas based on quite non-religious interests.

It is common, when referring to tensions and conflicts involving Christians and Muslims, to assume that religious revival, Islamic or otherwise, is a universal phenomenon which, to the extent it is politicised, puts at peril coexistence between communities. While it is true that some religious movements can foster war, some other movements see themselves as agents of peace in societies where the main actors in conflicts are motivated by ethnic and ethno-nationalist interests. Many of those who manifest a stronger religious commitment seem to position themselves on the moderate range of the political spectrum.

In the Muslim world, ideological thought patterns represent the West as selfish, materialistic and dominating. In the West, the equivalent thought patterns perceive Islam as irrational, fanatical and expansionist. In the age of global communication and migration, these thought patterns, in the variety of their subtle and not-so-subtle expressions, foster antagonism.

---

[5] See Peter L. Berger, 'The desecularization of the world: a global overview', in Peter L. Berger (ed.), *The desecularization of the world: resurgent religion and world politics*, Ethics and Public Policy Center, Washington DC: Eerdmans, 1999.

It is true that the issue of Islam and the West is more complex and more contingent upon contemporary concerns than either proponents and opponents of culturalist politics would imply. Many of the problems, such as foreign hegemony and intervention, terrorism and international threats, are confused and exaggerated. But they have become real issues although they are, in the main, relating to power of states, the treatment of migrant and minority groups and the balance of forces within many developing societies.[6]

But it is not less true that the end of worldwide ideological confrontations, and the globalisation of Islam,[7] has favoured the re-emergence of perceptions where Islam and the West exist as subjective, imaginary constructs, which influence the way each sees the other.

It is increasingly suggested that in the post-cold-war world, flags do count tremendously, as do other symbols of cultural and religious identity, and that marching under flags leads to war. For 'people seeking identity and reinventing ethnicity, enemies are essential, and the potentially most dangerous enmities occur across the fault lines between the world's major civilizations'.[8]

The world has entered an era of cultural struggle where wars and confrontations are no longer the result of clashes between individual nations or states. The clash between the 'West and the rest', we are told, is religious to the extent that religions shape civilisations, and they do so significantly. It is political as long as politics is determined by civilisational affinities instead of ideological options. The explosive force of such ideas lies in the reading of old hostilities between East and West into modern-day collective consciousness and the potential consequences of this in relation to world politics.

A significant number of Muslims see the wars in Palestine, Bosnia, Chechnya and Afghanistan as a continuation of the Crusades. What were called, widely and until the nineteenth century, the 'Frankish invasions' have gained the connotation of a global and trans-historical religious and political conquest. Western soldiers engaged in military operations against Iraq are Crusaders and so are Christian missionaries. This de-historicisation and amalgamation enforces the religious overtones of what had been, for a long time, but a major political and military confrontation in the history of Western expansion. The 1991 Gulf War was

---

[6] Fred Halliday, *Islam and the myth of confrontation*, London: I. B. Tauris, 1996, p. 127.

[7] See Yvonne Haddad, 'The globalisation of Islam: the return of the Muslims to the West', in John Esposito (ed.), *The Oxford history of Islam*, Oxford: Oxford University Press, 1999.

[8] Samuel B. Huntington, *The clash of civilizations and the remaking of world order*, London: Simon and Schuster, 1997, p. 20.

seen by many as a revival of the Crusades, despite the fact that many Islamic states joined the US-led Western military alliance. Western predominance in the Arab world, colonial and post-colonial, nurtured a historicist view of the Crusades, whereby Muslims see themselves retrospectively as victims despite their position of strength at the time. The serenity and fortitude which characterised Muslim reactions to the Medieval Crusaders or Franks is reinterpreted in terms of the military, political and economic subordination of the Islamic world today.

The imaginary has been an important factor in conflicts since 1991. Soon after the Gulf War, the majority in the West was fearful of the growth of Islamism on the southern shores of the Mediterranean. Thus many decision-takers and opinion-makers were prepared to turn a blind eye to the severe blow to democracy by the Algerian military, which led to a cruel civil war. Public images of Muslims as fanatical and violent revealed a dangerous congruence between many ideas in the secular and mainstream left or right, and the ultra-nationalist and xenophobic slogans warning against Islamic threats.

For their part, a number of Western historians have been trying to re-historicise, more intensively in the last few years and around the nine-hundredth anniversary of the first Crusade, a designation that has almost become a generic expression conveying the sense of a zealous campaign. This crucial work, which undoubtedly contributes to the healing of memories, is hardly paralleled when it comes to reading the history of Muslim peoples. Worse, reductionist approaches proposing the notion of *Jihad* as the key, and the only key, to interpret Muslim attitudes towards non-Muslims past and present, seem to receive a wide audience.

Thus, many Muslims overstate the religious character of political and military confrontations while many Christians, mainly, but not only, in the West fail to historicise *Jihad* and recognise its religious significance, not only as a legitimation of defence war but as the spiritual struggle in the way of God.

In addition to war-prone attitudes and fears that are fostered by the tendency to globalise Christian–Muslim relations, one could refer to the way in which the rights of Christian minorities in predominantly Islamic countries are often advocated in the West, including a call for reciprocity in the treatment of minorities, frequently heard in religious, and sometimes secular, circles. The logic of reciprocity, borrowed by religious communities from states, favours a worldview opposing an Islamic *Umma* with Christendom, no matter if both are not historical realities in the present time, each having a ramification in the 'abode' of the other. Asymmetrically diverse, minorities can be, and are, perceived as victims and not actors. Their ability to act as bridge-builders is severely jeopardised when they are forced into the situation of hostages.

Such a role of mediation, that many of them nevertheless are able to play, is put at risk when human rights violations are addressed selectively. Many of the interests of Christian minorities cannot be safeguarded and promoted unless in conjunction with those of the Muslim majorities amongst whom they live. Upholding the rights of Christians in the Muslim world in a way that suggests, or is looked upon as, a form of foreign intervention for the sake of protection, reinforces the perception that they are alien in their own countries or disloyal to them. Defending the rights of Christians in opposition to their Muslim co-citizens and neighbours, with whom they share culture and national identity, aggravates the suspicion of majorities towards minorities seen as an instrument of a real or potential threat instigated by foreign and powerful forces.

Moreover, there are cases where the amplification of a number of real problems faced by Christians may hide, in actual fact, an unwillingness to contribute effectively towards their solution. It may provide a justification for a policy of resignation announcing, at times, the imminent eradication of the concerned minorities.[9] What is seen as an irreversible process renders the Muslim world homogeneous, a radical other, which can be thrown into 'outside darkness'.

Christian–Muslim relations in the age of globalisation

In some parts of the world, the traditional nation-state model is subject to growing questioning. Some countries have fallen apart, as we have seen in the Balkans; others, e.g. in Western Europe, are constructing larger entities. States have become too small for some purposes and too large for others. It is often claimed that the future belongs to the infranational and supranational formations. In many post-colonial independent countries of Africa, the Arab world and Asia, nation-building projects remain incomplete, become fragile or are failing. This is also the case in post-Soviet countries. The conflict in Chechnya, for instance, represents a potential shattering of the ever-fragile post-Soviet federalism as much as it reflects the possible advance of politicised Islam in Eurasia.

The borders set by the old and new imperial powers, while mostly unchanged, could not gain universal acceptance. In some cases they are disputed. Claims to common nationhood have been countered by the

---

[9] See Jean-Pierre Valognes, *Vie et mort des Chrétiens d'Orient*, Paris: Fayard, 1994.

fact that ethnic, cultural and linguistic communities sometimes straddle
several state boundaries, while contributing to divisions within them.
The examples are many in the Caucasian and trans-Caucasian regions
and in the Balkans.

National governments are often far from having succeeded in deli-
vering on promises of genuine national independence and social and
economic advancement. Indeed, in many instances, early progress has
gone into reverse and large sections of the national population have sunk
deeper into poverty. This has provoked, or fuelled, many violent
upheavals in Algeria and in quite a few sub-Saharan African countries.
Official rhetoric of development, national unity, democracy and human
rights has often contrasted with reality and contributed to the erosion of
the credibility and legitimacy of political institutions.

The state is further weakened by a continuing globalisation of economic processes and of information, which is associated with greater
human mobility through migration, refugee movements and the growth
of transnational networks. The threat posed by a global culture to
national and local identities adds to the pressures on national and
regional loyalties. New relations between people across traditional ties
and webs of interests have created new loyalties and identities in which
local community has little meaning.

As many states are becoming weak, people are thrown back to identify
with, and rely on, traditional community structures and identities for
meaning and security. Conversely, when a state becomes oppressive,
people find protection in traditional community structures and identities. In both cases, the effects of globalisation leading to greater cultural uniformity invite, in many cases, a search for specificity and favour
a reaffirmation of traditional identities. We are before a paradox where
unprecedented homogenisation exacerbates the quest for distinction
and recognition.

When various human needs, personal or collective and material or
symbolic, are being met or expressed in *one* identity instead of many, the
borders between communal loyalties are mutually reinforced. Boundaries between oneself and the other are thus strengthened. They create
closed communities within which common and exclusive memories can
be developed and activated, the self and stranger are stereotyped and the
latter is easily demonised.

In such cases, differences in community size become an issue
of minority threatened by majority. In order to achieve political
empowerment, insecure communities in one place seek alliances with
others perceived to share a common identity. National governments and
political movements that are part of 'majority' communities consider

their suspicion towards 'minorities' justified and deepened. At the same time, some governments strengthen their power by managing communities and relations between them, exploiting mutual fears, mobilising one against the other and recruiting some in support and thus further undermining the security of others.

In many countries the logic of politics and culture seem to go the course of national fragmentation. The dynamics of globalisation limit substantially the exercise of power within the limits of a national territory. But this does not announce the universal demise of politics driven by national aspirations and considerations of national sovereignty. And of course there are in some countries manifestations of an awakened nationalism. As explained above, culturalist or primordialist understandings of the nation consider nationalism to be an archaism, something like a return of history and of ancestral hatred. Again, it is not ancestral hatred that is the cause of wars, but war that causes hatred. Ancestral hatred is, more often than not, fabricated rather than inherited. It is in many ways a creation of modernity and much less an expression of a continued history.

It is undeniable that relations between Muslims and Christians are strongly influenced by local and regional histories and events. But, as suggested in this chapter, broader developments also have a significant impact, especially when they contribute to destabilising societies previously characterised by peaceful relations and shared life. It is mostly in situations where uncertainties of change begin to be felt that mistrust and mutual apprehension can build up between communities, creating tensions leading possibly to conflicts.

When communities identify themselves, or are identified, exclusively or even exaggeratedly by their religion, situations become more explosive. Christianity and Islam carry deep historical memories, though in different ways that are region-specific. They appeal, albeit variably, to universal loyalties. The two faiths come to be seen as a cause of conflict while often they are not more than an intensifying feature of disputes whose main causes are outside religion.

There are cases where a conflict in one place, with its local causes and character, is perceived and instrumentalised as part of a conflict in another, with its separate and specific causes and character. So enmities in one part of the world spill over into situations of tension in other regions. An act of violence in one place is used to confirm stereotypes of the 'enemy' in another place or even to provoke revenge attacks elsewhere in the world. What is otherwise a remote conflict becomes a local problem. Neighbours hold each other accountable for the wrongs attributed to their coreligionists elsewhere. Unless they are prepared to dissociate themselves publicly from those with whom they share a common faith, they are accused of complicity with them.

It is therefore crucial to offer a possibility of counteracting processes which tend to globalise conflicts that involve Muslims and Christians. In other words, it is necessary to 'de-globalise Christian–Muslim tensions' as a vital step towards resolving them. Attention to the specific local causes of conflicts helps to identify solutions to be found in addressing, first and foremost, those local causes. This is not possible unless the leaders of both communities refuse to be drawn into others' conflicts on the basis of uncritical response to calls for solidarity among adherents to one faith. It is only in applying common principles of peace, justice and reconciliation that parties to local conflicts are helped to release Islam and Christianity from the burden of sectional interests and self-serving interpretations of beliefs and convictions. Christian and Islamic beliefs and convictions can then constitute a basis for critical engagement with human weakness and defective social and economic orders, in a common search for human well-being, dignity, social justice and civil peace.

Bibliography

Berger, Peter L., 'The desecularization of the world: a global overview', in Peter L. Berger (ed.), *The desecularization of the world: resurgent religion and world politics*, Ethics and Public Policy Center, Washington DC: Eerdmans, 1999.

Haddad, Yvonne, 'The globalisation of Islam: the return of the Muslims to the West', in John Esposito (ed.), *The Oxford history of Islam*, Oxford: Oxford University Press, 1999.

Halliday, Fred, *Islam and the myth of confrontation*, London: I. B. Tauris, 1996.

Hobsbawm, Eric, 'A new threat to history', in *The New York review of books*, vol. 40, no. 21 (December 16) 1993, pp. 62–4.

Huntington, Samuel B., *The clash of civilizations and the remaking of world order*, London: Simon and Schuster, 1997.

Lewis, Bernard, *What went wrong?: the clash between Islam and modernity in the Middle East*, Oxford: Oxford University Press, 2002.

Rupnik, Jacques (ed.), *Le déchirement des nations*, Paris: Seuil, 1995.

Striving together in dialogue: a Muslim–Christian call to reflection and action, The World Council of Churches, Interreligious Relations and Dialogue, no. 28, Geneva, 2001.

Valognes, Jean-Pierre, *Vie et mort des Chrétiens d'Orient*, Paris: Fayard, 1994.

Vidal, Gore, *Screening history*, Cambridge, MA: Harvard University Press, 1992.

3   The question of Euro-Islam: restriction or opportunity?

Jorgen Nielsen

In 2002 a group of senior journalists on the Danish daily newspaper *Politiken* published a collection of essays under the title 'Islam in Denmark: reflections on a third way'.[1] In their foreword they described the two positions between which they were positing a third way.

In one trench are the *xenophobes* who say 'no thank you to everything' regarding Muslims. They oppose the multicultural society, even though it is already reality. They are against further immigration, even though that is a condition for the continuing financing of the welfare state. They are sceptical about the immigrants' religion, customs, dress, etc., even though these are things which belong to the private sphere. The xenophobes prevail in large sections of the political parties and were especially visible in the general election campaign last autumn.

In the other trench are the so-called *progressives* who say 'yes please' to everything as regards Islamic culture. They see Muslims as inherently an enrichment of Danish culture. Any attempt to take a critical stand towards fundamentalist and reactionary tendencies in Muslim culture is automatically labelled racism and xenophobia.

Both stances are deeply problematical.[2]

The following year another collections of essays appeared, this time edited by a group of young Danish Muslims of immigrant heritage, interestingly including an introduction by yet another *Politiken*

Acknowledgment: this paper has been developed from one presented at the University of Wisconsin Madison in a conference on Islam in Europe held in March 2004.

[1] Adam Holm, Michael Jarlner and Per M. Jespersen (eds.), *Islam i Danmark: tanker on en tredje vej*, Copenhagen: Gyldendal, 2002.

[2] Ibid. pp. 7–8 (my translation; emphases in the original). The election campaign referred to in this quotation is the Danish general election in November 2001, which was characterised by a major debate about asylum seekers in response to the 11 September attacks in the US and led to a new, sharply right-wing coalition government.

journalist, Anders Jerichow.[3] In what might be considered a response to the above, the editors in their conclusion state:

> To dare to state that Islam is also a Danish religion, and thus distance oneself from the Middle East's monopoly on holiness, requires . . . that Muslims understand themselves as full citizens of the society in which they live . . . It particularly requires that Muslims in Denmark (and the rest of the West) become active participants in developing a feeling of 'being at home' in their societies and challenge the bi-polar perception of a world where Christianity and secularism are a western preserve and Islam an eastern, regardless of the fact that Islam and secularism by nature are universal and transnational.[4]

To many, such statements might seem uncontroversial. They certainly would not cause much in the way of raised eyebrows in Britain outside small extremist circles, whether among Muslims or on the political right. However, they do represent middle-ground views which are far from being shared across Europe, whether among Muslims or among the non-Muslim majority.

A term which has come into increasing use in recent years in this context is that of 'Euro-Islam'. Apart from its questionable aesthetic character, it is a term which, like so many short-hand terms, is in danger of disguising as much as it reveals. Professor Bassam Tibi claims to have been among the first to use it, but he uses it in a very particular sense. In his contribution to a series of round-table discussions held in Paris in 1992–3 under the title *Islams d'Europe: intégration ou insertion communautaire?*, Tibi called for 'an Islam integrated into European societies'.[5] He asserts that this integration is not a one-way process: 'the two parties must share in this and, as the third religious community of Europe, "Euro-Islam" must accommodate and assimilate the socio-cultural evolution which Europe has accomplished.' He then emphasises three aspects of this:

1. Tolerance 'but not in the Muslim sense', rather in the broader European sense.
2. Pluralism, by which he means that Muslims must abandon the Qur'anic sense of superiority (viz. Qur'an 3:110).
3. Secularism, namely the separation between religion and state.

---

[3] Mona Sheikh, Fatih Alev, Babar Baig and Norman Malik (eds.), *Islam i bevægelse*, Copenhagen: Akademisk, 2003.

[4] Ibid. p. 256 (my translation).

[5] Bassam Tibi, 'Les conditions d'un "euro-islam"', in Robert Bistolfi and François Zabbal (eds.), *Islams d'Europe: intégration ou insertion communautaire?*, Paris: L'Aube, 1995, pp. 230–4 (my translation).

According to Tibi, it is the duty of the European political structures (national governments and the European Union) actively to encourage the 'development of a liberal Islam and to defend its own [the European] identity'. More recently Tibi took up this discussion again, clarifying that by secularism he means *laïcité* and reiterating his points regarding tolerance and the abandonment of a sense of superiority. He takes the argument further, attacking the views of some that Muslims should be granted some form of protected status akin to that of the *dhimmi*, as well as the 'multiculturalists', arguing that the result of both policy directions would be ghettoisation.[6] His particular target here is the German orientalist Tilman Nagel who ventured this idea in a 1998 lecture,[7] but Tibi confuses Nagel's reference to 'protected minorities' (*dhimmis*) with the status of 'enemy alien' (*musta'min*). Nagel has not been alone in suggesting a *dhimma*-type solution; it has also been used by some Muslims to denote the kind of status they could see for themselves.[8]

There are several problems with this approach, but I will briefly point to two particular ones. Despite the assertion that both sides need to move, there is precious little discussion of how Europe is supposed to move, other than by encouraging change in the right direction by Muslims. More problematical are the assumptions being made about Europe implied in the direction which Muslims are expected to follow. On the one hand, demands are being made of Muslims to meet European standards which Europeans themselves have often not met. The expectation of religious tolerance is one which is blind to the continuing national and ethnic intolerance which remains endemic in European culture and continues to find expression in national legislation and policies. The implication that the European religious scene is one which acknowledges the equality of esteem of all religions in the public space is also open to question, especially in countries where some churches hold privileged positions in relation to the state and the tax-payer. This last point then takes one directly into Tibi's call for an Islamic *laïcism*. The term is commonly used to denote not only the very strict separation of church and state established in the French law of 1905 but also the more ideological French view that the citizen's

---

[6] Bassam Tibi, 'Muslim migrants in Europe: between Euro-Islam and ghettoization', in Nezar AlSayyad and Manuel Castells (eds.), *Muslim Europe or Euro-Islam: politics, culture and civilization in the age of globalization*, Lanham: Lexington, 2002, pp. 31–52.

[7] Reported in the *Frankfurt Allgemeiner Zeitung*, 10 June 1998, referred to by Tibi, p. 38 and note 27.

[8] I heard such views being expressed at the Islamic Foundation in Leicester in the 1980s, although it is a view no one there would espouse today.

relationship to the state is based exclusively on the individual's *citoyenneté* – the state does not relate to citizens as communities, especially not as religious communities. But if we take the term to mean simply the separation of religion and state, not only are Muslims being asked to be more European than the Europeans, but other Europeans are being asked to become like the French![9]

Here is the crux of the issue at hand. There is more than one way of being a European when it comes to cultural and religious practice and identity. There are therefore necessarily more ways than one for Muslims to become European. In raising the banner of 'Euro-Islam', its proponents stand accused of painting with a very broad brush indeed – in both the 'Euro' and the 'Islam' parts of the expression. It is this form of the concept which becomes restrictive. Too quickly and easily it shifts subtly from being a description of the complicated process of integration which Muslims of immigrant origin are passing through, to becoming a prescription which implies a dichotomy between 'good' and 'bad' Muslims, a dichotomy which is particularly dangerous at a time when Islam in the public space is too facilely viewed from the perspective of public security.[10] Ironically, while this approach appeals to a need for differentiation within Islam, in this case cultural and ethnic differentiation as between, for example, Arab and African Islam – so why not a Euro-Islam? – it merely concludes in establishing smaller but equally monolithic blocks, such as 'Europe'.

The point has already been made that Europe is not one, especially not when it comes to matters of religion, whether in the public or the private sphere. There are certainly those who, in the overall context of the so-called European project, have sought to apply the Treaty of Rome's 'ever closer union' also to these spheres, but here surely is a sphere where the principle of subsidiarity applies. Let me illustrate with some examples, first of all in Denmark where we started. This is a small country of only five million inhabitants, which until the Second World War had been a country of emigration. Denmark is also in many ways the archetypal nation-state as that creature was developed in the national–romantic movement of the nineteenth century. It had one language, one religion (Lutheranism), one sense of ethnic–national belonging, a core territory which had existed as one political entity for a thousand years (at least in the myths of collective memory and national historical narrative

---

[9] This is a view which Tibi expounds at greater length in chapter 12 of his *Im Schatten Allahs: der Islam und die Menschenrechte*, Munich: Piper, 1994, pp. 298–315.

[10] This is the concern, for example, behind a collection of articles on *Islamismus* published in 2003 by the German Ministry of the Interior in its series 'Texte zur inneren Sicherheit'.

of the school textbooks), and an unbroken line of monarchs throughout that period. It has had its glory days, but they are long since gone leaving only residual echoes in popular tourist sites. It had not been untouched by the outside world, so there were small Baptist, Methodist, Catholic, Jewish and other congregations. But to be Danish meant, essentially, to be Lutheran, something which was regularly reiterated in the public celebration of rites of passage, especially as confirmation classes were integrated into the annual cycle of the public-school year. The Lutheran church is literally a department of state, with its own cabinet minister, its civil service regulations, and priests as government employees. The church was the official registrar of births, marriages and deaths. Where other countries have birth certificates, Danes have baptism certificates.

But things have changed. Starting in the late 1960s the country experienced the immigration from outside Europe which had already become common in the previous two decades in many other parts of the region. While there were some smaller religious groups among these immigrants, the majority were of Muslim background. Unlike some of the other countries the immigration into Denmark was very mixed in its ethnic origins. Turks, North Africans and Pakistanis were later followed by Iraqis, Iranians, Palestinians, Lebanese, Somalis and Bosnians, giving a current total of over 150,000 or about 3% of the total population.[11] Gradually, the question marks which had traditionally been placed against the Danishness of Catholics or Baptists were transferred to the newcomers. As elsewhere, different parts of Danish society responded in different ways and at different speeds. Within the limitations set by official structures and regulations, schools were surprisingly fast to adapt. This was aided by a traditional ease of access to public funding for parent-led 'free schools' instituted in the nineteenth century to cater for the various revival movements which were appearing within the Lutheran fold. The facility had been used later by a number of free-thinking and humanist movements, movements attracted to alternative approaches to education, including Marxist groups. After the Muslim immigration started, Denmark was among the pioneers in the opening of Muslim schools.[12] On the other hand, the state church and the ministry of the interior were slow to adjust to the changing situation. It took some years before it was made possible for birth or naming certificates to be issued by a civil authority, rather than the Lutheran parish

---

[11] Brigitte Maréchal, Stefano Allievi et al., *Muslim in the enlarged Europe: religion and society*, Leiden: Brill, 2003, p. xxiv.

[12] The government's Humanities Research Council funded a project on Muslim schools in the mid-1980s: Asta Olesen (ed.), *Islam og undervisning I Danmark*, Århus: Århus Universitetsforlag, 1987.

priest whose function this had traditionally been. There was a struggle before the state would allow the registration of names not to be found on an official list of approved Danish first names. And by the 1980s the status of 'recognised religious community', laid down in the Constitution, was regarded as being redundant in the face of Muslim claims for such a status.[13]

Such resistance could not last, for a number of reasons. The sheer pressure of numbers was one dimension, especially in the three main cities where Muslims were concentrated: Copenhagen, Aarhus and Odense. More important probably was a combination of the growth of a new Danish-born and educated generation of Muslims – they have been called 'new-Danes' – more than capable of holding their own in the public debate and in the workplace, and the strengthening of a consciousness of traditions of democracy and equality of rights in the context of a very lively, and sometimes quite rough, public debate about Danishness and its ability to change and be more inclusive. This debate came to a head around the turn of the millennium with some politicians and public figures peddling scare stories about floods of asylum seekers, often termed 'illegal', and the electoral success in November 2001 of a coalition of right-wing parties entering government with the parliamentary support of the extreme right Danish People's Party. At the same time, the clergy and lay leaders of the state church had realised that they had to review the role of the church, after the similar state churches of Norway and Sweden had been disestablished. So just when the political lead has fallen into the hands of nationalist politicians, significant sectors of society – certain local governments, such as the second city of Aarhus, leading bishops and literary personalities – have engaged more actively in working with younger Muslim leaders and intellectuals towards a multicultural and cooperative approach to integration, a process in which both sides adapt.

I have paid possibly too much attention to a country of little significance to most. But it is an interesting case for our purposes precisely because it started almost as the model European nation-state. It was inevitable that there should be some kind of *Kulturkampf* in response to the settlement of significant new communities, a process in which a defence of the national identity potentially put the nation at odds with its equally strong democratic and cooperative identity.

---

[13] For further information about Denmark, see Jørgen Bæk Simonsen, 'Globalization in reverse and the challenge of integration: Muslims in Denmark', in Y. Y. Haddad (ed.), *Muslims in the West: from sojourners to citizens*, New York: Oxford University Press, 2002, pp. 121–130, and the index references to Denmark in B. Maréchal, S. Allievi et al. (eds.), *Muslims in the enlarged Europe*.

Let me then pay a little more attention to some better-known countries. It was in the United Kingdom in 1967 that an attempt was made by the political leadership to set a framework for the response to immigration and settlement. The then Labour Home Secretary, Roy Jenkins, sought to define the process of integration not as a process of levelling leading to uniformity but one which aimed at 'cultural diversity, coupled with equal opportunity, in an atmosphere of mutual tolerance.'[14] While much remains to be done to achieve this goal – and each of the concepts used by Roy Jenkins can be and has been problematised by academics – it still stands out as one of the most positive statements by any British politician in this field. In many ways, some of them often not admitted, this kind of view remains the benchmark of UK policy across the various sectors. (It is, of course, also an expression of the kind of 'communitarianism' which is often contrasted as a British model against the 'French model' of the *citoyenneté* of the individual under the law.) Despite the endless ideological debates of the 1970s and 80s around overarching concepts of race and racism understood within class analyses of society, public policy, as Kepel correctly records,[15] has always tended to find its way back to something like the Jenkins model.

What has changed is the terms of reference of cultural identities. As the idealised solidarity of 'black Britain' came under increasing strain, especially in the wake of urban street clashes in 1981 and 1985, so religious identities began to play a more active role. Various factors contributed to this. One is likely to have been the gradual withdrawal of public funding from voluntary organisations instigated by the Thatcher government. I have argued elsewhere that this opened the field for those organisations which had quietly grown up within the communities themselves, often hardly noticed by those groups whose existence was predicated on public funding. Such 'hidden' organisations were often the mosque and other religious associations.[16] There were a number of high-profile local political incidents, in which the city of Bradford featured prominently, including the Rushdie affair.[17] The Rushdie affair itself, quite apart from whatever else it may have been, was a symptom of the impact which the generation of the children of the immigrants was

---

[14] Quoted by Kenan Malik, 'The trouble with multiculturalism' in *Spiked-politics*, 18 December 2001, on http://www.spiked-online.com/Articles/00000002D35E.htm, accessed 27 May 2005.

[15] See Gilles Kepel, *A l'ouest d'Allah*, Paris: Seuil, 1994, pp. 322–5.

[16] Jorgen S. Nielsen, 'Islam, musulmani e governo britannico locale e centrale: fluidità strutturale', in J. Waardenburg et al., *I musulmani nella società europea*, Turin: Fondazione Giovanni Agnelli, 1994, pp. 143–56.

[17] See Philip Lewis, *Islamic Britain: religion, politics and identity among British Muslims*, London: I. B. Tauris, 1994.

beginning to have. In the 1981 Census, the group of children aged 6–15 in households headed by someone of Pakistani or Bangladeshi ethnic origin was markedly more numerous than any of the older ten-year age categories.[18] Through the protests against Rushdie they, for the first time, brought into the public sphere their own perspectives of how they see themselves and their communities. This new process of self-identification is more complex and variable than had been assumed to be the case previously, whether among the governing authorities or among the holders of power in the immigrant generation.[19]

But there is also another dimension of the British environment which must play a role. In many ways Britain did not share the mainland European experience of the construction of the nation-state. 'Englishness', however it plays out, preserves a conscious memory of at least some of the component parts which went into its construction. This is most obvious in the marriage of Anglo-Saxon and Norman which is a theme in the popular tales of Robin Hood and which Sir Walter Scott romanticised in some of his novels in, among others, the figure of King Richard I. 'Britishness', in its turn, is a conscious conglomerate of the various so-called nations of the British Isles, even though its relationship to the component nations, above all the English, remains complex and mobile. While religion did play a role in the formation of some of the nations of Britain, especially in the centuries-long strife over the place of Roman Catholicism in the body politic, there was never the foundational identification of one state with one religion which was constituted elsewhere in the settlement of Westphalia in 1648.[20] In fact, only the following year the execution of King Charles I in the Cromwellian revolution signified the categorical rejection of such a settlement. Britain, and above all England, became multireligious. Indeed, Cromwell welcomed Jews back to the country some five centuries after they had been expelled by Edward I. Although Roy Jenkins did not primarily have the religious dimension of culture in mind when he made his 1967 statement,[21] it is certainly an argument worth considering that his

---

[18] Office of Population Censuses and Surveys, Census 1981: Country of Birth, Great Britain London: HMSO, 1983.

[19] This is discussed significantly in Gerd Baumann's *Contesting cultures: discourses of identity in multi-ethnic London*, Cambridge: Cambridge University Press, 1996.

[20] Adrian Hastings argues that the religious dimension of, in particular, English nationalism should be traced rather further back, well into the medieval period, and its origins are almost quintessentially Christian; see his *The construction of nationhood: ethnicity, religion and nationalism*, Cambridge: Cambridge University Press, 1997.

[21] In fact, he expressed some doubts about his own principle when reflecting on the Rushdie affair over two decades later.

concept of 'multicultural integration' flows much more easily out of this historical background than it does from the background of the post-Westphalian princely state.

Can one undertake similar exercises with reference to other European countries? Undoubtedly, although I will not attempt to do so in such detail here. But it may be worth just drawing attention to the examples of Austria and Spain, both countries where Islamic community structures have been afforded legal recognition within an existing system of recognised religion status.[22] Austria still has an extant memory of being at the centre of a multiethnic and multireligious empire: recognition of Islam in 1979 was legally a re-enactment of an earlier recognition which had taken place in 1912 within the terms of the 1867 Constitution of the Habsburg dual monarchy. The recognition of Islam in Spain in 1992 was not only a consequence of post-Franco moves to making the newly democratic state neutral. It was also part of a conscious attempt to reorientate Spanish national identity towards a more inclusive view of its past and thence towards a more integrated place in the Mediterranean region; the year of the recognition was not a coincidence, being the 500th anniversary of the fall of Granada and the end of Muslim rule in the Iberian Peninsula.

However, there is another side to this discussion, namely the Muslim one. While I take the view that the histories, policies and legal structures of the various European countries impose varying constraints on the way Muslim communities and individuals orient themselves, this in no way means that Muslims have their choices dictated by these structures. In fact, without going into details, it is fascinating to observe the many different ways in which Muslims are constructing their sense of self and community, their relations to the wider society both locally and nationally, and imagining the directions they want to mark out for the future. They range from positions close to full assimilation, with religion and personal piety becoming limited to the private space (a position apparently close to what Bassam Tibi sees as desirable), through various forms of collective visibility and public participation, to various forms of the assertive and even aggressive public separation characteristic of certain radical extremist movements, at the edge shading over into a

---

[22] The question of relations between the state and Islam is covered in Silvio Ferrari, 'The legal dimension', in Brigitte Maréchal, Stefano Allievi et al., *Muslims in the enlarged Europe: religion and society*, Leiden: Brill, 2003, pp. 219–54. For Spain, see further J. Mantecón Sancho, 'L'Islam en Espagne', in R. Potz and W. Wieshaider (eds.), *Islam and the European Union*, Leuven: Peeters, 2004, pp. 105–42. For Austria, see M. Schmied and W. Wieshaider, 'Islam and the European Union: the Austrian way', in ibid., pp. 199–217.

willingness to use violence. Some years ago, I suggested a typology to capture this varied spectrum:

1. One result of social marginalisation is a growth in youth activity on the margins of the law. In the last few years, Asian youth gangs, some mobilising Islamic symbols, have appeared in certain districts of the main cities. One might call this the *random retaliation* option.
2. A large proportion of young people, especially in city districts with major concentrations of Muslims, are finding security in a process of quiet retrenchment within the family and clan networks of the community. The price of this support is loyalty to the collective norms of the community in question. This option is one of *collective isolation.*
3. A not insignificant number of young people have been successful at school and have gone into further and higher education. They are taking an active part in the wider economy but are keeping this strictly separate from their home and community lives, an option which might be called *limited participation.*
4. Many young people have, since the Rushdie affair, become increasingly involved in organising Muslim activities. A majority of such organisations are campaigning at local and national level for social and political space. Internally little attention is being paid to the adaptation of ways of life to the surroundings. This could be termed the *high profile separation* option.
5. A smaller but growing tendency is for groups of young Muslims to seek simultaneously to develop new cultural ways of being Muslim while at the same time attempting to find ways of constructive participation in the wider society: a *high profile integration* option?
6. Finally there is a small minority who have adopted a programme, at least in propaganda if very seldom in implementation, of radical Islamist political action. This is the option of *aggressive action.*[23]

While most public attention is directed to how these various trends relate to the public sphere and how they express themselves in the context of the various political events of recent years, less is being paid to the internal debates taking place. Here there is a range of philosophical and theological discussions, which in many ways remind one of the debates which ranged among Islamic theologians in the formative periods of the eighth–eleventh centuries. In the process of trying to explore what it means to be an authentically practising Muslim believer in a

[23] J. S. Nielsen, 'Muslims in Europe: history revisited or a way forward?', *Islam and Christian-Muslim relations*, 8, 1997, 135–43.

contemporary European environment, young Muslims are again having to work out principles of faith, approaches to textual hermeneutics, the nature and function of Sharia, the role of religious authority for the believer and the community, and their place in the universal community of believers, the *ummah*. This debate is but a small part of a global Islamic debate, one in which European – and North American – Muslim experiences potentially have something significant to contribute.[24] The debate is wide and thorough and comprises not just the conservative or 'fundamentalist' voices which grab the headlines but significant 'liberal' and 'moderate' ones (most of whom would reject such labelling).[25]

But that internal debate regularly comes under enormous pressure from outside. The two-dimensional worldviews encouraged particularly from Washington in the aftermath of the attacks of 11 September 2001 ('if you are not with us, you are against us') have made differentiated discussions within the Muslim world extremely difficult. The growing number of voices seeking to develop Islamic ideas of democracy and human rights – precisely the 'liberals' and the 'moderates' just referred to – have been forced onto the defensive. I have personally heard some of them bemoan that it is now much more difficult to discuss democracy in open forum without being accused of surrendering to a US agenda. A similar tone started emerging from the UK government within a few weeks of the London bombs of 7 July 2005. It was quite clear, and was confirmed by leading politicians to be so, that the alleged bombers, who attacked the London transport system that day and those who carried out the failed bombings two weeks later, neither represented nor had the support of the vast majority of the Muslim community – in fact the identities of some of them were provided to the police by family and community members. Despite this, pressure was very soon put on the Muslim community as a whole to re-emphasise their commitment to being British in ways which implied that their opposition to some aspects of government policy, in particular UK involvement in the war in Iraq, was potentially tantamount to treason. The effect in both instances has been to reinforce traditional Western views of a monolithic, threatening

---

[24] This potential contribution of Western Muslim experience is the theme of Tariq Ramadan's *Western Muslims and the future of Islam*, Oxford: Oxford University Press, 2004.

[25] See, for example, on Egyptian thinkers, Raymond W. Baker, *Islam without fear: Egypt and the new Islamists*, Cambridge, MA: Harvard University Press, 2003; on government, Gudrun Krämer *Gottes Staat als Republik*, Baden-Baden: Nomos, 1999; and on religious minority rights, J. S. Nielsen, 'Contemporary discussions on religious minorities in Islam', in *Islam and Christian–Muslim Relations*, vol. 14, no. 3, pp. 325–35.

Islam, and perversely to weaken the traditional internal pluralism of Islamic thinking.

This takes us back to where I started. If the concept of 'Euro-Islam' can be prevented from falling into the kind of restricted narrow and prescriptive role, which threatens in some quarters, and an open and plural conception of European Islam can gain the upper hand, then there are more opportunities than restrictions. This opens opportunities for both Islam and for Europe. Tariq Ramadan advocates

> a new and constructive posture which relies on a fine comprehension of Islam's priorities, a clear vision of what is absolute, definitively fixed and what is subject to change and adaptation and, finally, an appropriate understanding of the Western environment. The objective being to shape a European-Islamic identity out of the crisis. Before disputing the secondary aspects of Islamic legislation, it is thus imperative to protect the five elements constituting *maqasid* [objectives of] *ash-Sharià*: namely, Religion, life, intellect, lineage and property.[26]

I am aware that Tariq Ramadan is, in some circles, a controversial figure – for reasons which I personally think have mostly to do with wilful misunderstanding of what he is trying to achieve and ignorance of the tradition out of which he comes.[27] But he is just the most well-known of a growing number of Muslim intellectuals in Europe who are seizing the opportunity of an open society to engage in the kind of profound rethinking of Islam which the encounter with modernity provokes.[28] For Europe, the situation we are currently living through provides an opportunity to escape from the sterile and too often destructive dimensions of the nationalist heritage. The response from the extreme right in, for example, Austria's local and regional elections and in the French regional and presidential elections, seems to indicate that they feel themselves under threat from such a development.

But the opportunity stretches further. Kevin Robins has used the term 'interrupted identities' to encapsulate the processes which take place when a culture is challenged to reinvigorate itself through the encounter with another culture. 'History is created out of cultures in relation and interaction: interrupting identities', says Robins.[29] Nezar

---

[26] Tariq Ramadan, *To be a European Muslim*, Markfield: The Islamic Foundation, 1999, p. 101.

[27] For more detail see my discussion in 'New centres and peripheries in European Islam?', in B. A. Roberson (ed.), *Shaping the current Islamic reformation*, London: Cass, 2003, pp. 64–81.

[28] In a discussion with young Islamist intellectuals in Jordan in 1995, I was asked by one what they might be able to learn from that much broader encounter with modernity which young Muslims in Europe were experiencing.

[29] Kevin Robins, 'Interrupting identities', in Stuart Hall and P. du Gay (eds.), *Questions of cultural identity*, London: Sage, 1996, p. 82.

AlSayyad and colleagues take this further in the context of discussing urban spaces, arguing that these 'borderlands' or 'third places' where cultures and traditions meet are no longer the ignored zones of tension and mingling between, for example, coloniser and colonised.[30] Relating this explicitly to the position of Muslims in Europe, he proposes

that borderlands are no longer fragments anchored between two fixed and well-defined places, and that sites of the in-between, such as the Third place, no longer simply occupy the margins of the periphery. I now believe that the most hybrid of places have moved firmly to the centre of the core . . . Muslim Europe may be the new but quintessential borderland.[31]

Given the rather Danish atmosphere to the beginning of this paper, I will conclude with a statement from the Danish writer Vilhelm Grønbech (1873–1948), who died long before the developments discussed here took place. It is quoted at the beginning of their conclusion by the four young Danish Muslims cited earlier:

It is probably something which is repeated everywhere, that the most fertile cultures come into existence where peoples meet. It is not the pure, unmixed populations which dominate history, but precisely those populations, where different peoples, different cultures and ideas have fused.[32]

Bibliography

AlSayyad, Nezar, (ed.), *Hybrid urbanism: on the identity discourse and the built environment*, Westport: Praeger, 2001.
  'Muslim Europe or Euro-Islam: on the discourses of identity and culture', in Nezar AlSayyad and Manuel Castells (eds.), *Muslim Europe or Euro-Islam: politics, culture and civilization in the age of globalization*, Lanham: Lexington, 2002.
Baker, Raymond W., *Islam without fear: Egypt and the new Islamists*, Cambridge, MA: Harvard University Press, 2003.
Baumann, Gerd, *Contesting cultures: discourses of identity in multi-ethnic London*, Cambridge: Cambridge University Press, 1996.
Ferrari, Silvio, 'The legal dimension', in Brigitte Maréchal, Stefano Allievi et al., *Muslims in the enlarged Europe: religion and society*, Leiden: Brill, 2003, pp. 219–54.

---

[30] Nezar AlSayyad (ed.), *Hybrid urbanism: on the identity discourse and the built environment*, Westport: Praeger, 2001, esp. pp. 1–18.
[31] Nezar AlSayyad, 'Muslim Europe or Euro-Islam: on the discourses of identity and culture', in AlSayyad and Castells, p. 28.
[32] Quoted in Mona Sheikh et al., p. 253.

Hastings, Adrian, *The construction of nationhood: ethnicity, religion and nationalism*, Cambridge: Cambridge University Press, 1997.

Holm, Adam, Michael Jarlner and Per M. Jespersen (eds.), *Islam i Danmark: tanker on en tredje vej*, Copenhagen: Gyldendal, 2002.

Kepel, Gilles, *A l'ouest d'Allah*, Paris: Seuil, 1994.

Krämer, Gudrun, *Gottes Staat als Republik*, Baden-Baden: Nomos, 1999.

Lewis, Philip, *Islamic Britain: religion, politics and identity among British Muslims*, London: I. B. Tauris, 1994.

Malik, Kenan, 'The trouble with multiculturalism' in *Spiked-politics*, 18 December 2001, on http://www.spiked-online.com/Articles/00000002D35E.htm, accessed 27 May 2005.

Maréchal, Brigitte, Stefano Allievi et al. (eds.), *Muslims in the enlarged Europe: religion and society*, Leiden: Brill, 2003.

Nielsen, Jorgen S., 'Contemporary discussions on religious minorities in Islam', in *Islam and Christian–Muslim Relations*, vol. 14, no. 3, pp. 325–35.

'Islam, musulmani e governo britannico locale e centrale: fluidità strutturale', in J. Waardenburg et al. (eds.), *I musulmani nella società europea*, Turin: Fondazione Giovanni Agnelli, 1994, pp. 143–56.

'Muslims in Europe: history revisited or a way forward?', *Islam and Christian–Muslim Relations*, vol. 8, 1997, pp. 135–43.

'New centres and peripheries in European Islam?', in B. A. Roberson (ed.), *Shaping the current Islamic reformation*, London: Cass, 2003, pp. 64–81.

Office of Population Censuses and Surveys, *Census 1981: Country of Birth, Great Britain*, London: HMSO, 1983.

Olesen, Asta (ed.), *Islam og undervisning I Danmark*, Århus: Århus Universitetsforlag, 1987.

Ramadan, Tariq, *To be a European Muslim*, Markfield: The Islamic Foundation, 1999.

Western Muslims and the future of Islam, Oxford: Oxford University Press, 2004.

Robins, Kevin, 'Interrupting identities', in Stuart Hall and P. du Gay (eds.), *Questions of cultural identity*, London: Sage, 1996.

Sancho, J. Mantecón, 'L'Islam en Espagne', in R. Potz and W. Wieshaider (eds.), *Islam and the European Union*, Leuven: Peeters, 2004, pp. 105–42.

Schmied, M. and W. Wieshaider, 'Islam and the European Union: the Austrian way', in R. Potz and W. Wieshaider (eds.), *Islam and the European Union*, Leuven: Peeters, 2004, pp. 199–217.

Sheikh, Mona, Fatih Alev, Babar Baig and Norman Malik (eds.), *Islam i bevægelse*, Copenhagen: Akademisk, 2003.

Simonsen, Jørgen Bæk, 'Globalization in reverse and the challenge of integration: Muslims in Denmark', in Y. Y. Haddad (ed.), *Muslims in the West: from Sojourners to Citizens*, New York: Oxford University Press, 2002, pp. 121–30.

Tibi, Bassam, *Im Schatten Allahs: der Islam und die Menschenrechte*, Munich: Piper, 1994.

'Les conditions d'un "euro-islam"', in Robert Bistolfi and François Zabbal (eds.), *Islams d'Europe: intégration ou insertion communautaire?* Paris: L'Aube, 1995, pp. 230–4.

'Muslim migrants in Europe: between Euro-Islam and ghettoization', in Nezar AlSayyad and Manuel Castells (eds.), *Muslim Europe or Euro-Islam: politics, culture and civilization in the age of globalization*, Lanham: Lexington, 2002, pp. 31–52.

4   Muslim identities in Europe: the snare of exceptionalism

Jocelyne Cesari

Muslims are currently the largest religious minority in western Europe. This presence of Islam in Europe is a direct consequence of the pathways of immigration from former western European colonies in Asia, Africa, and the Caribbean that opened up in the early 1960s. Since the official end of work-based immigration in 1974, the integration of such immigrant populations has become irreversible.[1] Concerns regarding integration are connected with an increasing number of policies on family reunification that contribute to a noticeable increase in family size 'within the Muslim communities in' Europe. In such a context, asserting one's Islamic faith becomes a major factor in population sedentarisation. In each country, this increasing visibility of Islam is at the origin of many questions, doubts, and often violent oppositions.

We no longer seek to grasp, as certain culturalist-based approaches have sought to do, the traditional attributes that define an individual or group essence. Our aim here is to understand the practices of differentiation used by individual Muslims in certain social circumstances. Identity is to be conceived not as a structure, but as a dynamic process. Accordingly, it is more relevant to talk about *identification* than identity, and it is important to emphasise the fact that the ways an individual defines him-/herself are both multidimensional and likely to evolve over time.

When studying religious practices and the formation of identities of European Muslims, one must take into account relationships of domination which tend to impose a reference framework that permanently places Islam and the West in opposition. More than any other religion today, the forms of identifying oneself as a Muslim are profoundly influenced by a narrative (active from the local to the international level)

---

[1] In 1974, the OPEC oil embargo created an economic crisis that justified the end of labour immigration and signalled a turning point in the European economy.

that circulates a whole series of images and stereotypes portraying Islam as religiously, culturally, and politically foreign.

This *does not mean*, however, that all acts or choices to be adopted by Muslims within this context are predictable. The goal of our approach is to examine what seems to be a gap between the racialisation of national discourses and the meta-discourse on Islam as an enemy, on the one hand, and the diversity and fluid nature of Muslims' attitudes, on the other. In other words, while studying the way that Muslims respond to a reference framework that is both imposed on them and based on a relationship of domination, we should neither assume that Muslims are prisoners of this framework, nor that they model themselves according to the identity that has been assigned to them. Although often considered an 'exceptional case' (i.e. operating according to rules of exceptionalism), Muslims are not always such an exception.

Research on Islam in Europe has not always managed to avoid the snare of exceptionalism. For example, when I first began researching in France in the mid-1980s, almost all Muslims in Europe were immigrants and existing knowledge about Muslims came primarily from the sociology of immigration. Such early research focused on the ways Muslims integrated into French society. In contemporary France, as in the rest of Europe, this key question remains. Is the integration process for Muslims similar to other immigrant experiences, or does the Islamic origin of the immigrants introduce something new and specific?[2] Still, sociologists specialising in immigration matters in France (and in Europe in general) have been inclined to downplay that aspect of an individual's identity related to his or her being a Muslim as less worthy of detailed analysis. Other factors (one's position in the economic market place, as well as social and political factors) continue to be seen as more important than religion for any explanation of the Muslim condition.

Conversely, scholars of Islam and political scientists of the Muslim world, as well as certain sociologists and anthropologists, emphasise the role of Islam itself as a system of norms and values. This second approach, often criticised for being too culturalist, runs the risk of becoming essentialist and ahistorical, a fact that has been underscored by researchers working in the tradition of Edward Said's *Orientalism*.[3] However, given that the question of an individual's Islamic identity has progressively moved to occupy a prominent position on the public stage,

[2] Frank Buijs and Jan Rath, *Muslims in Europe: the state of research*, Report for the Russel Sage Foundation, New York, 2003.
[3] E. Said, *Orientalism*, New York: Pantheon Book, 1978.

and because of the increased visibility of Muslim action and activity, the specifically religious component of integration has come to be, over the years, a legitimate subject for research in France and Europe. And, of course, the relevance of such research has increased in the post September 11 context.

We should note that political interest in Islam in the European context was strengthened in the 1980s in response to the increased domestic influence of political movements linked to Islam (the Algerian FIS, *Milli Görüş*, etc.) and to the greater proximity between European States and certain Muslim States such as Algeria, Morocco, Turkey and Pakistan. This political interest soon began to shape Islamic identities and research on Islam. Let us recall that the term 'Islamophobia' appeared four years before the terrorist attacks of 11 September 2001 in the context of British public debate on discrimination towards Muslims.[4]

European researchers have been attempting to establish a general interpretative framework to understand the religious condition of Muslims in such a context.[5] For example, many researchers in Europe consider that being a minority within a democratic and secularised environment entails a decisive element in the transformation of Muslims' practices and relationships with Islam. However, this approach often amounts only to a mere description of the modalities according to which Muslims adapt to their new context.[6] Another (and more innovative) approach aims to explore the modes of interaction between Muslim groups and different segments of Western societies. Such a process-based approach to identities means refusing to essentialise both the minority and the dominant culture and leads to an

---

[4] Runnymede Trust, *Islamophobia: a challenge for us all*, London: Runnymede Trust, 1997. See also J. Cesari (ed.), *Muslims in Western Europe after 9/11. Why the term islamophobia is more a predicament than an explanation*. Report of the European Commission, 2006.

[5] Felice Dassetto, *La construction de l'islam européen: Approche socio-anthropologique*, Paris: L'Harmattan, 1996; Jan Rath, R. Penninx, K. Groenendijk and A. Meyer, *Western Europe and its Islam: the social reaction to the institutionalization of 'new religion' in the Netherlands, Belgium and the United Kingdom*, Leiden: Brill, 2001.

[6] T. Gerholm and Y. G. Lithman (eds.), *The new islamic presence in Western Europe*, London: Mansell, 1988; B. Lewis and D. Schnapper (eds.), *Muslims in Europe*, London: Pinter, 1994; G. Nonneman, T. Niblock, and B. Szajkowski (eds.), *Muslim communities in the New Europe*, Ithaca, NY: Ithaca Press, 1996; W. A. R. Shadid and P. S. van Koningsveld (eds.), *The integration of Islam and Hinduism in Western Europe*, The Netherlands: Kampen, 1991; W. A. R. Shadid and P. S. Koningsveld, *Religious freedom and the position of Islam in Western Europe*, The Netherlands: Kampen, 1995; W. A. R. Shadid and P. S. Koningsveld, *Muslims in the margin: political responses to the presence of Islam in Western Europe*, The Netherlands: Kampen, 1996; S. Vertovec and C. Peach (eds.), *Islam in Europe: the politics of religion and community*, New York: St. Martin's Press, 1997; S. Vertovec and A. Rogers (eds.), *Muslim European youth: reproducing ethnicity, religion, culture*, London: Ashgate, 1998.

understanding of the social construction of Muslim communities within the dialectic formed between surroundings and group resources.[7]

The multiplicity of identities follows from the fact that these identities are distributed according to age, gender and socio-economic level. In the case of Muslim minorities, it is also useful to underline the following particular dimensions of identity construction: the meta-discourse on Islam; the influence of dominant cultural and political frameworks; the complex interaction between religion and ethnicity; the influence of global Islam; the state of collusion between religion, ethnicity and social marginality; and the challenge of a theological revival.

Meta-narratives about Islam

In order to study the ways Muslims define and experience their identity, it is necessary to take into account the frameworks and structures that are imposed by dominant meta-narratives about Islam. Certainly, the importance of the way an individual is viewed by others and the significance of *interaction* in identity formation in general are well known. Muslims in Europe, perhaps more than the members of any other religious group, are no longer in control of this interaction, and a discourse about Islam is imposed upon them – a discourse that spreads across all levels of society from the micro–local to the international.

In the post-September 11 context, both European and American Muslims have faced relentless correlations between *Islam*, seen as an international political threat, and *Muslims* in general (even those living in democratic nations, as has been shown by the hostile reactions that followed the attacks of 11 September 2001). This suggests the permanence of an essentialist approach to Islam and Muslims which is rooted in several centuries of confrontation between the Muslim world and Europe. What we profess to know about Islam is to a large extent the product of a vision constructed upon centuries of discord, as much political as religious. The mobile and paradoxical reality of Muslims, both

---

[7] Jocelyne Cesari, 'Muslim minorities in Europe: the silent revolution' in John Esposito and François Burgat (ed.), *Modernizing Islam: religion in the public sphere in the Middle East and in Europe*, Rutgers University Press, New Brunswick, NJ, 2003, pp. 11–15; see also www.euro-islam.info; our work also borrows much from a strain of research that accords prime importance to the dialectic process in the analysis of interactions between groups and cultures, notably when the recognition of one group by another group is at stake. See N. Sakai, 'Modernity and its critique: the problem of universalism and particularism' in H. Harootunian and M. Myoshi (eds.), *Postmodernism and Japan*, Durham, NC: Duke University Press, 1989, pp. 93–122; R. Sakamoto, 'Japan, hybridity, and the creation of colonialist discourse,' *Theory, Culture and Society*, vol. 13 no. 3, (1996), pp. 113–128. See also J. Cesari, *When Islam and democracy meet: Muslims in Europe and in the United States*, Palgrave, New York (2nd ed.), 2006.

inside and out – from their most private behaviour to their most public – tends to disappear under the weight of perceptions that have been progressively deposited over the centuries. These perceptions are constructed out of specific historical moments and encounters that permanently crystallise different, even contradictory, sets of images such as violence, heresy and debauchery, or sensuality, brutality and cruelty.[8] This discourse tends to play on the confrontation between Islam and the West and positions Islam as a problem or obstacle on the path towards modernisation. Muslims are thereby pressed to make adjustments, particularly since 11 September 2001. Of course, no ethnic or religious group escapes stereotyping when it encounters other groups. What seems specific in the case of Islam is: (a) the historical moment at which the same network of representations is invested with meaning, from the micro–local to the international level; and (b) the strengthening of the stereotype by certain forms of the scholarly tradition that have been built up around Islam.

The essentialist approach, as described and criticised by Edward Said in his *Orientalism*,[9] remains pervasive. It is remarkable to note that, since the 1980s, the tendency to consider Islam as a risk factor in international relations has been legitimised by perceptions deposited over centuries, perceptions which would seem very familiar to any eighteenth-century gentleman or *honnête homme*. The same recurring attributes are activated and reformulated by changes in international and domestic circumstances. It seems that the attacks of 11 September 2001 have reinforced this interpretation that considers Islam an inherent risk to security.

Islamic identities are constructed at the heart of these contexts. There is an interstitial space between the act of representation and the actual presence of the community. It is within this gap that Muslims can act. In such a situation, where the relationship between the dominating and dominated has so many consequences, three scenarios are possible: acceptance, avoidance, or resistance.[10] These three possible attitudes

---

[8] Many such perceptions descend from the tradition of orientalism. While the more conspicuous forms of orientalism have been profoundly modified by sociology, anthropology and political science, its more latent forms (the result of amassed representations) still continue to operate. Edward Said is thus correct in asserting that the orient and Islam only exist as topoi, the collection of references and sum of characteristics linked to the imagination. Within such an interpretation, supported by actual quotes from religious texts, Islam is always presented as a closed system, thus denying Muslims and Islamic society any capacity for change. Such interpretations are clearly motivated in part by the same ideology that has sought to justify all attempts at dominating these parts of the world since the nineteenth century.

[9] Said, *Orientalism*.

[10] Gerard A. Postiglione, *Ethnicity and American social theory*, Lanham: University Press of America, 1983, pp. 181–2.

subtend the multiplicity of discourses and actions in the name of Islam, whether they are oriented towards Muslims or non-Muslims. Acceptance means that a dominant discourse is accepted and is accompanied by cultural amnesia and a definite will to assimilate. This trend is marginal amongst immigrant Muslims. Avoidance refers to behaviours or discourses that attempt to separate Muslims as much as possible from the non-Muslim environment by developing, for example, a sectarian usage of Islamic religious beliefs. Resistance means refusing the status given to Islam within dominant discourses and politics. Resistance need not be violent: it can involve, for example, taking a view opposite to that of dominant narratives, and producing a voluminous apologetic literature. As for practices, certain forms of resistance involve what Erving Goffman calls 'contact terrorism'. This means using certain Islamic symbols linked to clothing or behaviour in order to play on the other's fear and repulsion. Resistance can also take on more radical forms, such as an inclination towards certain violent Islamic movements. This tendency is demonstrated by the cases of Khaled Kelkal, a French citizen (born in France to Algerian parents), who was involved in the GIA battle, and others such as John Reid the 'shoe bomber', who joined the *Al Qa'ida* movement. However, there also exist positive forms of resistance through which Muslims reappropriate for themselves elements of Islamic practice, based on personal commitment and faith while still 'keeping up with the times'. In other words, in order to understand the space between the act of representation and the actual presence of the Muslim communities in Europe we must ask in relation to Islam, who? says what? and where? One element affecting an array of responses is the diversity of dominant political and cultural frameworks.

The diversity of dominant political and cultural frameworks

The ethnic diversity of European Muslims is often (and very rightly) underlined, but it is also important to take into account the diversity of national contexts: the status of religion within different societies, the modes of acquiring nationality, the presence or lack of acknowledgment of multiculturalism, and the specific characteristics of each European country, all have a direct influence on the dynamics of the formation of Muslim minorities and on the construction of identities. Thus, the secularisation of social relationships makes less valid any form of social or cultural action based on religious values. In other words, the actions of European Muslims should be contextualised within the range of opportunities made possible by the dominant elements of each society. There are many examples of such identity formation that are closely related to the characteristics of the dominant culture and political framework. In this way, Britain's multicultural policies have impeded the specifically religious dynamics of the Muslim minority, at least before the time of the Rushdie affair. Similarly, the introduction of religious instruction within state schools in Germany and Austria has motivated Muslims to create textbooks with the goal of transmitting the Islamic tradition in a way that is adapted to their status as a minority.[11]

The importance of the link between the local and the national level within the dynamics of Muslims' identification must be highlighted. For example, the visibility of a new generation of Muslim leaders is being reinforced based on the validity of action that has appeared at the local level. In a similar vein, disputes at the local level feed national debate about Islam and vice-versa, according to subtle dialectics between the two levels of visibility and Islamic activity. Moreover, such disputes are often inserted in the global debate regarding the political role of Islam. For example, the lack of permission to build a mosque at Lodi in 2002 became a topic of national public debate in Italy and was used to justify resistance towards the construction of other mosques all over the country. Public discourse of this nature has only been fuelled by the international situation following 11 September 2001.[12]

Ethnicity versus religion

Individuals' identification with Islam appears in most cases to be an element of emerging ethnic communities. From Turkish immigrants in Germany to British Indians and Pakistanis, or even (to a certain extent) Moroccans living in France, Islam is a vital element in the orchestration of ethnic identity within European societies – especially for the first generations of immigrants. Simultaneously over the last decade, more 'transethnic' forms of Islamic religion have begun to develop.[13] For example, in Great Britain, a new generation of Muslim leaders has

---

[11] Sean Macloughin, 'Recognising Muslims: religion, ethnicity and identity politics' in J. Cesari (ed.), *Musulmans d'Europe*, Cemoti 33, 2002, pp. 43–57; Irka-Christin Mohr, 'Islamic instruction in Germany and Austria: a comparison of principles founded in religious thought' in J. Cesari (ed.), *Musulmans d'Europe*, Cemoti 33, 2002, pp. 149–67.

[12] Chantal Saint-Blancat and Ottavia Schmidt di Frieberg in J. Cesari (ed.), *Musulmans d'Europe*, Cemoti 33, 2002, p. 91–106.

[13] Transethnic refers to the use of Islamic references insisting upon a universal meaning of religious bonds and dismissing the importance of cultures and ethnicity in the relationships between Muslims.

started to emerge who articulate positions distant from the ethnicised and often isolationist Islam dominated by the early Indian and Pakistani immigrants (following the precepts of *Barelvis* and *Déobandis*).[14] Since the Rushdie affair in particular, these new leaders have opened a dialogue with the national government.

The emergence of a new generation of leaders within Islamic associations and religious movements is a phenomenon that is spreading all over Europe. In fact, this development is indicative of a specific social phenomenon, namely the acculturation of Islamic references to a secularised context. The existence in certain European countries of a third or even a fourth generation of Muslims means that versions of Islam detached from the ethnic and national identifications of the first generations (cultural references, language, behaviour, interactions with non-Muslims, etc.) are already well established. In other words, there now exists a French Islam, an English Islam, a Belgian Islam, etc. This acculturation is realised through a contradictory double movement: the privatisation of Islamic references and the increase in the collective practices of Islam.[15] While we must be careful to keep in mind the gap between the reality of Islamic practice and theological or intellectual discourse, daily concrete practices reveal an acculturation to the secularised context. This kind of 'homemade' and personalised version of Islam takes relativism into account (something which is not always reflected in even secular intellectual debate, especially in Europe).

Global Islam

Globalisation is a cultural process that favours the development of non-territorialised cultures and communities based on race, gender, religion, or even lifestyle. In this respect, Islam is a powerful element in identity formation, weaving together solidarity between various groups that are separated by the constraints of diverse nations, countries and cultures.

Over the past two decades, two different globalised forms of Islam have attracted an increasing number of followers in different parts of the Muslim world and beyond. One form includes theological and political movements that emphasise a universal link to the Community of

---

[14] The *Déobandis* are followers of a fundamentalist movement that appeared in India in 1866. They emphasise extensive knowledge of the *Hadith* (deeds and sayings of the prophet Muhammad) and reject the innovations of Sufi practices and saints. The *Barelvi*, founded by Ahmed Reza (1856–1921), also emphasise the figure of the Prophet, but they believe that the immortal souls of the Prophet and saints act as mediators between believers and God.

[15] See the section below: 'The challenge of theological revival'.

Believers (*Ummah*). This form includes movements such as the Muslim Brotherhood, the *Jamaat Al-Tabligh*, or the Wahabi doctrine. Today, the conditions for communication and the free movement of people/ ideas make the *Ummah* even more effective. Unlike Protestantism, where a diversification in interpretations of religious belief led to the founding of separate communities and the proliferation of sects, the unity of the *Ummah* as an imagined and constantly renewed community based on an understanding of a shared fate is maintained.

It is important to make a distinction at this point between radicalism and fundamentalism. While radicalism is manifested in groups that advocate the use of violence and reject any kind of compromise with non-Muslims and especially Westerners, fundamentalism may come in the form of the desire to believe in an Islam based on a direct relationship to the divinely revealed text. This desire is often the cause of people's decisions to join Salafi and Wahabi movements.[16] Members of these movements are thus fundamentalists, in the sense that they refer back to the sources of the religion, the Qur'an and the *Hadiths*. The return to the source texts can be conservative or puritan, as is shown by the growing success of the *Jamaat Al-Tabligh* and the fact that portions of the new generations find inspiration in schools of thought such as the one built around Sheik Al-Albani, a specialist in *Hadiths*.[17] This return to the divinely revealed sources can also give rise to more open-minded interpretations that are in touch with the social and political facts and issues of various European contexts.[18]

The other form of global Islam refers to diasporic communities that are based on solidarity beyond the boundaries of nations and culture and that are often labelled 'transnational networks'. These networks consist of non-governmental participants such as religious leaders, immigrants, entrepreneurs and intellectuals who develop bonds and identities that

---

[16] Historically the Muslim Brothers (founded 1928) and the Wahabi movement (created by Ibn Abdel Wahab (1730–1792) and became the official doctrine of the Saudian monarchy in 1924) are part of the *salafist* current. The institutional and political evolutions of these two trends have made the term '*salafist*' a synonym for conservatism connoting a 'reactionary stance,' most notably within the European context. Wahabism is hostile to all forms of intellectualism, religious establishment and even mysticism. However, this is not true of all trends based on a return to the word of the religious texts. Not all Muslim Brothers, for example, are originally anti-modern or anti-intellectual.

[17] Al-Albani was a sheik at the University of Medina who died in 1999.

[18] For example, Muslim actors in Europe inspired by the Muslim Brotherhood are at the forefront of negotiations for the recognition of Islam in the public space of various European countries. They are also concerned by the development of a specific jurisprudence taking into account the minority condition of Muslims in European democratic and secular societies. See J. Cesari, *When Islam and democracy meet: Muslims in Europe and in the US*, New York: Palgrave, 2004.

transcend the borders of nation-states. To achieve transnational status, a group must possess three main traits: (1) awareness of an ethnic or cultural identity, (2) establishment of group organisations across different nations, (3) development of relations – whether monetary, political or even imaginary – linking people in different countries.[19]

The various forms of virtual Islam are part of this globalised Islam. 'Electronic religiosity' is contributing to the global expansion of Islam through the circulation of audio and videotapes, the broadcasting of independent television satellite shows, and (most significant of all) the creation of websites. In particular, bulletin boards, chat rooms and discussion forums on the internet are promoting alternative and even contradictory understandings of Islam where only nationally based understandings previously existed. In so doing, these websites have a significant impact on Islamic discourse and help break up the monopoly of control over sacred issues possessed by traditional religious authorities.[20]

Mobile dynamics thus lead to the autonomy of social groups in the field of international relations. Often, these social groups do not strive to assert themselves as collective participants in the transnational arena; instead, private interests push them into this unintended role. Family reunions, marriage arrangements and business activities, for example, are usually motivated by individual or family interests; yet, these activities often entail international mobility. Private decisions affect not only visiting rights, family groupings and monetary flows, but also religious, linguistic and cultural models, indirectly producing a collective result on the international scene.

A glimpse into the complex interaction of local, national and international groupings characterising Islam in Europe reveals some of the shortfalls of current scholarship on this subject. Because of the importance of transnational networks for Western Muslim communities, any

---

[19] Diaspora is one form of deterritorialised identity that links dispersed people with their country of origin. In the case of Muslims, even if their bond with their country of origin is strong, it is challenged by a broader solidarity with the Muslim world at large. See Sheffer Gabi, 'Whither the study of ethnic diasporas? Some theoretical, definitional, analytical and comparative considerations', in George Prevelakis (ed.), *The networks of diasporas*, Paris: L'Harmattan, 1996, pp. 37–46; Robin Cohen, *Global diasporas: an introduction*, Seattle: University of Washington Press, 1997.

[20] It would be misleading, however, to consider on-line Islam as an exclusive indicator of a new democratic public space without paying attention to specific social changes within specific Muslim contexts. In other words, to assess accurately what Muslim websites are accomplishing in terms of knowledge, perspective and affiliation, one must investigate how electronic religiosity is resonating with significant social changes in general. See Peter Mandaville, 'Information technology and the changing boundaries of European Islam', in Felice Dassetto (ed.), *Paroles d'Islam: individus, sociétés et discours dans l'Islam européen contemporain*, Paris: Maisonneuve et Larose, 2000, p. 281–97.

analysis that stresses Muslims' obligations to the host society – excluding international influences – fails to provide a balanced view. The adaptation of Islam to the democratic context is a two-dimensional activity, involving both the identification with global or transnational forms of Islam and with the national cultures of different host countries. As explained below, one major factor influencing adjustment to the national cultures is the socio-economic position in which Muslims find themselves in the European societies.

Islam, ethnicity and poverty: a set of 'dangerous liaisons'

The socio-economic condition of European Muslims is one of great fragility. The unemployment rate for immigrant Muslims is, as a general rule, higher than the national average: e.g. 31% and 24% for Moroccans and Turks respectively in the Netherlands. In 1995, INED (the French National Demographics Institute) showed that with equal levels of education, unemployment was twice as high for youth from Muslim immigrant backgrounds as for youth from non-Muslim immigrant backgrounds and the situation has not improved since then.[21] In this respect, the situation of Muslims in Great Britain is particularly critical. Those persons originating from Bangladesh and Pakistan have a level of unemployment three times higher than that of the minority communities considered to be the most disadvantaged. In British inner cities, almost half of all Bangladeshi men and women are unemployed. This marginality is passed on to the generation born and educated in Great Britain: in 2004, the unemployment rate (13%) was the highest for male Muslims and the highest for females as well (18%). This disadvantage is not limited to jobs requiring only basic qualifications, but also concerns high-profile domains such as medicine and education.

This socio-economic marginality is most often accompanied by residential segregation. Data from the British census shows that Pakistani immigrants tend to live in the most dilapidated or unhealthy housing conditions; ethnic concentration per residential area or per residence is also a factor that must be taken into consideration in the inner cities of the United Kingdom and Germany, as well as in France's poorer suburbs.

---

[21] Felice Dassetto, B. Maréchal and J. Nielsen (eds.), *Convergences musulmanes, aspects contemporains de la présence musulmane dans l'Europe élargie*, Louvain La Neuve: Academia Bruylant, 2001. A report of 2002 from the Consil Economique et Social describes discrimination practices on the job market.

Such a situation of relegation has important consequences for Islam in Europe. The temptation within the realm of politics is to associate Islam with poverty and to consider (although without any open acknowledgment of this) that the former is the cause of the latter. On the Muslims' side, there is a tendency to use Islam in a defensive or reactive way. Ethnicity thus becomes a trap when a collusion occurs between ethnicity, religion and poverty. This trap can in some situations lead to riots or a state of social unrest as has recurrently been the case in England where a team of researchers on community cohesion, established under the auspices of the Home Office, led an inquiry in the towns of Oldham, Burnley, Southall, Birmingham and Leicester where riots broke out in the spring of 2001. The results, published on 11 December 2001, are alarming.[22] They show whole groups withdrawn from society, experiencing an immense feeling of frustration, and faced with poverty and a lack of equal opportunities. 'You are the only white person I shall meet today,' said one Pakistani in Bradford who was interviewed for the report. Whether in the domain of housing, employment, education, or social services, the report describes an England segregated according to closely related factors of race and religion. The predominant anti-Muslim racism in British society is responded to by withdrawal and a reactive use of Islam. There is a marked lack of communication between ethnic groups and local political milieus, particularly concerning delicate questions of culture, race and religion. The British situation is reminiscent of that of black American Muslims as Islam has become an element that accentuates separatism.

Although similar levels of segregation are not reached, the ethnic perception of social differences is also pervasive within the urban space of France, Germany and Holland. In the case of France, this takes the form of concentrating the poorest populations (a majority of Muslims) in the suburbs. Ethnicity generally corresponds to a way of defining oneself or being defined by others, as Arab, Moroccan, or Muslim, based on factors that allow differentiation (facial features, religion) without being systematically realised by culturally specific behaviour.

The correlation between social problems and Islam can be cited as one reason for the political success of movements on the extreme right, not only in France (with the Front National's marked advance during the first round of the presidential elections on 28 April 2002), but also in

---

[22] Community cohesion, A Report of the Independent Review Team, Home Office, December 2001.

Belgium, Austria, and even Holland.[23] Indeed, the collusion between Islam and poverty accentuates the validity of hypotheses concerning the incompatibility of cultures and the threat constituted by the settling of Islam in the West.

One of the consequences of 11 September 2001 has been the intensification of stigma via the knotting together of Islam, the poor suburbs and terrorism. This and subsequent terrorist attacks have indeed hardened the discourse on immigration (in Austria, Denmark, Germany, Greece, Italy and Portugal) and security. The antiterrorist law ratified by George Bush on 26 October 2001 has been followed by comparable initiatives in Europe. In Great Britain, a law on antiterrorism, crime and security issues was passed on 14 December 2001 – giving rise to an intense debate on the restriction of public freedom: the law increases the power of the police in matters of collecting information on and monitoring of citizens. In Germany, two similar laws were introduced (one on 8 December, the second on 20 December, 2001). They increase both the funds available to police forces and their powers of investigation. Moreover, these new laws planned to place armed security agents in German planes and to review the privileged public corporation status of religious organisations.

The security debate has been subverted by the events of September 11 and by efforts to develop counter-terrorist measures. This much is evident in the French law promulgated on 15 November 2001. This law addressed security issues in daily life, but it also included a whole series of clauses that amalgamated interior (i.e. national) security, crime and terrorism; such actions combining approaches to terrorism and local crime increasingly ostracise Muslim youth living in the poor suburbs.[24] It is still too early to measure the consequences of these laws on the religious behaviour of Muslims in Europe, but it is very likely that they will result in an increase in the reactive and defensive use of Islam.[25]

---

[23] In March 2002, an openly xenophobic and anti-Islamic party led by Pim Fortuyn emerged in the parliamentary elections, and to general surprise, won a majority of votes in Rotterdam. The party leader was murdered under mysterious circumstances on 6 May 2002. Despite this loss, the party arrived in second place behind the Christian-Democrat party during the parliamentary elections of 15 May 2002, taking 26 out of 150 seats in the Houses of Parliament.

[24] Two measures in particular show no relationship with important crime issues or terrorism. The first concerns the maintenance of quiet in the entry halls of large apartment buildings, and the second villainises people who 'regularly' do not purchase a valid ticket when using public transport.

[25] The integration of Muslims in Europe in the Aftermath of 9/11, NOCRIME Conference, Paris: February 3, 2003 (see www.euro-islam.info).

The challenge of theological revival

Regarding the religious practices of Islam and the 'Europeanisation' of Islam, we might speak in terms of two phenomena that follow parallel paths. We have noted that ethnicity often plays a more important role than religion in the definition of Islamic identities. However, there also exists a scenario in which the relationship to Islam takes precedence over ethnic identities.

The dominant mode found within European Muslim populations is an attempt to reconcile a maximum amount of individual freedom with belief in a more or less well-defined form of transcendence that can be lived according to the constraints of one's own era (at least via observance of key rites of passage: circumcision, marriage and burial). People who follow such a mode will define themselves as 'non-practising believers'. Many such believers who do not really practise also do not reject the ethnic Islam which they inherited from their parents and which forms them within a festive and traditional relationship to Islam. They generally have little knowledge of the Islamic tradition or the rituals it prescribes. Most in this category will not have received any instruction in the Qur'an, either within or beyond the family (religious schools, etc.). In such a context, Islam means faithfulness to one's group of origin and implies no real feelings of belief or piety. This kind of loose identification with Islam is present in both the middle and upper social classes.

For those who defend Islam as a form of identity, the term 'Islam' is associated with ritual-like moments in family life, most notably the celebration of special feast days (for example *Aïd-El-Kebir*); such celebrations imply a break in the surrounding space and time. Furthermore, the word is associated with the respect due to parental beliefs and practices – although it does not imply the same conformism amongst those who show this respect. For these Muslims, Islam is conceived of as a cultural heritage inscribed within family traditions and behaviours linking them to their family's country or area of origin. In this way, Muslim identification operates as a 'marker' revealing cultural affiliation – thereby making Islam more a matter of culture than of religion.

On the other hand, a small minority of Muslims form a second group that is defined by a strict demand for respect of Islamic prescriptions. Religion in this case is invested in as an orthopraxis, i.e. as a concern for respecting religious prescriptions to the letter, and this group attempts to embody them in daily life. Identification with Islam offers the individual direct access to daily reality and provides a framework that s/he can use to structure life: the world can be sectioned off into the 'pure' and the 'impure', and all acts can be categorised according to the degree to which they are lawful or unlawful. All available evidence describes this behavioural conformity as a function of Islamic prescriptions (whether on the topic of food, clothing, or ritual acts).

Muslims in this second group are often involved in an individual search that takes the form of learning classical Arabic (a language which most Muslim children in the West do not understand); they begin active investigation of the divinely revealed texts, and they read general works on the founding and tradition of Islam (for the most part in translations into the language of the host country). The main European-language books that are available in almost all bookstores offer explanations of the pillars of Islam and prescriptions in different domains of life (social, economic, cultural, educational, etc.); they include biographies of the Prophet and tell of the exemplary lives of certain famous Companions; and they address such subjects as the status of women and the relationship between Islam and science.

The Europeanisation of Islam is thus built upon a paradox. The democratic context promotes a diversification of religious practices marked by the seal of individualisation and secularisation. However, given the lack of religious authorities and sufficient places for people to learn about Islam, the Islam that is learned about is still, in the majority of cases, dominated by the conservative trends of the Muslim world. Europe has become a chosen land for fundamentalist movements dominated by Saudi Wahabism and other trends grouped together as *salafist*. The growth of such groups can be explained by the fact that they are capable of quickly supplying a basic education in Islam to those who are not only lacking real knowledge on the subject, but who also lack the means to gain access to broader information. Where formal education is dispersed, it tends to be conservative and to promote a withdrawal from and rejection of the non-Muslim environment – especially amongst the most fragile layers of Muslim youth. When collusion occurs between Islam and marginality, the trend is to identify oneself with Islam in reaction to hostility or the underrating of one's surroundings. Of course, destructive use of the Islamic message does exist and is evident in the involvement of young European Muslims with *Al Qa'ida* and the attacks of 11 September 2001 in the United States as well as the Madrid bombing in 2004, the murder of Dutch film-maker Theo Van Gogh in 2004, and the London bombings of 2005. We must investigate the meaning of such commitments to a theology of hatred that is not always limited to the poorest members of society and is more specifically a European phenomenon. Explanations that rely upon nihilism or humiliation are insufficient.[26]

Alongside this radical and destructive trend, there is another unprecedented and opposing conception of Islam being formed: this Islam offers a source of morality and education while extolling the logic of individual choice (i.e. free will) and breaking away from the ethnicisation of religion. These European Muslims advocate an individual logic for decision-making that fits well with the increasing subjectivisation of religious affiliation. Within this logic, it is not enough to believe and to practise one's religion because one was born into a given tradition or belief system. It is necessary, rather, to express one's individuality and give personal meaning to the divinely revealed message by making a choice to be a practising believer. This results in the individual making his/her distance from his/her family – a move justified by the perception that the parents do not seem to understand what 'real' Islam is and that they have no 'true knowledge' but act only under the influence of customs and superstitions linked to their culture. This well-informed and logical search for a universal Islam highlights the unprecedented experience of reconstructing a religious tradition within the European context. It is important to emphasise at the same time the extreme difficulty of this process, as it often requires difficult ruptures with the family milieu, as well as the adaptation of elements of the Muslim tradition to the context of the Muslim community's minority status.[27]

Because of the increasing deterritorialisation of religious references, a gulf has been growing between fundamentalists and modernists regarding the interpretation of the Islamic tradition.[28] One fundamental

---

[26] Olivier Roy, *L'Islam mondialisé*, Paris: Seuil, 2002.

[27] These modes of identification with the Islamic tradition are also very visible (in different ways) in American society. However, we can observe that given the greater importance of the elite within American society, intellectual output is also more substantial there than in Europe. There is, in particular, one current that is critical of the emerging Islamic tradition. Taking a hermeneutic approach, it attempts to produce interpretations that question the traditional outlook on certain points: the relationship with non-Muslims, the relationship with secularism, and in particular the status of women. The question of the status of women is a key element in the divergence between modernist and conservative approaches. With one or two exceptions, the most vocal supporters of modernism have been in the United States (Khaled Abou El Fadl, Farid Esack Fazlur Rahman, Amina Wadud, etc). See Khaled Abou El-Fadl, *And God knows his soldiers: the authoritative and authoritarian in Islamic discourses*, Lanham, MD: University Press of America, 2001; Farid Esack, *Qur'an, liberation and theology: essays on liberative elements in Islam*, New Dehli, India: Sterling Publishers Ltd, 1990; Fazlur Rahman, *Islam and modernity: transformation of an intellectual tradition*, Chicago: The University of Chicago Press, 1982; Amina Wadud, *Qur'an and women*, Kuala Lampur, Malaysia: Penerbit Fajar Bakti Sdn Bhd, 1992.

[28] Fundamentalists as represented by Wahabism or the *Tabligh* movement recommend a return to the divinely revealed text in order to apply the principles of the Qur'an and the

distinction among Muslims and the way they relate to the European context will concern the status of the Islamic tradition. Muslims clearly follow two different ways of dealing with the revealed text and its interpretation: for one group it is an absolute that must be wholly accepted and never questioned, while for the other, still a minority, it is questionable and available for historical and hermeneutical critique. Such a polarised attitude goes hand in hand with an acceptance of the relativism and pluralism that are linked with a democratic and secular context. The current climate of Islamophobia in Europe does not facilitate the acceptation of such a relativism, and it is probable that tensions over religious and cultural issues in Europe will increase, thereby reinforcing the unity of Muslims around the perceived cause of their discrimination – their religious affiliation.

Bibliography

Buijs, Frank and Jan Rath, *Muslims in Europe: the state of research*, Report for the Russel Sage Foundation, New York, 2003.

Cesari, Jocelyne, 'Muslim minorities in Europe: the silent revolution', in John Esposito and François Burgat (eds.), *Modernizing Islam: religion in the public sphere in the Middle East and in Europe*, New Brunswick, NJ: Rutgers University Press, New Brunswick, NJ, 2003, pp. 11–25.

When Islam and democracy meet: Muslims in Europe and in the US, New York: Palgrave, 2004.

Cesari, Jocelyne and Jean McLoughlin, *European Muslims and the secular state*, London: Ashgate, 2005.

'The hybrid and globalized Islam of Europe', in (eds.) Yunas Samad and Kasturi Sen, *Islam in the European Union: transnationalism, youth, and the war on terror*, Oxford: Oxford University Press, 2007, pp. 108–22.

Cohen, Robin, *Global diasporas: an introduction*, Seattle: University of Washington Press, 1997.

Sunnah in daily life. They refuse any form of adapting Islamic principles to the modern world and to its culture. Several extremely varied currents exist, which range from the refusal of politics (e.g. *Tabligh*) to radicalisation (e.g. the Taliban or *Al-Qa'ida*). Alternately, there is a current of thought that recommends a return to the divinely revealed texts but that does not reject contemporary surroundings or modernity. This latter current is often referred to as reformist. I, however, prefer the term modernist, given its explicit objective of returning to the religious texts in order to find solutions to political and social problems of the time, as well as its explicit reflection on the philosophical principles of modernity. (This form of modernism should not be confused with the first vintage of modernists who recommended that the colonially dominated Muslim world should abandon Islamic principles in favour of a form of modernisation without God, following the Western model.) There are obviously significant differences between the founders of the Muslim Brotherhood, Hassan El Banna and Mohamed Iqbal, and Ali Shariati or Rached Ghannouchi.

Community cohesion, A Report of the Independent Review Team, Home Office, December 2001.

Dassetto, Felice, *La construction de l'islam européen: approche socio-anthropologique*, Paris: L'Harmattan, 1996.

Dassetto, Felice., B. Maréchal, and J. Nielsen (eds.), *Convergences musulmanes, aspects contemporains de la présence musulmane dans l'Europe élargie*, Louvain La Neuve: Academia Bruylant, 2001.

El-Fadl, Khaled Abou, *And God knows his soldiers: the authoritative and authoritarian in Islamic discourses*, Lanham, MD: University Press of America, 2001.

Esack, Farid, *Qur'an, liberation and theology: essays on liberative elements in Islam*, New Dehli, India: Sterling Publishers Ltd, 1990.

Gabi, Sheffer, 'Whither the study of ethnic diasporas? Some theoretical, definitional, analytical and comparative considerations', in George Prevelakis (ed.), *The networks of diasporas*, Paris: L'Harmattan, 1996.

Gerholm, T. and Y. G. Lithman (eds.), *The new Islamic presence in Western Europe*, London: Mansell, 1988.

The integration of Muslims in Europe in the aftermath of 9/11, NOCRIME Conference, Paris: February 3, 2003.

Lewis, B. and D. Schnapper (eds.), *Muslims in Europe*, London: Pinter, 1994.

Macloughin, Sean, 'Recognising Muslims: religion, ethnicity and identity politics' in Jocelyne Cesari (ed.), *Musulmans d'Europe*, Cemoti 33, 2002, 43–57.

Mandaville, Peter, 'Information technology and the changing boundaries of European Islam', in F. Dassetto (ed.), *Paroles d'Islam: individus, sociétés et discours dans l'islam européen contemporain*, Paris: Maisonneuve et Larose, 2000.

Mohr, Irka-Christin, 'Islamic instruction in Germany and Austria: a comparison of principles founded in religious thought', in Jocelyne Cesari (ed.), *Musulmans d'Europe*, Cemoti 33, 2002, 149–67.

'Network of Comparative Research on Islam and Muslims in Europe,' NOCRIME, http://www.nocrime.org.

Nonneman, G., T. Niblock, and B. Szajkowski (eds.), *Muslim communities in the New Europe*, Ithaca, NY: Ithaca Press, 1996.

Postiglione, Gerard A., *Ethnicity and American social theory*, Lanham: University Press of America, 1983.

Rahman, Fazlur, *Islam and modernity: transformation of an intellectual tradition*, Chicago: The University of Chicago Press, 1982.

Rath, Jan, R. Penninx, K. Groenendijk, and A. Meyer, *Western Europe and its Islam: the social reaction to the institutionalization of 'new religion' in the Netherlands, Belgium and the United Kingdom*, Leiden: Brill, 2001.

Roy, Olivier, *L'Islam mondialisé*, Paris: Seuil, 2002.

Runnymede Trust, *Islamophobia: a challenge for us all*, London: Runnymede Trust, 1997.

Said, E., *Orientalism*, New York: Pantheon Book, 1978.

Saint-Blancat, Chantal and Ottavia Schmidt di Frieberg in Jocelyne Cesari (ed.), *Musulmans d'Europe*, Cemoti 33, 2002, 91–106.

Sakai, N., 'Modernity and its critique: the problem of universalism and particularism', in H. Harootunian and M. Myoshi (eds.), *Postmodernism and Japan*, Durham, NC: Duke University Press, 1989, pp. 93–122.

Sakamoto, R., 'Japan, hybridity, and the creation of colonialist discourse', *Theory, Culture and Society*, vol. 13, no. 3, 1996, pp. 113–28.

Shadid, W. A. R. and P. S. van Koningsveld (eds.), *The integration of Islam and Hinduism in Western Europe*, The Netherlands: Kampen, 1991.

Religious freedom and the position of Islam in Western Europe, The Netherlands: Kampen, 1995.

Muslims in the margin: political responses to the presence of Islam in Western Europe, The Netherlands: Kampen, 1996.

Vertovec, S. and C. Peach (eds.), *Islam in Europe: The politics of religion and community*, New York: St. Martin's Press, 1997.

Vertovec, S. and A. Rogers (eds.), *Muslim European youth: reproducing ethnicity, religion, culture*, London: Ashgate, 1998.

Wadud, Amina, *Qur'an and women*, Kuala Lampur, Malaysia: Penerbit Fajar Bakti Sdn Bhd., 1992.

5 From exile to diaspora: the development of transnational Islam in Europe

Werner Schiffauer

Islam in Europe faces the challenge of defining a role for Islam outside the classic Islamic countries, the *dar al Islam*. This means resituating Islam in three respects: with reference to the country of immigration, to the country of origin, and to global Islam. Situating Islam in the immigration society and in Europe in particular, is complicated by two distinctive features. On the one hand, there is a long tradition (nurtured again and again by both sides) of situating oneself in a structure of alterity, i.e. posing an antagonistic relationship between a purportedly 'Islamic' and a purportedly 'Judeo-Christian' value system. On the other hand, the layers of society supporting Islam are for the most part worker migrants and their descendants. They are newcomers to Europe who assumed their position at the bottom of the professional ladder and slowly worked their way up over generations. Thus, Islam is not only the other religion per se, it was also often the religion of the worker, of the *underclass*, the outsider, and the ghetto-dweller. These two aspects distinguish the situation of Islam in Europe from its situation in other regions where Islam is in the minority.

Secondly, one must establish a reference to the country of origin. The country of origin, and the role religion plays in it, are viewed from the outside and are projected onto the screen of differences to the society of immigration. Things which are not questioned in the home country because they are well established by tradition and on-going practice lose their self-evident character. Thirdly, a new reference to global Islam develops. At least in the countries of the Near and Middle East, there exists an ethnocentric, conditioned and little-considered identification between nation and Islam. While there is a well-established presence of Islam outside the Arab or Turkish nations, being Muslim and Arab-ness or Turkish-ness, respectively, have often been identified with one another. Such linkages begin to disintegrate with migration: in Europe, one is identified as a Muslim and held responsible for events in the entire

Islamic world. One must explain one's positions on corporal punishment, the veil and September 11 even when these phenomena play no role in one's own practice of Islam or in one's country of origin.

Corresponding to the diversity of its references, the Islam being established in Europe also provides extremely diverse images of itself. Attempts to situate itself have given rise to a number of solutions. Indeed, as demonstrated also in the present volume, Islam does not speak with one, but with many voices.[1] However, it is time to take another step beyond the customary (and in the meantime somewhat boring) detection of plural identity or multivocality. Indeed, the diverse voices and positions developing do not stand beside each other without connection, but refer to, supplement, or contradict one another. For this reason alone, they cannot ignore one another because, as Zygmunt Bauman has pointed out, the majority society views them as a collective person, as a community of shared responsibility. They are held accountable for one another. Since the statements or deeds of individual Islamic communities threaten to reflect back on all other Muslims, they must take a position, or even distance themselves, as the case may be. This becomes particularly clear with extreme occurrences, such as the book burning in Bradford or September 11, but it also applies in less dramatic cases. Because this is so, these many voices constitute a place of debates, or fields of discourse. These fields of discourse can be analysed by identifying controversial key issues and describing the constellation of positions derived from them.

This text is concerned with the debates about situating Islam in Europe. It refers in particular to Turkish immigrants in Germany as an example, though the patterns identified here may be found in Muslim communities throughout Europe. The thesis is that the first generation's debate focused on other points, had other themes, and led to other group constellations than did the second generation's debate. In a first step I will examine the attempts by the first generation to define an 'Islam in exile'. For this generation, Europe was *gurbet*, or foreign. The factions that developed reflected perceptions of the role that Islam should play in Turkey. Even if this Islam was Turkey-oriented, it clearly distinguished itself from Turkish Islam, above all in terms of the pointed bitterness with which the factions confronted each other. I will then turn to diaspora Islam which is currently emerging among second-generation immigrants. The debates in the second generation

---

[1] On the promotion of polyphonic anthropology, see, among others, J. Clifford, 'On ethnographic allegory', in J. Clifford and George E. Marcus (eds.), *Writing culture. The poetics and politics of ethnography*, Berkeley: University of California Press, 98–121.

confront the necessity 'to come to terms with the new cultures they inhabit, without simply assimilating to them and losing their identities completely'.[2] I want to demonstrate that faction-building arises in this second generation's grappling with the problem of recognition in the host society similar to that typical of other diaspora communities: namely, producing wings with ultra-orthodox, orthodox and individualised positions. Herein lies one of the differences between the present work and that of such authors as Hall, Bhabha, Clifford and Gilroy, to whom, as will become clear, I otherwise owe a great deal. They see the core of diaspora identity in hybridity and view ethnic or religious fundamentalism as a regrettable slip-up. I, on the contrary, view the coexistence of these wings as an almost essential characteristic of diaspora identity.

A theoretical note

My theoretical interest is to draw on the important insights developed on the relationship between power and identity in the discussion of post-colonialism and to render them fruitful for an understanding of the development of Islam in Europe amongst the second and third generation of immigrants. This entails more than applying a theory to a new field. It is indeed not by accident that Islam has up to now been handled as a sort of stepchild in the discussion of diaspora. This neglect is connected with a frequent confusion of normative and empirical content which is in turn a result of the theory's political emphasis. For many theoreticians of post-colonialism, the breaks, complex schisms, distractions, alienation, etc. characteristic of the diaspora situation seemed to provide a chance to overcome the traps of that subject-focus Foucault analysed. The diaspora offered a chance for a creative, cosmopolitan existence, and thus an opportunity to emancipate oneself. The Afro-Caribbean diaspora became in this regard a favourite child; it produced forms of protest in which the European Left could recognise itself, because of the proximity between them. Academics influenced by the student movement could project themselves into it as something they could be enthusiastic about from a leftist revolutionary perspective. The result was a systematic ethnocentric bias of post-colonial theory.

This bias becomes especially clear in the treatment of the culture developed among Muslim immigrants. This diaspora culture was no less radical than that of the Caribbean immigrants. But it was clear that Islamic forms of protest were not those that the European Left associated

---

[2] S. Hall, 'The question of cultural identity', in Stuart Hall, David Held and Tony McGrew (eds.), *Modernity and its futures*, Cambridge: Polity Press 1992, p. 310.

with emancipation. An exemplary demonstration of this can be made with reference to the role Paul Gilroy ascribes to the staging of bodiliness in the protest culture:

The body has become, in various ways, a cultural locus of resistance and desires. A sense of the body's place in the natural world can provide, for example, a social ecology and an alternative rationality that articulates a cultural and moral challenge to the exploitation and domination of the 'nature within us and without us'.[3]

All of this can be precisely applied to the politics of veiling. Yet, it was clearly not *this* form of body politics about which Gilroy spoke so enthusiastically.

Turning to Islamic forms of protest can help overcome the ethno-centric bias of post-colonial theory. It can contribute to a separation of empirical content from normative valuations and thus lead to a more precise empirical analysis. A comparative approach allows for distance and promotes a certain sobriety. The following is based on material collected during a span of over twenty years, mainly in the study of the Turkish diaspora in Germany. However, a recently completed com-parative study[4] shows that numerous insights can, with certain restric-tions, also be applied to other European countries.

Islam in exile

The key term for understanding first-generation migrants' religious sen-timents is the word *gurbet*, or foreign.[5] The experience of foreignness has several facets. One is fear of self-loss. The migrant, who is often single, moves into a space in which no one knows him or her. Often used to a high measure of social control, the migrant suddenly finds him or herself in a realm in which social control is practically non-existent. This often leads to feelings of disorientation. Among first-generation migrants, stories circulated about Turkish workers who had 'gone to the dogs' in Germany (i.e. had relationships with women, become alcoholics, and thus lost their perspective on life). Islam offered a certain stable point

---

[3] P. Gilroy, 'Urban social movements, "race" and community', in Patrick Williams and Laura Chrisman (eds.), *Colonial discourse and post-colonial theory. A reader*, Hemel Hempstead: Harvester, 1993, p. 407.

[4] W. Schiffauer, Gerd Baumann, Riva Kastoryano, and Steven Vertovec (eds.), *Civil enculturation. nation-state, school and ethnic difference in The Netherlands, Britain, Germany and France*, New York, Oxford: Berghahn Books, 2004.

[5] On *gurbet* as key term for first-generation migrants, see M. Greve, *Die Musik der imaginären Türkei. Musik und Musikleben im Kontext der Migration aus der Türkei nach Deutschland*, Stuttgart Weimar: Metzler-Verlag, 2003.

against this trend of anomic experiences, not least because one found, in Islam, a community of like-minded people who could give each other mutual support. A second facet of this experience of foreignness was a crisis of meaning. Practically every migrant asks him- or herself at some point what s/he is actually doing in the foreign world which causes so much pain and whether it would not have been better to stay at home. Turkish migrants often expressed this feeling by complaining about the 'coldness' of Europe. Here, too, a religious orientation helps to deal with this question better, even if not to answer it. For example, such disorientation could somehow be eased with the argument that it does not make a difference for a Muslim where he fulfils his religious duty. And of course a community offers a certain degree of 'warmth'. A third, and indeed the most essential, aspect of the experience of the foreign was connected with the beginning of family reconstitution in the early 1970s. This meant, on the one hand, that one was preparing for a longer stay in Europe. On the other hand, it meant that one was now confronted with having to rear children in a foreign environment. One could no longer, as in Turkey, rely on one's children picking up one's own norms and values from the broader environment. *Gurbet* here stands for the fear of losing one's children. In brief, the migration situation forced a refocusing on one's own norms and values. Islam seemed perfect for this:

There is a really big difference between children [who go on the Koran course] and others, as far as upbringing is concerned and respect for their fathers and for you [as a guest]. When a guest comes into the house, the child will respect him. But another child will start babbling on for no reason and it will get on your nerves, even make you angry . . . So, it's all about our traditions and customs. A child learns them at the Koran course. A child doesn't learn them in school.[6]

All of the above gave the first generation's religiosity a decidedly defensive touch; they focused on the maintenance and protection of their own values and life designs in a foreign environment.

These needs were reflected by the founding of mosques everywhere in the Federal Republic of Germany. In many cases, the initiative came from the bottom, from migrants who were not otherwise institutionally organised. The initiators quickly faced the problematic fact that founding an organisation in a foreign environment requires know-how. They had to found an association, formulate by-laws for it, obtain legal advice, etc. This need for practical action was taken up by organisations whose origin was in Turkey and which became active in Germany.

---

[6] Interview conducted by me with a Turkish migrant in Augsburg Germany 1978. The quotation is found in W. Schiffauer, *Die Migranten aus Subay. Türken in Deutschland: eine Ethnographie*, Stuttgart: Klett-Cotta, 1991, p. 243.

Important among them were the *Süleymancı*, the *Nurcu*, the *Milli Görüş*, and the Idealist Associations often better known as 'Gray Wolves'.

The *Süleymancı* and the *Nurcu*, forbidden in Turkey, stem from Islamic-brotherhood religiosity. They were founded already in the first years after the Kemalist revolution to posit an Islamic upbringing against what they felt to be an impoverishment of Islam, and they henceforth operated undercover. The *Milli Görüş* was founded in the 1960s with the aim of Islamification of Turkey under the slogan 'The Just Order' (*adil düzen*). From this, a series of Islamic-conservative parties have developed (the Party of National Order, the National Salvation Party, the Welfare Party, the Virtue Party, and finally the Party of Well-Being). The sequence of names reflects the precarious legal position of this group in Turkey; its political formations have again and again been prohibited and re-founded under new names. Along with these three Islamist organisations came the Idealist Associations (e.g. the Gray Wolves), the European branch of the rightist nationalistic National Movement Party, which advocates a synthesis of Turkishness and Islam. The *DİYANET*[7] did not take action on its own in the early years (even if the faithful could turn to the office for help in founding mosques). Thus, the Turkish state largely left this realm to the communities of political Islam. This changed only in the beginning of the 1980s, when Turkey shifted from a policy of effectively ignoring the migrants to a conservative cultural policy whose aim was to increase the tie of Turks abroad to the Turkish state.[8] The *DİTİB* ('*Diyanet İsleri Türk Islam Birliği*' – 'Turkish Islamic Union of the State Office for Matters of Belief') was founded as the European branch of the *DİYANET*. It stands for an Islam that understands the role of religion as strictly restricted to the private realm. Finally, as the last organisation, came the radical Islamist community of Cemaleddin Kaplan, the later Caliphate State, which split off from the *Milli Görüş* in 1983. It strove for an Islamic revolution in Turkey according to the Iranian model.

By the mid-1980s, the field had been sorted out. Nearly all mosques had classified themselves under one or other organisation. The representation of the Islam of the worker migrants by organisations which (with only one exception) all stemmed from Turkey had far-reaching consequences. The need for a defensive religiosity that turned its back on Europe was taken up and honed into a clear orientation towards Turkey. The communities were distinguished by what role they saw for

---

[7] *DİYANET* - The Turkish State Office for Matters of Belief, the administration of Kemalist Islam.

[8] On the change of state policy, see A. Çaglar, 'Encountering the state in migration driven transnational fields: Turkish immigrants in Europe', unpublished Habilitation thesis, Free University, Berlin, 2003.

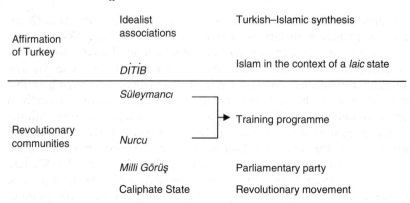

Figure 5.1 The socio-political outlook of major Muslim organisations in Germany in the 1980s.

Islam in Turkey. Those communities with an affirmative position toward a *laic* (strictly secular) Turkey distanced themselves from those communities which, at least in the 1980s, strove for an Islamist refashioning of the country (see figure 5.1). The latter were individually distinguished among themselves in terms of the strategy they contemplated for the introduction of the *Sharia*. The *Nurcu* and the *Süleymancı* emphasised consciousness raising through Koran courses and training programmes; the *Milli Görüş*, the parliamentary process; and the Caliphate State, in turn, revolution.[9]

With respect to this Turkey-oriented perspective, promotion of a role for Islam to play in Germany was of only secondary importance. This becomes especially clear in the failed attempts to establish religious education in German schools. Such education would have been completely in line with a defensive religiosity. It would have been possible to have German society accept it as well, if the Islamic communities had come together and appeared in unity as a bargaining partner with German institutions.[10] Yet, the opposing interests they had with reference to Turkey made this impossible. This also contributed to the fact that they did not perceive the immigration country as their 'own' country, as a space that they could somehow actively participate in shaping. Germany was and remained *gurbet*, the painfully perceived foreign.

[9] It must also be pointed out that in the 1990s, with the exception of the Caliphate State, all communities renounced the introduction of the *Sharia* in Turkey.

[10] W. Schiffauer, 'Islam as a civil religion: political culture and the organization of diversity in Germany', in Tariq Modood and Pnina Werbner (eds.), *The politics of multiculturalism in the new Europe*, London and New York: Zed Books, 1997.

Although oriented toward Turkey, Islam in exile distinguished itself clearly from Islam in Turkey. Above all, the large number of communities competing with one another in Europe in the attempt to represent Islam played a significant role. The monopoly enjoyed by *DİYANET* in Turkey was broken in Europe, even if the largest number of Turkish Muslims remains faithful to it. An already existent latent fractionalisation of Islam found expression in Europe. Due to reasons mentioned above, there was, secondly, a certain shift of power, with groups such as the *Süleymancı* or even the *Milli Görüş* proportionately more strongly represented in Europe than in Turkey. A third remarkable difference was the establishment of the Caliphate State, as there is no corresponding organisation in Turkey. This is a phenomenon that, echoing Anderson's 'long distance nationalism',[11] could be called 'long distance religiosity'. With the security and distance of the migration situation, a portion of the faithful developed non-compromising positions that were implausible in Turkey itself.

Pluralism of this sort provokes a more reflexive relationship with religion than exists in Turkey, as one has an option between various communities. Thus, a situation of competition between religious offers unfolds in Europe, which Peter Berger[12] views as characteristic of modern religiosity.

Greater institutional splintering, however, had a negative impact on the culture of debate. In Turkey, where the political groups existed underground, there was a lively exchange of positions and vigorous culture of debate. In Europe, where the political groups were manifest, the exit option[13] increased. The boundaries between groups were emphasised as they distanced themselves from, and battled with, one another. So while the disputes between positions were often conducted discursively in Turkey, they were often non-verbal in Europe. The splintered nature of European Islam was at that time viewed with amazement in Turkey.[14]

The idea of an exile Islam was explicitly stated, articulated by the various communities during these years. In the *DİTİB* mosques, it assumed the form of a homeland rhetoric. The transmission of Islamic norms and values was identified with socialisation as a Turk and

---

[11] B. Anderson, *Long-distance nationalism: world capitalism and the rise of identity politics*. Amsterdam: University of Amsterdam Centre for Asian Studies (= The Wertheim Lecture 1992).

[12] P. L. Berger, *Zur dialektik von religion und gesellschaft*, Frankfurt am Main: Fischer 1973.

[13] A. O. Hirschman, *Exit, voice and loyalty*, Cambridge, MA: Harvard University Press, 1970.

[14] See for example U. Mumcu, *Rabita*, Istanbul: Tekin, 1987.

transmission of love of the fatherland. Thus, in religious instruction, educational units were offered on topics such as 'We love our fatherland' or 'Loving the fatherland / Duties to the fatherland / Even abroad we think of the fatherland'. The *Milli Görüş* expressed the difference between the 'own' and the 'foreign' with the telling opposition between *dar al İslam*, 'land of Islam' and *dar al harb*, literally, land of the enemy. The dominant term in this opposition is *dar al İslam*. With reference to Turkey, it formulated a political programme. Islam in Turkey enjoys a majority status, but it has been alienated by the Kemalists; the battle for Islamification is more easily conceived as a legitimate one, as it is a matter of repossessing one's own realm. The secondary term, 'land of war', which sounds more militant than is perhaps intended, expresses the fact that in Germany one was in principle in an inimical land, a country to which one could not lay claim and, therefore, could not hope to shape. One need not feel committed to that country. A third formula which raised the point of exile Islam was the term *Hegira*, which was especially popular in the Caliphate State. *Hegira* refers to the young Islamic community's act of emigration to Medina in the year 622, an act made necessary by political repression. Ten years later, this emigration found its conclusion with the triumphant return to Mecca. This definition was particularly popular among Islamic refugees during the state of emergency in Turkey from 1980 to 1983.[15]

The development of diaspora Islam

Against the background of the first generation's exile Islam, the second generation's significantly more complex diaspora Islam unfolds. It is more complex because the fractionalisation resulting from Turkey-specific perspectives is maintained, but now overlaid with positions arising from confrontations with the immigration society. As should be demonstrated in the following with the example of Muslims in Germany,[16] the battle for recognition is decisive for the development of this position.[17]

---

[15] In 1980 the military ended the civil unrest at Turkish universities. The clashes between left and right had left over 10,000 dead. A state of emergency was declared and all political parties were forbidden. Many leftist, rightist and Islamist activists were imprisoned or fled to Europe.

[16] The question of the Islamic immigrant's recognition has not been resolved in any European country. The concrete spelling out of the struggle, however, depends on the various political cultures. On this, see Schiffauer et al., *Civil enculturation*.

[17] On the central role of recognition, see above all C. Taylor, 'Die politik der anerkennung', Charles Taylor (ed.), *Multikulturalismus und die politik der anerkennung*, Frankfurt/Main: Fischer, 1992, 13–78; A. Honneth, *Kampf um anerkennung. Zur*

Second- and third-generation Muslims are confronted with the situation that they, unlike their parents, are Europeans. They grew up in one European society or another, passed through its institutions and have built diverse relationships to the society. They are German, English, or French Muslims and not just Muslims in Germany, England, or France. This is nothing to be taken for granted, but a practical relationship, a task or project. They must situate themselves in the given society and develop an understanding of themselves in that situation. However, two factors complicate this task. First, both the immigration society and the first generation of migrants construct the relation between 'European culture' and Islam as a relation between the familiar and the foreign, and thus place it in an oppositional, rather than a complementary, relationship. The second complicating factor is that this relation is not between two parties on an equal footing but is dominated by the European side. Those newly arrived who are struggling to establish a place for their religion are always in a structurally disadvantaged situation with respect to those occupants who define the conditions for admission.

The construction of the 'Muslim Other' has been analysed again and again and therefore need only be briefly mentioned here. Today, it relies primarily on two areas which are considered central to the European community of values. First, there is a suspicion of an inability to embrace democracy and of incomplete enlightenment. It is insinuated that separation of politics and religion is essentially foreign to Islam. The second large area concerns equality of men and women. The Islamic family is seen as a hotbed of authoritarianism, patriarchy, misogyny and domestic violence, as the exact counter model to the 'egalitarian' and 'liberated' European family. Though Islam is principally accorded value as a world religion, at the individual level most Europeans have trouble imagining what valuable contributions Islam could make to European civil society or what Europeans could learn from Islam. Here, distrust is coupled with fear about their own identity; many Europeans are afraid of growing Muslim influence. Perhaps it will help to quote one such perspective, as it comes from a Social Democratic politician with a generally positive position on migration:

I think the question of Islam and Islam classes alike, something I sense as a politician, provokes great fears and concerns in the population. You can sense that in particular when you take part in discussions in Berlin neighborhoods.

moralischen grammatik sozialer konflikte, Frankfurt am Main: Suhrkamp, 1992; and A.G. Düttmann, *Zwischen den kulturen. Spannungen im kampf um anerkennung*, Frankfurt am Main: Suhrkamp, 1997.

There are, to formulate it crassly, concerns that Islam, people of Islamic religion in Germany, when they go into the schools, may somehow slowly change the art and nature of our culture, which is completely western.[18]

These patterns of thinking determine the debate on very disparate levels. A basic suspicion expressed in most debates on the admission of Turkey to the EU is that the Judeo-Christian value system is incompatible with the Islamic one. The generalised suspicion that Islam is prone to fundamentalism has intensified since September 11. However, it may well be especially decisive that the discourse on alteration has profoundly marked reality in the education system in at least some European countries.[19]

All of the above leads to a widespread feeling among the second generation that they are doubly discriminated against, both as immigrants and as Muslims. Europeans would sooner or later come to terms with the immigration of secular Turks or Arabs, but not with the immigration of professing Muslims, a young Muslim of the second generation told me.[20]

Yet, this debasement would be less problematic if it were not connected with a difference of power separating new arrivals from occupants. This is a matter of demands made by a minority which must be pushed through against prevailing assumptions and wrung from a sceptical majority and often against that majority's opposition. On its own, this would not be so problematic. However, in contrast with many other minorities, Muslims confront an astonishing societal solidarity against them. Unlike other questions concerning immigrants, the Muslim situation has no coalition partner on the left. On the contrary, as far as Islam is concerned, the objections from the left, fed by a mixture of secularism and feminism, are often more intense than those from the right. Thus, many Muslims often feel they are running head-on into a wall when they raise demands, beginning with the construction of mosques, which must be pushed through against the explicit opposition of the neighbourhood and sometimes of the state authorities, continuing with the right to wear Islamic clothing to school or at work, up to the desire that their limits of modesty be respected in swimming and gym

---

[18] Klaus Böger, Senator for School, Youth-Affairs and Sport, quoted in: Senatsverwaltung für schule, jugend und sport, (ed.), *Islamischer religionsunterricht an Berliner schulen – probleme, fragen, antworten*, Friedrich-Ebert-Stiftung: Berlin, 2000, p. 4.

[19] Schiffauer et al., *Civil enculturation*.

[20] The picture would, however, be incomplete if one did not also observe that the first immigrant generation fashioned equally distorted images of the West. 'European culture' was constructed as the inversion of their own Islamic–Turkish culture, a hotbed of sexual permissiveness, alcohol and drug abuse, and decayed family ties.

classes. In all these areas, Muslims experience scepticism, reserve, and not infrequently opposition to their demands. It is not at all unusual that they are put off by state agencies despite clear legal requirements, or that they attain their clear legal rights only after long and wearying court battles. The confrontation with power in such disputes also frequently means an encounter precisely with the power of definition. In such disputes, they as Muslims must often tolerate non-Muslims classifying and judging their request, and even themselves, according to whether they conform to the 'true humane Islam' or are 'perverted by fundamentalism'.

It is my thesis that, under the conditions described above, the search for recognition must almost by necessity lead to an agonising conflict-oriented *fight for recognition*. The relation between power and opposing power becomes central in such situations. It makes the development of an identity impossible which is not constantly under pressure to define itself in opposition. Before we turn to the material, we must first briefly sketch out the problem.[21]

The search for recognition is connected with a precarious relationship between same and equal, on the one hand, and other and different, on the other. One wishes to be recognised as equal, because every expression of inequality means exclusion and discrimination. Yet one also wishes to be perceived as something special and unique, or at least to be respected in one's difference. It is clear that tension is present in this double desire for recognition. Indeed, it may well be something impossible to achieve. No sooner is one seen as different and special, than the problem of equality arises; and no sooner is one treated as an equal, than the question arises about the right to be different, the dismay that the dissimilar is handled as similar. This is sometimes raised as a paradox;[22] I would not go that far. The relation between equality and difference is indeed unproblematic when the special meets with recognition or at least well-meaning openness and curiosity. That is the case when, as Charles Taylor[23] put it, one's contact with other cultures is based on the assumption that each

---

[21] It is not possible, in the framework of this text, to go into all questions that have been discussed in the extensive socio-philosophical literature on the problem of power and recognition. Especially important here are E. Goffman, *Stigma*, Frankfurt am Main: Suhrkamp, 1980; H. Bhabha, 'Remembering Fanon: self, psyche and the colonial condition', in P. Williams and Laura Chrisman (eds.), *Colonial discourse and post-colonial theory. A reader*, Hemel Hempstead: Harvester 1993, p. 112–23. J. Butler, *The psychic life of power: theories in subjection*, Stanford: Stanford University Press, 1997, F. Fanon, *Die verdammten dieser erde*, Frankfurt am Main: Suhrkamp, 1981.

[22] eg. by Düttmann, *Zwischen den kulturen*.

[23] Taylor, 'Politik der anerkennung'.

individual culture has a value (which does not mean according to Taylor that one must ultimately reach the same conclusion). Zen Buddhism, for example, enjoys basic recognition in Europe and certain practices growing out of this background can count on a basically positive reaction from a large portion of the public.[24] Someone who belongs to this religious group can play out his uniqueness without the question of equality ever arising. When things are not seen this way, as in the case of conservative Islam, the recognition of difference and the recognition of equality enter into an almost irresolvable dilemma. For then, emphasis on uniqueness occurs at the expense of equality, and vice versa. Emphasis on uniqueness is then no longer viewed as a special or possible contribution to the 'value system', but as a violation of its principles. The next step, exclusion, is then easy to take. With this schema, one easily takes the position that the search for recognition per se is misguided because it leads nowhere.

This sketch must suffice here. The argument allows us to approach the identity dilemmas of the second generation in its confrontation with European society. To drive the point home, European societies make it almost impossible to avoid convolutions, distortions, or self-denials when a Muslim living in Europe seeks to define him or herself as a European Muslim. I would like to demonstrate this by examining the ideal–typical identity options the second generation has developed in their confrontation with European society. In Weberian tradition, I shall let the positions themselves comment on and criticise each other. It should thereby become clear that each position can be read as an answer to the difficulties resulting from the other positions, only to lead to another dead end.

Option 1: The struggle for equality

Perhaps the most obvious demand of a religious minority is the struggle for equality and equal rights. The demand that one's own voice must be taken just as seriously as those of others refers to individual participation in an open civil society. These individual rights include an 'equal treatment, directed by the citizens themselves, of their identity ensuring contexts of life', as Jürgen Habermas put it.[25] Indeed, one has the impression that the supporters of this position largely share Habermas'

---

[24] See among others Sigrid klinkhammer, *Moderne formen islamischer lebensführung*, Marburg: Diagonal 2000, p. 253.

[25] J. Habermas, 'Anerkennungskämpfe im demokratischen rechtsstaat', in C. Taylor (ed.), *Multikulturalismus und die politik der anerkennung*, Frankfurt/Main: Fischer, 1992, p. 158.

dream when one examines their statements for an implicit ideal of society. This position places the struggle against discrimination, against any form of unequal treatment, in the foreground.

This position is especially plausible for Muslims who regard Islam as a private matter, a matter between the individual and God: in other words, for Muslims who feel somehow close to the DİTİB. Aylin Gencel's[26] description of such a family is illustrative. The family members profess a 'conscious' Islam. By that they mean an Islam to which one turns by one's own decision and above all an Islam that one acquires individually and independently. The 'conscious' Islam is contrasted with a traditional ('village') Islam taken over from one's parents without reflecting and examining very much on one's own. The family members deduce from their individual devotion to God that there is no compulsion in Islam. 'And it is also not so that one forces the other to anything. Why do I pray the namaz? For my own peace of mind. Why do I fast? I don't fast for you, my mother, the children, or my husband. No, I fast for myself.'[27] In family practice, women with traditional veils and women without veils live together, the older members pray regularly, the younger ones don't. The children are sent to Koran class, but the family also tolerates it if a daughter marries a non-Muslim. Such families are sceptical about too strong a position for Islamic communities. They see them as institutions that principally position themselves between the individual and society and often make directorial claims. They accuse the community members of trusting authority too much, of blindly following the imams without thinking for themselves. According to them the dogmatism which reigns in the communities is not compatible with their form of the individual learning of faith.

The ideal of an individual reader formulated here is widespread, even if many would admit that they, unfortunately, do not have time to put it into practice. This goes along with a mutual respect for different readings of Islam. This all serves as a prerequisite for Islam to develop further in a way that fits modernity, which is also the prerequisite for demonstrating the importance of Islam's contribution to modernity. 'The West lags behind the Koran, but we lag behind the West'; this popularly used figure of speech expresses this idea quite well.

For this vision of an individualised religious practice to develop into a convincing model, however, it would be necessary for the aforementioned problem of power and discrimination to be resolved. European

[26] A. Gençel, 'Images of Islam in the diaspora – an ethnographic study of a Turkish family in Berlin'. Unpublished Master thesis, Fakultät für Kulturwissenschaften. Europa-Universität Viadrina Frankfurt Oder (2003).
[27] ibid. 44.

societies would have to accept Islam as a voice to be taken seriously. This would require, among other things, a willingness to accept Habermas' demand to separate the universal contents of constitutions from local and particularistic traditions, assuming that such is possible at all.[28] In principle, British society, with its attempts to redefine Britishness, has gone further in this than any other European country. In the continental societies, such trends are hardly visible.

This vision of an 'individualised Islam' is closely related to the school of 'liberal' reformism. According to Tariq Ramadan this school is characterised by a strong emphasis on rationality and on the prime value attached to the individual. Adherents of this school express the opinion that because of historical development, Koran and *sunnah* cannot be taken as the basis for social conduct any more, and that applied reasoning has to formulate the criteria for social behaviour.[29] This type of Islam would accept a pluralism of norms and values and accept individualised paths to the truth. This vision however can only fully develop if the problem of power and discrimination is solved. If this is not the case this position will easily be associated with self-denial, assimilation and weakness. Islam has to be accepted as a voice which has to be taken seriously by European societies if this school is to flourish. This would imply living up to the demand formulated by Habermas to emphasise the universalist contents of the constitutions and not their local and particularist background.

The experience of exclusion and powerlessness confronts supporters of an 'individualised Islam' with the problem of having to fight for their positions. As we shall see in the presentation of the next position, this would, however, mean having to sacrifice some of their basic principles. If they are not prepared to do so, it leads to a rather resigned withdrawal. They then live their Islam in private, as does the family Aylın Gençel described. There, they live in a nearly perfect Turkish world (with a decidedly urban character). They live in Berlin and maintain functional relations with German society. They categorically reject any and all demands to conform:

Well, as for conforming . . . Why should I be obliged to conform? OK, as far as the language is concerned, I can understand . . . But as far as work and living are concerned, and what do I know to what degree I should conform. I don't know, but when I hear that, I feel resistance in myself.[30]

---

[28] Habermas, 'Anerkennungskämpfe', p. 166.
[29] T. Ramadan, *Muslimsein in Europa*, Marburg: MSV, 2001, p. 300.
[30] Unpublished interview by A. Gençel 2002.

Option 2: The struggle for the right to difference

Supporters of the second position, labelled 'collectivist committed', start at precisely this point. They consider the individualised position hopeless. Is it really realistic to believe one can live out and maintain his difference in his private space? Hasn't one then already lost from the very outset? This would mean hiding Islam like some sort of stigma of which one must be ashamed. It is clear that European society could easily live with individualised Muslims. Then it does not even have to deal with Islam and will therefore not change. With respect to recognition, in standing up for one's right to wear a veil, for example, one makes no progress this way. A girl with a veil will simply remain isolated. It is therefore necessary to struggle for a public position for Islam. Islamic spaces must be created. Islam must become an accepted way of life in European society. People must come to take Islamic clothing just as much for granted as they do a necklace with a crucifix. An Islamic girl must be able to wear her veil with confidence and pride. Only then will Islamic dress be perceived as something special and no longer as only different, an otherness that one must exclude. In short, while supporters of the first position start with the demand for equality, collectivist committed Muslims put the primary focus on the right to difference and derive from it the demand for equality. They insist on being different and having a right to be different, and they expect the majority society to show respect for this difference. The fight for collective rights for the religious community is central to this position.

Only through collective effort does one have a chance to win the struggle for rights. In contrast, one is lost as an individual. From this point of view, supporters of this position tend from the very beginning to stress solidarity more strongly than do the supporters of the first position. As in other groups as well, community building seems a possible form of resistance politics. What Paul Gilroy notes for 'black Britain' also applies to Islamic communities:

Community, therefore, signifies not just a distinctive political ideology but a particular set of values and norms in everyday life: mutuality, cooperation, identification and symbiosis. For black Britain, all these are centrally defined by the need to escape and transform the forms of subordination which bring 'races' into being.[31]

A strong emphasis on the significance of community life is the conclusion from this. A lively Islam without a lively community life seems

---

[31] Gilroy, *Urban social movements*, p. 414.

unthinkable for the collectivists; in the individualised position, they see a pale imitation of a spiritually inspired (*şuurlu*) Islam.

As Anthony P. Cohen[32] has shown, community construction requires the construction of symbols on which one has agreed and with which one delineates the boundaries of the collective identity. For collectivist Islam, body symbolism is central. By means of clothing, especially for women, a strong symbol of the difference to the majority society, and to individualised Islam as well, is created. The marker is especially the 'turban', the special form of Islamic veiling that, in Turkey, arose after 1980 and which is clearly distinguished from the traditional veil.[33] This symbol generally stands for a profession of Islamic familialism. What however may appear homogeneous from the outside (and also in self-perception) turns out to be very heterogeneous upon closer observation. As in all other communities, the dress codes provide a commonality of *form*, but much less commonality of content. Thus, one can demonstrate that there are many hidden motives behind the decision to wear the turban,[34] which can sometimes be combined, but can also sometimes be separated. The turban can stand for criticism of Western sexual morals and in particular promiscuity, for an ascetic bodily technique, or for a perceived need to profess Islam openly. Especially interesting, and important for our purposes, are contexts in which wearing the turban becomes a prerequisite for argumentative rebellion. This is the case with committed feminist Muslims. At one *Milli Görüş* event, for example, several female speakers took stands clearly and massively against domestic violence and against arranged marriages, and called for women to be active in public life and, to make that possible, for men to participate in housework. It was quite clear that these arguments went too far for many of the men present. Yet the symbolic clarity the women produced with their clothing forced the men to deal with their demands. After the basic point of loyalty was settled one could get down to business with all the more pressure.

A collectivist position is closely related to neo-orthodoxy or *Salafi* Reformism (Ramadan). The emphasis on strong ties to the communities has often a legalist touch. This however is not static. In its self-description it aims at a balance between rationality and revelation. By *ijtihad* one tries

---

[32] A. P. Cohen, *The symbolic construction of community*, London, New York: Routledge, 1985.

[33] N. Göle, *Republik und schleier. Die muslimische frau in der modernen Türkei.* (Berlin: Babel Verlag, 1995).

[34] J. Jouili, 'Islamische weibliche identitäten in der diaspora: frauen maghrebinischer und türkischer herkunft in Deutschland und Frankreich'. Application for a PhD thesis, Europa-Universität Frankfurt/Oder (2001).

to find legally correct solutions for the new challenges of the life in Europe. The struggle for the right to difference corresponds to a religious orientation toward the law as it was revealed to Muhammed (as the necessity to insist on the difference is derived from it) and at the same time to accept the necessity of taking into account the new circumstances of a life in Europe when putting religious law into practice. The aim is to maintain Muslim identity and ritual practice, to recognise the European constitutions and to engage oneself in the country in which one lives.[35]

Such community building is not infrequently accompanied by a strong emphasis on group solidarity. Anyone fighting for collective rights tends to see an important aspect in the development of a counter force in internal unity. As a rule, internal criticism, especially of the community leadership, falls by the wayside. Intense social control is often accompanied by sanctioning of outsiders and dropouts. For fear of exclusion, contradiction is often not publicly formulated, but at best expressed behind one another's backs. It would be a misunderstanding to reduce this to some kind of control from above. This control indeed comes from below and is quite voluntarily exercised, namely by community members who see a guarantee for the cohesion of the community in an intact leadership. In such situations, to borrow Bourdieu's formulation, one of the 'genuine political modes' – in this case the independent formation of one's own opinion – is withdrawn in favour of the other one, the delegation of authority, i.e. the 'choice of speakers and authorities in the sense of a decision for certain ideas, convictions, designs, programmes, plans, which, because incarnated in their reality and credibility in personalities, indeed also depend on the reality and credibility of these "personalities"'.[36] The symbolic construction of community and the sanctioning of deviance lend this position a decidedly 'orthodox' imprint.

This tendency to 'defer oneself' seems to be connected with the insight that individualisation represents an important mechanism for a regime to execute discipline.[37] The profession of individuality, of independent formation of opinions, can under certain circumstances weaken a cause because it contributes to the isolation, surveillance and individualisation of the individual subject.

Yet here, the dilemmas surrounding collective self-assertion become clear. It arose to build up a counter force in the face of powerlessness and discrimination. Nonetheless, there is a problematic tendency to

---

[35] Ramadan, *Muslimsein in Europa*, p. 298.

[36] P. Bourdieu, *Die feinen unterschiede. Kritik der gesellschaftlichen urteilskraft*, Frankfurt/Main: Suhrkamp, 1982 p. 665. Examples from the communist party, ibid. p. 667.

[37] M. Foucault, *Überwachen und strafen. Die geburt des gefängnisses*, Frankfurt am Main: Suhrkamp, 1991.

copy the power structures on the inside, and all the more markedly the greater the pressure of the society that one is reacting to. Precisely this lets these communities easily become sites of internal authoritarianism. Neo-orthodoxy's very 'trust in authority' frequently appears problematic to supporters of an individualised Islam. On the other hand, according to supporters of neo-orthodox Islam, the individualists' position leads to surrender of self.

Option 3: The rejection of the struggle for recognition

The third position to be found among Muslims of the second generation can be characterised as an anti-hegemonic position. It reproaches both the individualised and the collectivist positions for their search for recognition, whether in the form of recognition of equality or of difference, because it always leads to a dead end. This position is extremely sensitive to the problem of power and identity, as has most clearly been developed by subject-theoretical thinkers.[38]

As soon as one seeks *any* recognition from the antagonistically oriented society, whether recognition as an equal or as different, one has already surrendered. For then one abandons to the other – to someone who does not belong to the community – the power of defining who is considered a good and who is considered a bad Muslim. This is not only offensive, but also a spiral at whose end lies self-denial because one has ultimately subjected oneself to the value judgements of the other religion. What, however, ask the supporters of this position, legitimates the majority society to usurp the role of judge over Islam at all? Certainly not moral superiority. Indeed, one of the central themes of the magazine *D.I.A.* ['The Islamic Alternative'], which is published by the Caliphate State[39] and provides a forum for the revolutionary variant of this position, is to attack the West's moral self-righteousness. What society produced fascism and colonialism and committed genocide against the Jews? The violence characteristic of the West throughout its history, according to the supporters of this position, is today primarily directed against Islam. Israel, Chechnya, Afghanistan and Iraq are again and again raised as examples of imperialist policy. The aim of this policy, they say, is to crush the only voice that opposes the globally valid hegemonic discourse. Anyone who tries to come to terms with the hegemonic power (or to settle down in its shadow), as do the individualists and the neo-orthodox, will

---

[38] Butler, *The psychic life of power.*

[39] The magazine appeared from 2001 to 2003, when it was closed down due to increased police pressure.

ultimately squander Islam's potential to be a radical alternative. This can also not be theologically justified. One must maintain the absolute non-negotiability of Islamic positions.

This anti-hegemonic position is related to ultra-orthodoxy. It emphasises purity and authenticity and sets itself apart from positions which are less puristic. The boundaries which are drawn vis-à-vis majority society are also drawn vis-à-vis other Muslims. They are criticised for accepting the rules of the game and betraying Islam. Boundary drawing to the outside produces dogmatism and a tendency to sanction all deviance. This position has a revolutionary and a quietist variant. The revolutionary variant, as represented by communities like the Caliphate State and similar movements,[40] insists on a revolution in the Islamic world in order to restore the true and pure Islam. These dreamers of a radical global restructuring see Europe as a base for their struggle. Among the Turkish population, the quietist variant is mainly represented by the *Süleymancı* Community.[41] The ultra-orthodox quietists differ from the orthodox communities in their understanding of *tağdid* (resumption): The former interpret resumption as revival, which requires a return to the origins and strict observance, whereas the latter interpret it as renewal. They emphasise the need for reinterpretation in order to answer the challenges of present society.[42]

The two other positions decisively criticise the ultra-orthodox position. According to the criticism of an individualised Islam, this position is unrealistic. It is an illusion to think one could opt out of society. Indeed, the anti-hegemonic position denies that living as Muslims in European society means, as Stuart Hall put it, that 'they are irrevocably the product of several interlocking histories and cultures, belonging at one and the same time to several "homes" (and to no one particular "home")'.[43] One might also point out that the ultra orthodox are (at least to a certain degree) deceiving themselves in their emphasis on cultural purity and religious absolutism. As has repeatedly been shown,[44] the proactive revolutionary ultra-orthodox deal with their own

---

[40] For example, the *Hizb-al Tahrir*, which have been particularly active in Great Britain and recently also in Germany. S. T. Farouki, *A fundamentalist quest: Hizb-al Tahrir and the search for an Islamic caliphate*, London: Grey Seal, 1996.

[41] Among migrants with Arab or south Asian background in France and Britain, the *Tablighi* movement is the most influential quietist ultra-orthodox community.

[42] G. Jonker, *Eine wellenlänge zu Gott: der verband der islamischen kulturzentren in Europa*, Bielefeld: Transcript; 2002, p. 179.

[43] Stuart Hall. 'The question of cultural identity', in Stuart Hall, David Held and Tony McGrew (eds.), *Modernity and its futures*, Cambridge: Polity Press, 1992, p. 310.

[44] A. Al-Azmeh, *Islams and modernities*, London: Routledge, 1993; G. Kepel, *Les banlieues de l'Islam*, Paris: Editions du Seuil, 1987; W. Schiffauer, 'Islamism in the diaspora. The fascination of political Islam among second generation German Turks',

tradition with the know-how they have acquired at European schools and universities. This has a lasting impact on their language and style of thinking. This becomes most apparent when their choice of wording and their positions take up the rhetoric of the radical Left, sometimes down to the last detail. As anybody else, the ultra orthodox are, as Hall puts it, 'irrevocable translators'.

The second criticism from representatives of an individualised Islam concerns the sectarian intolerance of supporters of the revolutionary anti-hegemonic position. An emphasis on purity and authenticity is indeed usually accompanied by a clear policy of exclusion of less pure positions. The ultra orthodox not only draw a border between themselves and the majority society, but also between themselves and other Muslims whom they accuse of getting involved in the system and thus betraying Islam. This demarcation between them and the outside produces an inward dogmatism and places sanctions on all possible deviations from the pure and true faith.[45] Precisely this tendency towards separation and intolerance appears to other Muslims as a contradiction of Islam's commandment of unity and the principle of openness connected with it.

The collectivist neo-orthodox Muslims would agree with the individualists' criticism in part; however, they would also criticise anti-hegemonic politics for being completely illusory. It would be positively counter-productive for any policies to attempt to create a space for Islam. Ultimately, anti-hegemonic politics would only play into the hands of Islam's enemies.

Ultra-orthodox Muslims gladly counter this criticism with a reference to God's will. God simply cannot want a portion of the faithful to become Westernised and another portion of the faithful to relinquish important positions simply to get on the good side of Islam's enemies. From this perspective, one can hope that God will support those who take God's revelation seriously.

Figure 5.2 lists the three positions of diaspora Islam of the second generation and summarises the criticism.

Supporters of an individualised Islam criticise orthodoxy for its authoritarianism. Authoritarianism contradicts individualised Muslims' conceptions of a 'conscious' Islam that does not accept direction from authorities but is instead characterised by individual and critical learning

Oxford: Transnational Communities Programme – Working Paper Series, http://www. transcomm.ox.ac.uk, 1999; W. Schiffauer, *Die gottesmänner. Türkische Islamisten in Deutschland. Eine studie zur herstellung religiöser evidenz*, Frankfurt am Main: Suhrkamp, 2000.

[45] Schiffauer, *Gottesmänner*, especially pp. 155–203.

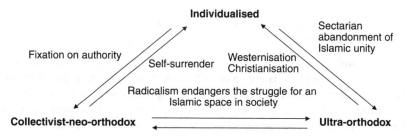

Figure 5.2 The three positions of diaspora Islam. The texts summarise the criticisms of each position. The direction of the criticism is shown by the arrowheads.

of the scriptures. They criticise ultra-orthodoxy for its sectarian and intolerant spirit, which contradicts what they consider the core of Islam: namely engagement for peace, tolerance and openness.

Supporters of neo-orthodoxy criticise individualised Islam, on the other hand, for its 'liberalism' where 'anything goes'. Individualised religious practice, the neo-orthodox argue, ultimately leads to conformity, loss of self and dissolution. They criticise ultra orthodoxy above all for its unrealistic political stance, in addition to its sectarianism. Ultra-orthodoxy's politics would ultimately make a politics of positioning in Europe completely impossible.

Supporters of ultra-orthodoxy criticise individualised Islam for its 'Westernisation'. For them, the positions taken by the individualists have nothing to do with Islam anymore. Profession of a private religion would correspond to Christianity, but not to Islam. Though orthodoxy principally opposes these phenomena of dissolution, it nonetheless submits to the definitive authority of non-Muslims. The ultra-orthodox say the orthodox will sooner or later assume positions that have nothing to do with Islam.

Each of these positions has its own inner logic, and is entangled in contradictions that the other positions mention. My interest was to show that this contradictory nature reflects the inner turmoil of the migration situation and the devaluation Islam experiences in Europe. This leads to an extremely unstable situation. One does not hold one position for good but rather moves from one position to the next. Much depends on the attitude wider society takes vis-à-vis the Muslim community. Exclusion and discrimination will strengthen the ultra-orthodox positions which emphasise that a dignified Islamic life is only possible within an Islamic state and society.

The reception of diaspora Islam
in the communities

The second generation's three positions have not (yet) achieved any organisational form, as is the case with corresponding communities of the Jewish diaspora. Much more, there are supporters of all positions in all communities that were established in the first years of migration to Europe. In each community, there are individuals with individualised, orthodox and ultra-orthodox opinions, if in varying proportions. The individualised stance is primarily to be found in the *DİTİB*, and indeed because of this community's avowed profession of an Islam that views religion as a private matter between man and God. The orthodox collectivist committed position, on the other hand, is mostly to be found in the *Milli Görüş*. The ultra-orthodox anti-hegemonic position is represented in the Caliphate State. So while the attitude toward Turkey still remains decisive on the level *between* the organisations, *within* the communities (usually), members of the second generation support positions they developed with reference to the host society. Thus a complex web pattern is woven which also offers the possibility for new coalitions.

The organisations have reacted to this shift in religious 'demand' in varying degrees. The *DİTİB*, which as far as its adherents are concerned could actually be the natural trustee of an individualised Islam, has failed so far with regard to the development of convincing positions of a diasporic Islam. This is because of its character as a state agency and its close ties with the Turkish state. This makes it more difficult for it to develop its own positions in reaction to developments in Europe. It is typical that in 2000, when lively discussions about the establishment of religion courses in Berlin's schools took place, the *DİTİB* found itself unable to participate in the debates. In central questions, such as whether the courses should be in Turkish or German, the organisation was not able to reach a consensus.

In contrast, a change in leadership has occurred in the *Milli Görüş* since the mid-1990s. Leading positions have been systematically filled with members of the second generation, who grew up in Europe. Since then, the top leaders of the *Milli Görüş* have attempted to develop an orthodox diaspora Islam. They have declared the Turkey-related conflicts that divided the communities in the 1970s and 80s to be outdated. Today's task is to create a place for Islam in European public life. In this connection, the community began to make a name for itself with a series of remarkable positions. It advocated courses in Islam in the German language, started a campaign among its adherents for them to acquire German citizenship, and issued statements encouraging the faithful to send their children (boys as well as girls) to German educational institutions, especially to the higher secondary schools (Gymnasiums). In internal discussions, they tried to determine the role of Islam in the constitutional secular state, their relationship to Christianity, and the role of women in Islam. The difference between diaspora and exile Islam was explicitly driven home when Mehmet Sabri Erbakan, who was the organisation's chairperson from 1999 to 2002, proclaimed in his inaugural address that Muslims in Europe have a privileged situation, because 90 per cent of all Muslims live in conditions of state oppression, material misery, or war. The privilege enjoyed by European Muslims, he said, entails a responsibility towards Islam throughout the world. In the *Milli Görüş*, the impression one gets concerning the development of a diaspora Islam is the opposite of the one created by the situation in the *DİTİB*. While the *DİTİB* lags behind developments in the communities, the leadership of the *Milli Görüş* is on the front line in these developments. At times, one got the impression that the compromises made in an effort to establish itself as an interlocutor went too far for the community's first generation.[46] The leadership emphasises its growing independence from the Turkish parent party, the current Party of Well-Being (*Saadet Partısı*, SP).

The ultra-orthodox positions are represented above all in the Caliphate State (revolutionary variant) and in the *Süleymancı* community (quietist variant). The Caliphate State, in spite of its prohibition in Germany in December, 2001, is still active. The Caliphate State stands for an Islamist revolutionary pan-Islamism. The dream of its founder, Cemaleddin Kaplan, was an Islamic revolution in Turkey, the re-establishment of the Caliphate, and through it the worldwide re-establishment of 'authentic Islam'. In the Turkish Language Association newspaper *Ümmet-i Muhammed* ('The Community of Mohammed'; renamed *Asr-i Saadet* ['The Age of Bliss'] after the prohibition of the community in Germany in 2001), the worldwide repression of Islam is portrayed with special attention to Turkey. Europe plays hardly any role at all in this newspaper; the choice of topics has much more to do with those of a global Islam. This is totally different in the German-language monthly publication *D.I.A.* (*Der Islam als Alternative*, or 'Islam as an Alternative'). The sequence of topics handled alone demonstrates the development of

---

[46] Given the leadership crisis in the *Milli Görüş*, it remains to be seen how this development will continue. The charismatic Mehmet Sabri Erbakan resigned in October 2002, officially for reasons of health, but, according to a report in the newspaper *Hürriyet*, because of an affair. His successor, Yavuz Celik Karahan, respected for his theological competence in the communities, is continuing his policies. Yet rumors have arisen that he, too, is involved in a scandal.

an anti-hegemonic position in dealing with Europe. With 'Protection of the five basic values', 'People with rights / People without rights', 'Foreigner', 'Jihad', 'Global Capitalism', and 'Nationalism', the articles address issues that play a central role in European debates. In the *Süleymancı* community, members of the second generation attempted an opening toward society between 1998 and 2000: a move that would have ultimately led the community closer to orthodox positions. These developments were stopped when a leadership change occurred in Turkey in 2000. Ahmed Arif Denizoglun, who now heads the transnational organisation, accused the Muslim communities of Europe of investing their energies in the founding of academies for inter-religious dialogue and neglecting their central task (teaching children in the classical Islamic sciences).[47]

Outlook

As a rule, in discussions on this subject the development of a European Islam is associated with the assimilation of Islam; European Islam will be 'our' Islam, open to negotiation, tolerance and open-mindedness. The aim of this text was to show that such a development is unlikely under conditions of de facto discrimination. Even individualised Islam (which still has the most similarities to the European phantasm) will, in view of the European stance, maintain its resistance, even if this resistance may often be hardly visible since it is expressed through withdrawal. Alongside that, collectivist orthodox and anti-hegemonic ultra-orthodox positions will further develop. There is no such thing as *the* European Islam, but instead a multiplicity of voices implicitly or explicitly dealing with the situating of Islam with reference to Europe, to the homeland, and to global Islam. Yet, there are not only numerous voices, but there are also the dynamics of a process-based nature. This results from the fact that every position developed in search for situation in Europe brings its own problems along with it. But these problems are but thorns that drive the search further.

And yet with all this, this text has not delved into a special source of religious pluralism in Europe. When we have talked about 'Europe' here, we have indulged in a problematic over-generalisation. Actually, the migrants are confronted with very different political cultures in Europe. While the exile Islam of the first generation developed very similar positions throughout Europe, because on the whole it turned its back on Europe, this no longer applies for the positions of the second

[47] Jonker, *Wellenlänge*, p. 136ff.

generation. The differences between individualised, collectivist orthodox, and anti-hegemonic ultra-orthodox Muslims will in all probability develop differently in England than in France; and in The Netherlands, differently than they will in Germany. The gradual replacement of Turkish, as the language in which the debates are conducted, by the language of the country inhabited will drive this diversification yet further. European Islam, then, will not only continue to have a multiplicity of voices, but it will indeed have an *increasing* multiplicity of voices.

Bibliography

Al-Azmeh, Aziz, *Islams and modernities*, London: Routledge, 1993.

Anderson, Benedict, *Long-distance nationalism: world capitalism and the rise of identity politics*, Amsterdam: University of Amsterdam Centre for Asian Studies (= The Wertheim Lecture 1992).

Atacan, Fulya, *Kutsal Göc. Radikal Islamci bir grubun anatomisi*, Ankara: Baglam Yayincilik, 1993.

Bauman, Zygmunt, *Modernity and ambivalence*, Cambridge: Polity Press, 1991.

Berger, Peter L., *Zur dialektik von religion und gesellschaft*, Frankfurt am Main: Fischer, 1967/1973.

Bhabha, Homi, 'Remembering Fanon: Self, psyche and the colonial condition', in Patrick Williams and Laura Chrisman (eds.), *Colonial discourse and post-colonial theory. A reader*, Hemel Hempstead: Harvester, 1993, 112–23.

Bourdieu, Pierre, *Die feinen Unterschiede. Kritik der gesellschaftlichen Urteilskraft*, Frankfurt/Main: Suhrkamp, 1982.

Butler, Judith, *The psychic life of power: theories in subjection*, Stanford: Stanford University Press, 1997.

Çaglar, Ayse, 'Encountering the State in migration driven transnational fields: Turkish immigrants in Europe', unpublished Habilitation thesis, FU Berlin, 2003.

Clifford, James, 'On ethnographic allegory', in James Clifford and George E. Marcus (eds.), *Writing culture. The poetics and politics of ethnography*, Berkeley: University of California Press, 1986, 98–121.

Cohen, Anthony P., *The symbolic construction of community*, London and New York: Routledge, 1985.

Düttmann, Alexander G., *Zwischen den kulturen. Spannungen im kampf um anerkennung*, Frankfurt am Main: Suhrkamp, 1997.

Fanon, Frantz, *Die verdammten dieser Erde*. Frankfurt am Main: Suhrkamp, 1981.

Farouki, Suah Taji, *A fundamentalist quest: Hizb-al Tahrir and the search for an Islamic caliphate*, London: Grey Seal, 1996.

Foucault, Michel, *Überwachen und strafen. Die geburt des gefängnisses*, Frankfurt am Main: Suhrkamp, 1991.

Gençel, Aylın, 'Images of Islam in the diaspora – an ethnographic study of a Turkish family in Berlin', Unpublished Master thesis, Fakultät für Kulturwissenschaften, Europa-Universität, Frankfurt Oder, 2003.

Gilroy, Paul, 'Urban social movements, "race" and community', in Patrick Williams and Laura Chrisman (eds.), *Colonial discourse and post-colonial theory. A reader*, Hemel Hempstead: Harvester, 1993, 404–20.

Goffman, Erving, *Stigma*. Frankfurt am Main: Suhrkamp, 1963/1980.

Göe, Nilüfer, *Republik und Schleier. Die muslimische Frau in der modernen Türkei*, Berlin: Babel Verlag, 1995.

Greve, Martin, *Die musik der imaginären Türkei. musik und musikleben im kontext der migration aus der Türkei nach Deutschland*, Stuttgart/Weimar: Metzler-Verlag, 2003.

Habermas, Jürgen, 'Anerkennungskämpfe im demokratischen Rechtsstaat', in Charles Taylor, *Multikulturalismus und die politik der anerkennung*, Frankfurt/Main: Fischer, 1992, 147–96.

Hall, Stuart, 'The question of cultural identity', in Stuart Hall, David Held and Tony McGrew, *Modernity and its futures*, Cambridge: Polity Press, 1992.

Hirschman, Albert O., *Exit, voice and loyalty*. Cambridge, MA: Harvard University Press, 1970.

Honneth, Axel, *Kampf um anerkennung. Zur moralischen grammatik sozialer konflikte*. Frankfurt am Main: Suhrkamp, 1992.

Jonker, Gerdien, *Eine wellenlänge zu Gott: Der verband der islamischen kulturzentren in Europa*, Bielefeld: Transcript, 2002.

Jouili, Jeanette, Islamische weibliche identitäten in der Diaspora: Frauen maghrebinischer und türkischer Herkunft in Deutschland und Frankreich, application for a PhD thesis. Europa-Universität, Frankfurt Oder, 2001.

Kepel, Gilles, *Les banlieues de l'Islam*, Paris: Editions du Seuil, 1987.

Klinkhammer, Grit, *Moderne Formen islamischer Lebensführung*, Marburg: Diagonal, 2000.

Ramadan, Tariq, *Die Muslime im Westen*, Marburg: MSV Verlag, 2001.

Mumcu, Ugur, *Rabita*, Istanbul: Tekin, 1987.

Schiffauer, Werner, 'Migration and religiousness', in Lithman Gerholm (ed.), *The new Islamic presence in Western Europe*, London: Mansell Pub. Ltd, 1988.

    Die Migranten aus Subay. Türken in Deutschland: Eine Ethnographie, Stuttgart: Klett-Cotta, 1991.

    'Islam as a civil religion: political culture and the organization of diversity in Germany', in Tariq Modood and Pnina Werbner (eds.), *The politics of multiculturalism in the new Europe*, London and New York: Zed Books, 1997a.

    'Islamic vision and social reality – the political culture of Sunni Turkish Muslims in Germany', in S. Vertovec and C. Peach (eds.), *Islam in Europe – the politics of religion and community*, London: Macmillan, 1997b.

    Islamism in the diaspora. The fascination of political Islam among second generation German Turks, Oxford, 1999.

    Die Gottesmänner. Türkische Islamisten in Deutschland. Eine Studie zur Herstellung religiöser Evidenz, Frankfurt am Main: Suhrkamp, 2000.

Schiffauer, Werner, Gerd Baumann, Riva Kastoryano, and Steven Vertovec, (eds.), *Staat–schule–ethnizität*. Münster: Waxmann Verlag, 2002.

    Civil enculturation: nation-state, schools and ethnic difference in the Netherlands, Britain, Germany and France, New York, Oxford: Berghahn Books, 2004.

Senatsverwaltung für Schule, Jugend und Sport, (ed.), *Islamischer religionsunterricht an Berliner schulen – probleme, fragen, antworten.* Podiumsdiskussion am 29.3.2000 in der Friedrich-Ebert-Stiftung. Berlin, 2000.

Seufert, Günter, *Café Istanbul. Alltag, religion und politik in der modernen Türkei*, München: Beck, 1997.

Taylor, Charles, 'Die politik der anerkennung', in Charles Taylor (ed.), *multikulturalismus und die politik der anerkennung.* Frankfurt/Main: Fischer, 1992, 13–78.

6   Bosnian Islam as 'European Islam': limits and shifts of a concept

Xavier Bougarel

Because of the Yugoslav wars, the 1990s were marked by the rediscovery of an ancient and autochthonous Muslim presence in Europe. Bosnian Muslims,[1] in particular, have become the symbol of a European Islam that had been covered up by the Cold War and forgotten by Western Europe, as well as by the Muslim world. However, present insistence on the European dimension of Bosnian Islam has created as many problems as it has solved for a better understanding of the religious identity of Bosnian Muslims and of their position in the complex relations between Europe and Islam.

Bosnian Muslims are, undoubtedly, Europeans, just like their Serbian and Croatian neighbours. They have their own way of expressing their Muslim identity, as illustrated by the work of the anthropologists William Lockwood, Cornelia Sorabji and Tone Bringa.[2] But the notion of 'European Islam' often encompasses phenomena that are quite distinct, or even largely opposed to one another. For example, the *sufi* (mystic) or syncretistic practices present in traditional Bosnian Islam are of Ottoman origin. Meanwhile, the deep secularisation of contemporary

---

[1] As of 1993, the national name of 'Bosniac' (*Bošnjak*), has officially replaced the term 'Muslim' (*Musliman*), currently used since the end of the nineteenth century. However, for the purpose of clarity, we have chosen to continue using the term 'Muslim', except for the translation of quotations explicitly using the term 'Bosniac'. Finally, it is important not to confuse the term 'Bosniac', which applies only to Bosnian Muslims, with the term 'Bosnian' (Bosanac), referring to all the inhabitants of Bosnia-Herzegovina. On these identity and linguistic questions, see Xavier Bougarel, 2002, 'Comment peut-on être Bochniaque?' [How can one be Bosniac?], in Alain Dieckhoff and Riva Kastoryano (eds.), *Nationalismes en mutation en Méditerranée orientale* [Changing nationalisms in the Eastern Mediterranean], Paris: CNRS éditions, pp. 173–93.

[2] See William Lockwood, *European Moslems. Economy and ethnicity in Western Bosnia*, New York, London: Academic Press, 1974; Cornelia Sorabji, *Muslim identity and Islamic faith in Socialist Sarajevo*, University of Cambridge (unpublished PhD dissertation), 1988; Tone Bringa, *Being Muslim the Bosnian way. Identity and community in a Central Bosnian village*, Princeton: Princeton University Press, 1995.

Bosnian society, reflected by the frequency of mixed marriages and the widespread consumption of alcohol, is a result of fifty years of Communist modernisation. In some cases, the idea of Balkan Islam as a genuine 'European Islam' is even based on false assumptions: in 2001, a well-known American think tank stated that 'Wahhabi practices find little support from the essentially Bektashi Balkan [Muslim] communities',[3] whilst a large majority of Balkan Muslims – including Bosnian ones – are in fact Sunni Muslims belonging to the *hanefi* rite, and *Bektashis* are mainly present in Albania, where they represent only 20 per cent of the Muslim population.[4]

More generally, the will to present Bosnian Islam as a sort of positive cultural exception sometimes entails a conception of this 'European and tolerant' Islam as homogeneous and *sui generis*, set in opposition to another, implicit Islam, considered 'intolerant since non-European', which is located beyond the Bosporus and the Strait of Gibraltar, or represented by the 'non-autochthonous' Muslim populations living in Western Europe. Therefore, the idea of an insurmountable opposition between Europe and Islam is not deconstructed by such use of the Bosnian example, but simply silenced, only to be perpetuated elsewhere.[5]

In fact, heterodox practices, rules for peaceful religious coexistence and processes of secularisation, can be met in many parts of the Muslim world, and the realities of Bosnian Islam cannot be understood without taking into account its various and long-lasting links with the rest of the Muslim world. Moreover, in Bosnia-Herzegovina as elsewhere, Islam represents a plural and changing reality that cannot be grasped independently of the cleavages which run through it and of the social actors which give life to it day after day. This appears clearly in the various political and religious debates that have divided the Bosnian Muslim community and its religious institutions since 1878.[6]

---

[3] International Crisis Group, *Bin Laden and the Balkans: the politics of anti-terrorism*, Brussels (9 November), 2001, p. 2.

[4] Sunni Muslims, who claim to be the true representatives of the tradition (*sunna*), represent approximately 90 per cent of the Muslims in the world. The remaining 10 per cent are mainly Shi'a Muslims. *Hanefism* is one of the four *madhhab* (legal schools) existing within Sunni Islam. *Bektashism* is a heterodox sufi order incorporating some elements of Shi'a Islam in its doctrine. About Wahhabism, see note 34.

[5] For insight into such implicit orientalist discourses, see e.g. Milica Bakic-Hayden, 'Nesting orientalisms. The case of former Yugoslavia', *Slavic Review*, vol. 65, no. 4 (Winter), 1995, pp. 917–31.

[6] From 1878 to 1918, the occupation of Bosnia-Herzegovina by the Austro-Hungarian Empire marked the end of four centuries of Ottoman presence in this part of the Yugoslav space. Later on, Bosnia-Herzegovina was incorporated into the Kingdom of the Serbs, Croats and Slovenes (1918–41), the Independent State of Croatia (1941–5), and the

All of these debates can be boiled down to a central issue: that of the relationship between Islam and Western modernity. More concretely, they deal with the compatibility of the notions of *umma* (community of the faithful) and nationhood, the status of *shari'a* (Islamic law) in the modern state, the reform of traditional religious institutions, such as the *madrasa* (religious schools) and the *waqf* (religious endowments), or the adaptation of certain dietary and dress precepts.[7] But such debates are in no way restricted to Bosnia-Herzegovina, even if the specific situation of the Bosnian Muslims, reduced after 1878 to a religious and ethnic minority living within a non-Muslim European state, gives them a particular tone. Moreover, the conflicts that pit the *'ulama* (religious scholars) against the secular intellectuals or, within the *Islamska Zajednica* (Islamic Community) itself, the reformists against the traditionalists, cannot be explained without taking into consideration outside influences such as the religious reformism of Muhammad Abduh at the end of the nineteenth century, the revivalism of Rashid Rida and the pan-Islamism of Shakib Arslan in the 1930s, or the 'Islamic socialism' of Muhammad Iqbal and the radical Islamism of Sayyid Qutb in the 1960s and 1970s.

In the 1990s, the disappearance of the Yugoslav federation and the independence of Bosnia-Herzegovina, followed by its violent partition, deeply transformed the context in which these debates were taking place.[8] Having proclaimed their own political sovereignty, Bosnian Muslims attracted the attention of the whole Muslim world and thus rendered such debates more significant than ever.[9] But the war and post-war circumstances have not allowed their open and dispassionate formulation. Until December 1995, Islam was largely considered a

---

Federal Socialist Republic of Yugoslavia (1945–91). Following the disintegration of Yugoslavia at the beginning of the 1990s, Bosnia-Herzegovina became an independent state in March 1992. See e.g. Noel Malcolm, *Bosnia: a short history*, Basingstoke: Macmillan, 1994.

[7] See Fikret Karčić, *Društveno-pravni aspekti islamskog reformizma* [Social and legal aspects of Islamic reformism], Sarajevo: Islamski teološki fakultet, 1990; Šaćir Filandra, *Bošnjaci i moderna* [Bosniacs and modernity], Sarajevo: Bosanski kulturni centar, 1996.

[8] Between April 1992 and December 1995, Bosnia-Herzegovina experienced a particularly violent war, with a death toll of 200,000 persons, and the forced displacement of more than half of the pre-war population. In December 1995, the Dayton Peace Agreement confirmed the division of Bosnia-Herzegovina into two ethnic entities, the Croat–Muslim Federation and the Serb Republic. See Steven Burg and Paul Shoup, *The war in Bosnia-Herzegovina. Ethnic conflict and international intervention*, New York/London: Sharpe, 1999.

[9] See, among others, Tarek Mitri, 'La Bosnie-Herzégovine et la solidarité du monde arabe et islamique' [Bosnia-Herzegovina and the solidarity of the Arab and Islamic world], *Maghreb-Machrek*, no. 139 (January), 1993, pp. 123–36.

taboo issue within the Bosnian-Muslim community.[10] While Serbian
and Croatian propagandas referred to all Bosnian Muslims as 'fundamentalists' and '*mujaheddins*', Bosnian Muslims themselves put their
hopes in a foreign military intervention, and tried therefore to appear as
the unanimous defenders of democracy and multiculturalism. The end
of the war, on the contrary, sparked an outburst of grievances and
disagreements which had remained latent up until then, and Islam
became one of the main sources of conflict in the newspapers and
electronic media, as well as in everyday conversations. But the vigour of
these polemics could not compensate for their poor articulation, as
slogans and anathemas often replaced elaborate arguments.

At the same time, political power in the Muslim-held territories was
being monopolised by the Party of Democratic Action (*Stranka
Demokratske Akcije* – SDA), a nationalist party created by the representatives of a pan-Islamist stream that first appeared in the 1930s and
reorganised in the 1970s.[11] The will of the SDA to re-Islamise the
national identity of Bosnian Muslims actually resulted in a paradoxical
'nationalisation' of Bosnian Islam.[12] Meanwhile, the party's efforts to
reintroduce certain religious prohibitions in everyday life came up
against the multiform resistance of a largely secularised society.[13] These
inner dynamics of the Bosnian Muslim community, which are unusual
and most often implicit, have escaped the attention of most external
observers, or have been reduced to an inevitable consequence of the
war. Since 1996, the transformation of Bosnia-Herzegovina into a de
facto international protectorate has limited the room for manoeuvre of
the SDA leaders, suggesting this time an equally inevitable and spon-
taneous 'return to normality'. In any case, the internal diversity of
Bosnian Islam, the issues and cleavages along which this diversity is
structured, and the agency of Bosnian Muslims themselves have been
largely ignored.

[10] See X. Bougarel, 'L'Islam et la guerre en Bosnie-Herzégovine: l'impossible débat?'
[Islam and the war in Bosnia-Herzegovina: an impossible debate?], *L'Autre Europe*,
no. 36–7 (Winter), 1998, pp. 106–16.

[11] On this pan-Islamist stream, its links to the Egyptian Muslim Brothers and its interest
for the Pakistani and Iranian experiments, see X. Bougarel, 'From "Young Muslims" to
the Party of Democratic Action: the emergence of a pan-Islamist trend in Bosnia-
Herzegovina', *Islamic Studies*, Islamabad, vol. 36, no. 2–3 (Summer–Autumn), 1997,
pp. 533–49.

[12] See X. Bougarel, 'Comment peut-on être Bochniaque?' [How can one be Bosniac?].

[13] See X. Bougarel, 'Le Ramadan, révélateur des évolutions de l'islam en Bosnie-
Herzégovine' [Ramadan revealing the evolutions of Islam in Bosnia-Herzegovina], in
Faribah Adelkah and François Georgeon (eds.), *Ramadan et politique* [Ramadan and
politics], Paris: CNRS éditions, 2000, pp. 83–96.

Instead of describing this diversity in all of its complexity and concrete expressions, we will attempt here to present its main cleavages by using a few emblematic figures of contemporary Bosnian Islam.[14] The three authors referred to below have been chosen for various reasons. Quite apart from their political and religious responsibilities, they are mostly known for their writings. Despite their different intellectual backgrounds and personal questioning, they are equally interested in the question of the relationship between Islam and Western modernity. Each of them represents one of the definitions of Islam along which Islam in Bosnia-Herzegovina can be categorised: namely, Islam defined as an individual faith, as a common culture and as a discriminatory political ideology. These three definitions of Islam in Bosnia-Herzegovina, embodied by Fikret Karčić, Enes Karić and Adnan Jahić, will form the basis for our consideration later of the specificity of Bosnian Islam, and its place in today's or tomorrow's 'European Islam'.

Fikret Karčić: Islam as individual faith

Fikret Karčić was born in Višegrad (eastern Bosnia) in 1955. He studied at the *madrasa* of Sarajevo, from where he graduated in 1973. He went on to study law and wrote an MA thesis on 'The Shari'a Courts of Justice in Yugoslavia 1918–1941' in 1985, followed in 1989 by a PhD dissertation on 'The movement for the reform of the Shari'a and its influence in the first half of the 20th century'.[15] In 1978, he began teaching *fikh* (Islamic jurisprudence) at the Faculty of Islamic Theology of Sarajevo. Fikret Karčić was elected president of the Assembly of the *Islamska Zajednica* (Islamic Community) of Bosnia-Herzegovina in the late 1980s, and began taking on important religious responsibilities. In 1989, after the Islamic religious institutions experienced a serious internal crisis linked with the end of the Communist regime, he was one of the authors of the new constitution of the *Islamska Zajednica* of Yugoslavia, and became a close adviser to the new *Reis-ul-Ulema*[16] Jakub

---

[14] For a more elaborate analysis of the evolution of Bosnian Islam in the 1990s, see X. Bougarel, 'L'Islam bosniaque, entre identité culturelle et idéologie politique' [Bosnian Islam between cultural identity and political ideology], in Xavier Bougarel and Nathalie Clayer (eds.), *Le nouvel Islam balkanique: les musulmans comme acteurs du post-communisme, 1990–2000* [The new Balkan Islam: Muslims as actors of post-communism 1990–2000], Paris: Maisonneuve & Larose, 2001, pp. 79–132.

[15] See F. Karčić, *Šeriatski sudovi u Jugoslaviji 1918–1941* [The Shari'ah Courts of Justice in Yugoslavia 1918–1941], Sarajevo: Islamska Zajednica, 1986; F. Karčić, *Društveno-pravni aspekti islamskog reformizma*.

[16] The function of *Reis-ul-Ulema* (chief of the *'ulamas*) was created by the Austro-Hungarian authorities in 1882, four years after they occupied Bosnia-Herzegovina. Its authority was extended to the whole Yugoslav territory in 1930.

Selimoski. Finally, shortly after the outbreak of the war, he left Bosnia-Herzegovina for Malaysia, where he became associate professor at the International Islamic University of Kuala Lumpur.

It is firstly through his role as a legal adviser that Fikret Karčić has developed his own conception of Islam. Beyond his co-authorship of the new constitution of the *Islamska Zajednica*, he was also in charge of defining an official Islamic stance on the introduction of a multiparty system. In a text published in January 1990, he writes that 'the religious communities and their members are not only objects of the democratisation process, but are also active participants in it', because 'the members of each religious community . . . represent an important part of the electorate, whose political commitment is a necessary condition for the construction of a democratic society'. Against this background, he considers that it is 'essential for religious communities to define the "rules of the game" for religious institutions and functionaries'.[17]

Karčić believes in particular that the *Islamska Zajednica*, while supporting the democratisation process and demanding the restoration of various religious rights, should proclaim its political neutrality. For him, the introduction of a multiparty system is a good opportunity to put an end to the political instrumentalisation of religious institutions: 'In a monistic system, if one did not want or could not act within the framework of the party in power, they did so within one of the [other] existing institutions. Sometimes, it was the religious community. In a system with several political parties, this is out of the question.' Therefore, Karčić wants to forbid the *'ulamas* to exercise any political responsibility, thus leaving the choices concerning party affiliation and vote to 'the conscience of each believer. The believers will then use the following criterion as guidance: to what degree does the programme of a party integrate the general values and principles of Islamic teachings?'.[18] He is, above all, resolutely against the creation of a Muslim or Islamic party:

The rule of neutrality of the I[*slamska*] Z[*ajednica*] should be particularly applied in regard to 'Muslim' parties or, if the case arises, to 'Islamic' parties. The history of political life in pre-war Yugoslavia and in some contemporary Muslim countries is full of examples of party struggles being imported from the political field into the religious institutions, of 'Muslim' parties fighting for influence upon the Islamic institutions, bodies and foundations. Such a situation has systematically had negative consequences.[19]

---

[17] F. Karčić, 'Islamska Zajednica i reforma jugoslovenskog političkog sistema' [The Islamic Community and the reform of the Yugoslav political system], *Glasnik Rijaseta IZ-e*, vol. 52, no. 1 (January–February), 1990b, pp. 7–13.
[18] Ibid.
[19] Ibid.

Although the positions elaborated by Fikret Karčić have been taken up in various official statements of the *Islamska Zajednica*, they were difficult to implement in reality after the creation of the SDA by the representatives of the pan-Islamist stream, its instrumentalisation of Islamic symbols for nationalistic purposes, and the widespread and conspicuous support this party enjoyed among the *'ulamas*.[20] These positions, however, remain significant, insofar as they point out two issues that are central in Karčić's writings: namely, the separation of religion from the state and the resulting individualisation of the faith.

In his works on the *shari'a*, Karčić is first of all interested in the possible ways to adapt the *shari'a* to the modern world and, more specifically, to the secular state. In 1985, he notes that 'after the abolition of the *shari'a* courts of justice [in 1947], the essence of certain institutions and principles of the *shari'a* continue to exist in the form of the moral and religious principles and practices of the Yugoslav citizens of Islamic faith'.[21] Six years later, during a conference on legal principles in Islam, he draws a contrast between the Muslim states, in which the *shari'a* constitutes a territorial law applying to everyone, and states with a Muslim minority, in which the *shari'a* is only a personal status, or a mere 'individual moral code for practising Muslims'.[22] Finally, in response to criticism from the Serbian press, he considers that 'the secular state . . . is the best model for the organisation of the relationship between political and religious authorities in multi-religious societies'; he declares himself to be 'reserved towards any ideological state'; and he considers that 'the idea of an "Islamic republic" in Bosnia-Herzegovina does not have any theoretical or practical basis'.[23]

Drawing on the Bosnian case, Fikret Karčić expands his analyses to the Muslim world in general. In his PhD dissertation, he writes that

the social functions of any law, including the *shari'a*, depend on the state of social relations in given societies. The *shari'a* consists of elements that can have various social, economical, cultural and political consequences. The social functions of this law will depend on which elements are emphasised. *Shari'a* can serve social modernisation, democratisation of the political and legal system and opening towards other cultures, or reactionary processes that may result in dogmatism, conservatism, political totalitarianism and cultural autarky.[24]

---

[20] See X. Bougarel, , 'From "Young Muslims" to the Party of Democratic Action'.
[21] F. Karčić, *Šeriatski sudovi*, p. 155.
[22] Presentation at the conference "Law in Islam", organised by the Zagreb mosque in April 1991, quoted in *Muslimanski Glas*, vol. 1, no. 2 (3 May 1991), p. 14.
[23] F. Karčić, 'O "islamskoj republici" u BiH' [On the "Islamic Republic" in Bosnia-Herzegovina], *Preporod*, vol. 21, no. 3 (February 1st), 1990c, p. 3.
[24] F. Karčić, *Društveno-pravni aspekti*, p. 195.

Later on, in his typology of contemporary legal interpretations of Islam, Karčić distinguishes four main tendencies: *secularists*, for whom 'Islam is a religion in the generally accepted sense of the term, whose legitimate field of expression is the personal, private sphere of the individual. They underline the moral values of Islam but no longer consider its teachings as the foundation of the social, political and legal system'; *traditionalists*, for whom 'Islam is defined as "religion and law"', but [who accept] the historical transformations of its social function and of the field of validity of Islamic law. The differentiation between religious norms and institutions and secular ones is accepted as a product of history, as well as the *de facto* domination of secular institutions'; *Islamic modernists*, who consider that 'updated Islamic teachings can represent an appropriate ideological foundation for public life in Muslim countries, and that a reformed *shari'a* can become the base or an important constituent part of positive law'; and *revivalists*, who 'try in particular to construct a complete ideology based on the main sources of Islamic teachings and on early Muslim history', and 'give to the experience of the original Muslim community of Medina a normative character, considering it as a model rather than a historical example of the fulfilment of Islam'.[25]

Finally, Karčić's reflection on the interpretation and modernisation of the *shari'a* led him toward an outline of an Islamic justification of the principle of secularism. In a text entitled 'Meaning and expression of Islam in the secular state', he considers that with the separation of religion from the state, 'religious communities lose many privileges . . . but, at the same time, become free to manage their own affairs without state intervention' and 'gain the possibility to devote themselves entirely to their original mission: the satisfaction of the religious needs of their members'. According to Karčić,

in a secular state, every religion is treated as the private affair of citizens, is excluded from politics, and has no influence on law. This is the status that Islam has and should have, in accordance with the principle of equality between religions . . . Islam can only be a religion and its legitimate field of expression is the private life of citizens.

In this context, he makes clear that 'some parts of the Islamic message take on a different meaning', and that 'the value judgements expressed in prescriptions concerning the *mu'amelat* [social relations] survive only

---

[25] F. Karčić, 'Razumijevanje islamskog vjerozakona (šeriata) u savremenom muslimanskom svijetu' [The understanding of Islamic law (shari'a) in the contemporary Islamic world], in Nusret Čančar and Enes Karić (eds.), *Islamski fundamentalizam. Šta je to?* [Islamic fundamentalism. What is it?], Sarajevo: Biblioteka 'Preporoda' i 'Islamske misli', 1990d, pp. 37–43.

insofar as they are carried on into the customs or the personal moral choices of individuals'.[26]

In this text which summarises his thinking, Fikret Karčić also tries to break with the classic Islamic representation of the world, pointing out that

it would be unjustified at the theoretical level, and anachronistic from an historical point of view to apply to contemporary international relations the categories of the 'house of Islam' [dar-al-islam] and 'house of war' [dar-al-harb],[27] or to place the situation of Muslims living in countries with a secular social order in this last category.

It is on this issue of the representation of the world – and the place of Bosnian Muslims in it – that Karčić focuses his attention during the war. From 1992 onwards, he seems to interrupt his reflection on the *shari'a*, without ever renouncing his former writings. But his priority is to present the reality of the Islamic renewal in the Balkans – i.e. 'mainly related to the religious and cultural spheres'[28] – and to denounce the biased representations coming from Serbia or Western countries.[29] Behind these endeavours, directly motivated by the war, there is a more general concern: Fikret Karčić counters Samuel Huntington's thesis about the 'clash of civilisations' by stating that 'if there are today in Bosnia-Herzegovina some elements of civil war, religious war or civilisational conflict, they are deliberately created in order to conceal the essential issue: aggression, territorial conquest, genocide'. Karčić concludes his critique of the Harvard University professor in the following way:

Apparently, certain influential circles in the West see in Bosnia-Herzegovina an ongoing conflict between civilisations. The Bosniacs [Bosnian Muslims] who accept such an interpretation or who would start to behave in accordance with it would indeed confirm this hypothesis. This seems paradoxical, but the nation which is accused of fundamentalism is fighting against the estrangement of

---

[26] F. Karčić, 'Značenje i iskazivanje islama u svjetovnoj državi' [Significance and expression of Islam in the secular state], in E. Karić (ed.), *Suvremena ideologijska tumačenja Kur'ana i islama* [The modern ideological interpretations of the Qur'an and Islam], Zagreb: Kulturni radnik, 1990e, pp. 29–36.

[27] The *'ulama* generally divide the world into two 'houses', the 'house of Islam' (*dar-al-islam*), covering all Muslim states in which the *shari'a* is implemented, and the 'house of war' (*dar-al-harb*), embracing the non-Muslim states. Some add a third 'house', the 'house of contract' (*dar-al-ahd*), which comprises the non-Muslim states allowing their Muslim minorities to practise their religion.

[28] F. Karčić, 'Islamic revival in the Balkans', *Islamic Studies*, Islamabad, vol. 36, no. 2–3 (Summer/Autumn), 1997, pp. 565–81.

[29] F. Karčić, 'Distorted images of Islam: the case of former Yugoslavia', *Intellectual Discourse*, Kuala Lumpur, vol. 3, no. 2, 1995a, pp. 139–52.

civilisations, is fighting so that the 'fault lines' become the lines of a fruitful coexistence, and not the lines of an inevitable confrontation.[30]

Despite the war, Fikret Karčić's concern to reconcile Islam with Western modernity and to encourage its individual, rather than its collective expression, remains intact.

Enes Karić: Islam as common culture

Enes Karić was born to a religious family in Travnik (central Bosnia) in 1958. Like Fikret Karčić, he also studied at the *madrasa* of Sarajevo, and he participated in the informal discussion circle created by Husein Đozo in the 1970s.[31] He graduated from the *madrasa* in 1978 and studied journalism and literature. He started teaching *tafsir* (interpretation of the Qur'an) at the Faculty of Islamic Theology in Sarajevo in 1982, and in 1989 he completed a PhD dissertation on the 'Hermeneutical problems in the translation of the Qur'an into Serbo-Croatian'.[32] During that same period, he played a leading part in the intellectual renewal of the *Islamska Zajednica* by publishing the journal *Islamska Misao* [Islamic Thought], by editing two books on *The contemporary ideological interpretations of the Qur'an and Islam* and *The Qur'an in the contemporary time*,[33] and by translating the works of Seyd Hussein Nasr, Fazlur Rahman and Mohamed Arkoun. Due to his intellectual independence, he rapidly got into trouble with the religious hierarchy and, in March 1991, he was removed from the editorial staff of *Islamska Misao* by Salih Čolaković, president of the *Islamska Zajednica* of Bosnia-Herzegovina and a close associate of the *Wahhabi* networks supported by Saudi Arabia.[34]

Enes Karić continued his religious activities after 1991, as shown by his translation of the Qur'an into Bosnian in 1995.[35] But from 1992 onwards, he became known mainly through his political activities. He

---

[30] F. Karčić, 'Ubijanje naroda u sjeni "sudara civilizacija" ' [The massacre of a nation in the shadow of the 'clash of civilisations'], *Ljiljan*, vol. 4, no. 111 (1 March), 1995b, pp. 32–3.

[31] See: X. Bougarel, 'From "Young Muslims" to the Party of Democratic Action'.

[32] E. Karić, *Hemeneutika Kur'ana* [Hermeneutics of the Qur'an], Zagreb: Biblioteka Filozofska istraživanja, 1990b.

[33] E. Karić, *Suvremena ideologijska tumačenja*; E. Karić, *Kur'an u savremenom dobu* [The Qur'an in contemporary time], Sarajevo: Svjetlost, 1991.

[34] Wahhabism is a neo-fundamentalist Sunni movement founded at the end of the eighteenth century by Ibn Abd al-Wahhab. It is especially hostile to Shi'a Islam, sufi orders and religious reformism, and constitutes the official religious doctrine of Saudi Arabia since its creation in 1932.

[35] *Kur'an sa prijevodom na bosanski jezik* [The Qur'an, with Translation into Bosnian], Sarajevo: Bosanska knjiga, 1995.

was an active contributor to *Muslimanski Glas* ('The Muslim Voice', the unofficial organ of the SDA) and, in December 1992, was elected vice-president of the new Council of the Congress of Muslim intellectuals. In June 1994, he was appointed Minister of Education and Culture by the Prime Minister Haris Silajdžić. He supported the Prime Minister in his growing disagreements with the SDA leaders and, in January 1996, left the government and joined the Party for Bosnia-Herzegovina (*Stranka za Bosnu i Herzegovinu* – SBiH) launched by Silajdžić. After the electoral defeat of this party in September 1996, he put an end to his political career and devoted himself to the *Ibn Sina Foundation*, a philosophical and religious foundation supported by Iran.

In the same way that the reflections of Fikret Karčić are based on the *shari'a*, the Qur'an inspires Enes Karić's thinking. In his PhD dissertation, he insists on the open, polysemic and irrevocably mysterious nature of the Qur'an. Upon this basis, Karić tries to show that the translation of the Qur'an is always an interpretation of it, and to justify the plurality of these interpretations, depending on both the historical ('because of the exceptionally open character of this structure, every era has its own way of reading the Qur'an, its own way of uttering it and, therefore, its own way of translating it')[36] and the geographical contexts:

The destiny of Islam lies in 'minor' or 'regional' theologies. Historically, the numerous regional theological systems of Islam have benefited and still benefit from a great autonomy, thanks to these multiple interpretations and 'faces' of the Qur'an. We are thus dealing with several correct readings of the Qur'an, which resulted in the appearance of many 'regional theologies' . . . We have in Islam a 'plurality of theologies' that denies any theology with a capital 'T'.[37]

According to Karić, Islam is one, but the Muslim cultures deriving from it are diverse, changing and irreducible to one culture. At the beginning of the 1990s, he already calls for a renewal of the *ijtihad* (interpretation efforts), and declares his hostility towards Islamic fundamentalism that 'ignores the limit between the source of faith and the historical translation of this source', that 'attributes divine qualities to something that is only a past human interpretation' and, more concretely,

---

[36] E. Karić, *Hemeneutika Kur'ana*, p. 219.

[37] Ibid., p. 247. A similar remark can be found in the commentary of Enes Karić on his own translation of the Qur'an: 'the Qur'an was given once and for all as the Word of God, but the understanding and the interpretation of the Qur'an have not been sealed for ever. Today's Muslims should know that every new interpretation of the Qur'an is at the same time an active interpretation of the world and a search for a worthy place in it. Every new fertile rainfall comes from clouds that are differently disposed in the same sky' ('Kur'anski univerzum (pogovor prijevodu)' [The Universe of the Qur'an (translation postscript)], *Kur'an sa prijevodom*, p. 1269).

reduces Islam, a universal religion, 'to the religion of two cities [Mecca and Medina], linking it with a specific soil, limiting it to the Arabs'.[38] In a similar way, Karić favours the introduction in school curricula of comparative science of religions. According to him, a separate religious teaching would underline the 'polemical and, thus, exclusive features' of the great monotheistic religions. Moreover, he considers that the true place for religious education is not the public school, but the mosque or the church, since 'faith is, first and foremost, an intimate and deep feeling, a personal feeling that cannot be expressed outside its own frameworks, atmospheres, spaces and temporalities'.[39]

For Karić, faith is an individual feeling, but can only remain lively if embedded in a common tradition and culture. This insistence on 'Islam as faith and culture'[40] explains the positions he takes during the war. Unlike Fikret Karčić, he does not hesitate to attribute a religious dimension to war: he compares the struggle of Bosnian Muslims to that of the Prophet against the infidels at Badr,[41] and states that through their struggle, 'the Bosniacs have illuminated the face of the *umma*'.[42] Karić even considers that 'the pious books, starting with the Qur'an, speak of the *jihad* as the various activities that contribute to safeguard the free expression of Islam, to protect goods, life, honour, and dignity . . . If Muslims need a state in order to defend these values, then the building of this state represents – from a religious point of view – a *jihad* par excellence!'.[43] However, Karić never ceases emphasising that Bosnian

---

[38] E. Karić, 'Fundamentalizam Prokrustove postelje' [Fundamentalism: The Bed of Procruste], in N. Čančar and E. Karić, *Islamski fundamentalizam. Šta je to?*, pp. 89–93.

[39] E. Karić, 'Dvosjekli mač vjeronauke u školi' [The double-edged sword of religious teaching in school], *Muslimanski Glas*, vol. 2, no. 10 (28 June), 1991a, p. 15. This personal position of Enes Karić is different from the position of the *Islamska Zajednica*, who was in favour of a separate religious teaching and managed to impose this formula on Karić in 1994.

[40] E. Karić, 'Značenje i iskazivanje islama u budućoj Bosni i Hercegovini' [Significance and expression of Islam in the future Bosnia-Herzegovina], in *Kongres bosansko-muslimanskih intelektualaca* (22 December 1992), Sarajevo: Bosnagraf, 1993, pp. 97–100. The title of this text by Enes Karić is obviously an allusion to the text published two years earlier by Fikret Karčić.

[41] E. Karić, 'Bosna je bošnjački Bedr' [Bosnia is the Bosniac Badr], *Ljiljan*, vol. 3, no. 58 (23 February), 1994b, p. 31.

[42] E. Karić, 'Bošnjaci su Ummetu osvjetlali obraz' [The Bosniacs have illuminated the face of the umma], *Ljiljan*, vol. 3, no. 61 (16 March), 1994c, p. 31.

[43] E. Karić, 'Agresija na Bosnu i Hercegovinu i pitanje džihada' [The aggression against Bosnia-Herzegovina and the question of jihad], in *Duhovna snaga odbrane* [The spiritual force of Defence], Sarajevo: Vojna biblioteka, no. 5, 1994a, pp. 73–77. Being an experienced linguist and philologist, Enes Karić goes back to the polysemy of the term 'jihad' before observing that, from a religious point of view, 'what the fighters of the Bosnian Army are doing is indeed a highest-level jihad', but that 'some fighters [do it] out of patriotism, others out of patriotism and religious inspiration, still others out of courage and heroism, or to protect their family and property'. In this context, Karić

Muslims have two homelands, 'the European one – their native soil, their country – and the spiritual, Islamic and oriental one'.[44] He reminds those who are tempted by anti-Europeanism that 'Europe is our homeland in a broader sense. We are Europeans by origin, by language and by many elements of our culture. The European identity of the Bosniacs does not contradict their Muslim identity.'[45]

As Minister of Education and Culture, Karić tries to reinforce the national Muslim identity by launching the publication of new text-books, entrusting the formalisation of a distinct Bosnian language to a group of linguists, and encouraging the activities of the Muslim cultural association *'Preporod'* ('Renaissance'). His activism costs him some criticism from the non-nationalist parties, when, for example, he sup-ports textbooks putting side by side Darwin's evolutionist thesis and the religious interpretation of the creation of the world, or when he forbids the broadcasting of music produced in Serbia or in Croatia. But Karić rejects the kind of multiculturalism these parties are referring to, 'a hybrid and artificial model that means belonging to no particular cul-ture', and proposes instead a 'Bosnian multiculturalism [that] is the natural product of the traditional cultures of Bosnia',[46] a 'genuine multiculturalism and multireligiosity . . . created in everyday life intercourses, and not meant to be shown to the world as a museum curiosity'.[47]

However, if Enes Karić occasionally sneers at the 'multiculturalist safaris' of some Westerners,[48] his harshest critiques are directed at the foreign *Wahhabi* missionaries. He constantly denounces the way these missionaries and their local followers insist on a sterile religious form-alism and deny the culture of Islam that is specific to Bosnian Muslims. In an important text entitled 'Our Bosniac identity and our Muslim identity', Karić writes that

the Muslim identity and the Islam of the Bosniacs are being attacked from all sides, but first of all by those neophyte and aggressive local Muslims working for [Islamic] humanitarians with dubious intentions. They attack the Islam as

considers that 'it would not be advisable to crush the diversity of these motivations that make up the mosaic of the heroic Bosniac resistance, and especially not by imposing something that could be unfavourably received by the fighters, or at least some of them' (ibid.).

[44] E. Karić, 'Značenje i iskazivanje islama u budućoj Bosni i Hercegovini'.

[45] E. Karić, 'Naše bosanstvo i naše evropejstvo' [Our Bosnian identity and our European identity], *Ljiljan*, vol. 6, no. 263 (January), 1998a, p. 20.

[46] E. Karić, 'Suze, stepe i pustinje' [Tears, steppes and deserts], *Ljiljan*, vol. 3, no. 100 (14 December), 1994d, p. 53.

[47] E. Karić, 'Značenje i iskazivanje islama u budućoj Bosni i Hercegovini'.

[48] E. Karić, 'Suze, stepe i pustinje'.

practised by the Bosniacs exactly where it contributes the most to the affirmation of our national identity and our spiritual matrix.[49]

To such a 'reduction of Bosnian Muslim identity to a coarse and sterile faith', Karić sets in opposition 'the Bosnian way of living Islam as a faith, a culture, a civilisation, a source of inspiration and a spiritual identification . . . the tolerant affirmation of all the traditional and – why not say this – Bosniac ways of living Islam in Bosnia'. For Karić, 'Arabs have their own traditional ways of living the universality of Islam, and we have ours. Moreover, no Muslim nation, if it is a nation, can be Muslim without these particularities that have been preserved for centuries, together with the universality of Islam.'[50]

While Karić's hostility towards Wahhabism is logical and constant, the evolution of his relations with the leaders of the SDA and the *Islamska Zajednica* is more unexpected. In the early 1990s, his definition of Islam as a common culture prompted him to join them in the reaffirmation and re-Islamisation of the national Muslim identity. But the same definition urges him more and more to deplore the artificial and vulgar features of the new religious kitsch, and to resist the political instrumentalisation of Islam by the SDA.

Already in 1992, Enes Karić links his definition of 'Islam as faith and culture' with the acceptance of the 'principle of the secular state and the separation of religion and state'.[51] According to him, this principle is not only necessary for the coexistence of the different religious communities in Bosnia-Herzegovina, but also for Bosnian Muslims themselves: 'What this principle ensures is the fact that Islam is their common treasure, as a religion, as a culture and as a tradition. In this way, the tolerance between Muslims is guaranteed and Islam cannot become the property of some of them.'[52] Three years later, he develops this reasoning in a text where his split with the SDA leaders is already perceptible:

It is very important that Bosnian Muslims have for long accepted the principle of Islam being practised and expressed within a secular society and a secular state. In today's European context, this principle helps Bosnian Muslims since it assures them an expression of Islam without any ideological *diktat* and without any political and ideological fiat on what the "true Islam" is. Islam in Bosnia is the common treasure of all Bosniacs, this precious treasure from which they have drawn for centuries their multiple religious, cultural, artistic, literary, urban, architectural inspirations. According to this conception . . . Islam cannot

---

[49] E. Karić, 'Naše bošjnastvo i naše muslimanstvo' [Our Bosniac identity and our Muslim identity], *Ljiljan*, vol. 6, no. 264 (4 February), 1998b, pp. 20–2.
[50] Ibid.
[51] E. Karić, 'Značenje i iskazivanje islama u budućoj Bosni i Hercegovini'.
[52] Ibid.

become anybody's property or monopoly, nor can it become the object of pragmatic adaptations to the political imperatives of the day. Bosniacs have to protect themselves against themselves, and against all forms of religious, traditional, political or cultural ostracism.[53]

From the affirmation of the specificity of Bosnian Islam to the defence of its internal pluralism, Enes Karić's approach is in fact quite coherent: it is precisely because he defines Islam as a common culture that he refuses to see it reduced to a discriminatory political ideology.

Adnan Jahić: Islam as a discriminatory political ideology

Unlike Fikret Karčić and Enes Karić, Adnan Jahić did not receive any formal religious education, despite the fact that he comes from a family of local notables and *'ulama*. He was born in Tuzla in 1967 and studied philosophy and journalism in Sarajevo. During his studies, he wrote an MA thesis on 'The history of the relations between religion and philosophy, from the ancient times to the time of Abu Nasr al-Farabi'. In 1995, he also published a book praising the Muslim military formations that collaborated with the German troops during World War II, and in which some members of his family seem to have played an important part.[54]

However, Adnan Jahić has become famous thanks to his journalistic and political activities, rather than his philosophical or historical works. In Tuzla, he was one of the main columnists of *'Zmaj od Bosne'* ('The Dragon of Bosnia'),[55] the unofficial organ of the local SDA during the war, and he was the chief editor of the monthly publication *'Hikmet'* ('Wisdom'),[56] launched by the new Mufti of Tuzla in 1993. While *'Hikmet'* dealt mainly with religious issues, *'Zmaj od Bosne'* became famous for its virulent attacks against the municipality of Tuzla, led by the non-nationalist parties, and was even criticised by Tadeusz Mazowiecki, the Special Rapporteur of the UN Commission on Human Rights, for its threats against the local Serb population. This did not prevent Jahić from

---

[53] E. Karić, 'Islam u suvremenoj Bosni' [Islam in contemporary Bosnia], in E. Karić, *Bosna sjete i zaborava* [Bosnia recalls and forgets], Zagreb: Durieux, 1997b, pp. 88–95.

[54] A. Jahić, *Muslimanske formacije tuzlanskog kraja u drugom svjetskom ratu* [The Muslim formations of the Tuzla area during World War II], Tuzla: Bosnoljublje, 1995e.

[55] This title alludes to Husein-kapetan Gradačević, an important figure from Gradačać, in the region of Tuzla, who led an uprising against the administrative and military reforms imposed in 1831 by the central Ottoman authorities, and whose war name was 'Zmaj od Bosne'. Since the 1990s, Bosnian Muslim historians have tended to present this uprising as one of the first signs of the Bosnian Muslim national awakening.

[56] In the interwar period, *'Hikmet'* was the organ of the traditionalist *'ulama*, who were opposed to the religious reforms of the Reis-ul-Ulema Džemaludin Čausević. See F. Karčić, *Društveno-pravni aspekti islamskog reformizma.*

enjoying a rapid political rise: having been a member of the regional direction of the SDA since 1994, he was elected to the Parliament of Bosnia-Herzegovina in September 1996, where he became president of the SDA parliamentary group. One year later, he had to resign from this function, but became then the official spokesperson of the SDA.[57]

Jahić's education is reflected in his strong interest in the relationship between Islam and philosophy. Among other things, he condemns the 'Cartesian turn through which the individual Self has a methodological, and then an ethical, axiological and overall primacy', permitting the emergence of a 'philosophical pluralism in the sense of an ideological diversity of goals and ends', and leading little by little to 'materialism, scientism, existentialism and the other forms of philosophical thinking in the modern world'. To these various streams of modern Western philosophy, he opposes an Islamic philosophy that, 'by definition, can only be one, and whose central theme has been and still remains God and His Revelation, that is, the divine and the human in the light of the Revelation'. According to Jahić, 'in no case should this kind of monolithism be considered as an imperfection, but as a quality and a sign of coherence in the original intention'.[58]

In the same way, Jahić contrasts the Western concept of democracy with the Islamic one. In the Western concept,

human rights and liberties constitute the greatest value of the community. Here lies the fundamental weakness of the Western society: there is no active relation between the state and the society, there is no progress at the spiritual and ethical level. Good as content exhausts itself in politics as form.

On the contrary, Islamic democracy refers to the principle of *tawhid* (uniqueness of God), and insists on 'the ethical perspective of

---

[57] In September 1997, the deputies of the three main nationalist parties (the Muslim SDA, the Serb SDS and the Croat HDZ) in the Parliament of Bosnia-Herzegovina elected as president of the Commission for Human Rights, Refugees and Asylum Velibor Ostojić, a high-ranking leader of the SDS, suspected to have taken an active part in the 'ethnic cleansing' of the town of Foča (eastern Bosnia) in 1992. Faced with protests by non-nationalist parties and independent media, the SDA changed its mind, claiming that the vote of its deputies was a mere 'misunderstanding', and Adnan Jahić had to resign from the presidency of the SDA parliamentary group.

[58] A. Jahić, 'Baqir As-Sadr i naša filozofija' [Baqir As-Sadr and our philosophy], *Hikmet*, vol. 8, no. 8/92, (August), 1995a, pp. 360–3. More precisely, Adnan Jahić acknowledges a certain 'confining [of medieval Muslim thinking] within obsolete methodological frameworks . . . which prevented any possibility of intellectual renewal and enrichment of the philosophical discipline in the Muslim world'. But he prefers a 'reinforcement of the [Islamic philosophical] approach, in a methodical and rational way, which would definitely welcome certain Western experiences', to some 'inarticulate efforts of superficial adaptation and fundamental reconciliation with certain philosophical themes of Western origin' (ibid.)

democracy': 'Islam is not primarily interested in formal democracy (even if it is in no case hostile to it), but rather in its principles and positive ethical values that will contribute to the fulfilment of the Islamic idea within the community.' According to Jahić, 'there will never be a place in Islamic political thinking for Western-style liberal democracy, which does not care about the general good of its own society, about its spiritual and ethical condition'.[59]

Therefore, unlike Fikret Karčić and Enes Karić, Adnan Jahić perceives the relationship between Islam and the West in terms of a structural opposition. He believes that the aim of the Western world is the 'total annihilation of the Muslim world',[60] and invites the latter to rid itself of 'Western secularism and nihilism, of positivism and existentialist materialism in philosophy and science, and of hedonism and utilitarianism in the field of ethics and morality'.[61] He recognises that, as Bosnian Muslims, 'we belong to the West in terms of geography and, partly, in terms of civilisation'. But immediately after that, he reminds his readers that 'in no case do we belong culturally and spiritually to the West', and he deplores the Western influence on Bosnian society, as reflected by widespread sexual promiscuity and hedonism, as well as the ideas of 'multiculturalism, human rights and tolerance'.[62] In his eyes, the war in Bosnia-Herzegovina is therefore 'the final confrontation between the autochthonous national and cultural values of the Bosniacs and the alien ones, imported from the West, which have been imposed on us [and presented] as our own for a long time'.[63]

This attitude of Adnan Jahić towards the West inevitably influences his reflections on the relationship between Islam and nationhood, and between Islam and politics. He rejects the penetration of the Western concepts of nationhood and secularism in the Muslim world, and sets against them 'the political unity of the *umma* and the Islamic social order'.[64] In both cases, however, Jahić soon comes up against reality, and his reflections become more hesitant. In some texts, he calls for the

---

[59] A. Jahić, 'Zavičajnost demokratije u islamskom političkom mišljenju' [The embeddedness of democracy in Islamic political thinking], *Hikmet*, vol. 9, nos. 9–12/105–108 (November), 1996b, pp. 247–54.

[60] A. Jahić, 'Bošnjaci i Zapad – principi budućih odnosa' [Bosniacs and the West – principles of future relations], *Hikmet*, vol. 8, no. 4/88 (April), 1995b, pp. 148–50.

[61] A. Jahić, 'Neke opservacije o političkim perspektivama islamskog svijeta' [Some observations on the political perspectives of the Muslim world], *Hikmet*, vol. 8, no. 6/90 (June), 1995f, pp. 248–53.

[62] A. Jahić, 'Bošnjaci i Zapad'.

[63] A. Jahić, 'Znamo, a nećemo?!' [Do we know, but we do not want?!], *Hikmet*, vol. 8, no. 2/86 (February), 1995g, pp. 52–3.

[64] A. Jahić, 'Neke opservacije'.

reinforcement of the unity of the *umma* against all 'political, national, civilisational, linguistic, socio-cultural and ideological particularisms'.[65] Elsewhere, he states on the contrary that 'Bosniacs as well as the other Muslims have their own culture based on Islam, enriched by different national traditions'.[66]

His most elaborate reflection on the national question is probably a text entitled 'Islam and nationhood in the light of the current events in the Muslim World'.[67] In this text, published in 1995, Jahić reaffirms the pre-eminence of the *umma* as an ideal which surpasses that of the nation as a worldly reality. But he considers also that it is essential to take this reality into account, and to reconcile it with Islam. What Jahić therefore rejects is the secular definition of the nation, and in particular any attempt to underplay the role of Islam or to emphasise the importance of pre-Islamic elements in the identity of Muslim nations. Furthermore, he denounces the national instrumentalisation of Islam and its reduction to a mere cultural legacy. According to him, only the restoration of the autonomy and transcendence of Islam can give rise to a true complementarity between Islam and nationhood:

Nationhood needs Islam, which complements it and orients it at the semantic level, gives it its *raison d'être*.[68] However, even religiosity cannot exist without a worldly base, without a solid and powerful medium, namely this national feeling, this innate sense of one's own belonging . . . This is why Islam and nationhood are in some way complementary. It is a complementarity of method, of function. It is not a complementarity of content. Islam, in its content, is perfect. In its relation to nationhood, it can ennoble it, embellish it, but cannot receive anything from it. However, nationhood is necessary to Islam in the way the painter needs the canvas on which he will paint his work of art.[69]

Having set the idea of both a complementarity and a hierarchy between Islam and nationhood, Jahić can envision the 'struggle for Islam and against excessive nationalism' as a gradual process, in which priority is given to the struggle against secularisation. The relationship between Islam and identity is thus closely related to the relationship between Islam and politics since, according to Jahić, 'the harmonisation of the relationship between Islam and nationhood . . . opens the way to a happier

---

[65] Ibid.

[66] A. Jahić, 'Bošnjaci i Zapad'.

[67] This text is the transcription of a talk held at an international conference organised in October 1995 by the Zagreb Mosque, under the title 'The Muslim world today'.

[68] In French in the text.

[69] A. Jahić, 'Islam i nacionalitet u svjetlu suvremenih prilika u islamskom svijetu' [Islam and nationhood in the light of contemporary circumstances in the Muslim world], *Hikmet*, vol. 8, no. 10–11/94–5 (November), 1995c, pp. 448–52.

Islamic society, without which a true and consistent Islamic state is out of the question'.[70]

At first sight, the positions of Adnan Jahić on the relationship between Islam and politics seem relatively clear, since he rejects the Western, formalist and permissive democracy, and praises an Islamic democracy based on 'positive ethical values', as well as the principles of *khalifa* (representation of God on Earth), *shura* (consultation) and *ijma'* (consensus).[71] However, Jahić also has difficulties in defining concretely these values and principles, and acknowledges that it is necessary to 'move from the ideal of political theory towards the reality of what is workable and possible'.[72] Against this background, he considers that 'we have to reinforce the democratic process in the Muslim world, since . . . democracy is, under the present circumstances, the most direct way to Islamic power'.[73] Beyond this tactical issue, he states also that 'the only possible way to establish an Islamic power, a state based on the norms and rules of the *shari'a*, is to start from a healthy and free Islamic society, that is to say a dominant Muslim population that consciously supports such a type of power'. Finally, since 'an Islamic power with no popular support cannot be legitimate',[74] he considers that it should submit itself regularly to the free vote of the population, and that, 'in case it loses the elections, power should be reorganised according to the preferences of the winner'.[75]

Adnan Jahić never openly sets the divine Law in opposition to popular sovereignty; nor does he assert that the former is superior to the latter. His criticisms are less directed at the institutional frameworks of Western democracy than at their secular character. In fact, most of his writings deal with this issue of secularism. Jahić also encourages *ijtihad*, but insists much more than Fikret Karčić or Enes Karić on its necessary limitations: 'we cannot conceive of *ijtihad* outside its Islamic context, nor think that it is possible to interpret it in a secular perspective'.[76] In a similar way, he deplores the way 'Islam, with the adoption [in the Muslim world] of the Western plans for a deeply secularised society and state, has started being excluded from all fields of political and social life', and the way secularisation has gradually 'expanded from the field of state politics to the field of culture and education', since

---

[70] Ibid.
[71] A. Jahić, 'Zavičajnost demokratije'.
[72] A. Jahić, 'Neke opservacije'.
[73] Ibid.
[74] A. Jahić, 'Zavičajnost demokratije'.
[75] Ibid.
[76] Ibid.

'spiritual secularisation is much more dangerous than political secular-isation'.[77] Taking up a distinction made first by *Reis-ul-Ulema* Mustafa Cerić, he tries then to clarify his own position by contrasting two types of secularism:

We are against a metaphysical secularism, which would draw us away – as a nation – from our faith, Islam; we are in favour of a political secularism, which is normal, and which implies that religious institutions and organs do not meddle in politics and in the affairs of the state. As a result, we are in favour of a secular state in the traditional political sense, and against a secular state in the con-temporary political sense of the term. We are in favour of a state that is separated from religion in its form, but we are against a state that would be also separated from religion in its content. This is the reason why we do not want a secular society, we do not want Bosniacs to be secular . . . We want Islam to be our moral, cultural and intellectual impetus, as we do not consider that it could be the Western culture and civilisation, whose goals we know, as well as those of their local supporters. This is the reason why it is important to understand that Islam is a collective issue and not an individual one, an issue requiring the largest possible consensus, and not any subjective free will.[78]

Finally, Adnan Jahić is also led to ponder the very definition of Islam. Obviously, he rejects the definition of Islam as individual faith: he proposes a collective and public morality rather than the individual and inner ethic put forward by Fikret Karčić. But he also criticises the definition of Islam as common culture, and denounces this part of the Muslim intelligentsia 'that is conscious of the role of Islam in the national awakening of its people, but gives it first of all a cultural and traditional meaning, and very little real significance in [everyday] life'.[79] In his eyes, 'those who believe that it is possible to be linked with Islam in an irregular and superficial way, to apply some of its precepts and to neglect others, should be aware of their inconsistency, and even of a certain hypocrisy. If some of its elements are not implemented, Islam cannot exist, nor can Muslims, and those who claim to be Muslims but avoid going to the mosque or fasting cannot be Muslims'.[80] According to the definition given by Enes Karić, Islam brings together all members of the Muslim community. For Jahić, on the contrary, Islam has a dif-ferentiating function within this community.

However, if Islam – or, to be more precise, the 'true Islam' – becomes a criterion of differentiation within the Muslim community, Jahić has no

---

[77] A. Jahić, 'Islam i nacionalitet'.
[78] A. Jahić, 'Islam – pitanje zajednice' [Islam, a collective issue], *Hikmet*, vol. 8, no. 9/93 (September), 1995d, pp. 390–1.
[79] A. Jahić, 'Znamo, a nećemo?!'.
[80] Ibid.

other choice but to entrust its implementation to the political power, and
the 'positive ethical values' to which he refers become nothing other than
an implicit state ideology. This process of differentiation on a religious
basis leads inevitably to social and political discrimination among Muslims, and the distinction between the separation of state and religion in
terms of form on the one hand, and in terms of content on the other hand,
is a mere tool permitting the discrete restoration of a party-state within
democratic institutional frameworks. As Jahić acknowledges himself,

> the preservation and reinforcement of Islam will depend in the first place on
> the extent of its presence in state school curricula, in the media, in popular
> literature and in other fields of social activity. The state does not need to be
> explicitly Islamic in order to encourage such forms of subtle Islamisation of the
> society.[81]

Adnan Jahić's determination to turn Islam into a discriminatory political ideology appears even more conspicuously in a text which provoked
much debate in Bosnia after its publication in September 1993. In this
text, entitled 'A sturdy Muslim state',[82] Jahić not only breaks a taboo by
declaring himself in favour of the creation of a Muslim ethnic state on
'the territories where our Bosnian army will remain after the war'.[83] He
also claims that 'Islam, by nature, knows no separation between religion
and society. Moreover, Islam is not a "religion", but a political and
religious ideology, a complete *Weltanschauung*. Islamic principles are
never limited to the surface of individual consciences and private religious
feelings. Original Islam tries to embrace the society in which it exists and,
therefore, the political and state structures themselves'.[84]

According to Jahić, the future Muslim state 'will have a Muslim
ideology based on Islam, on Islamic legal–religious and ethical–social
principles, but also on elements of Western-European origin that are not
in conflict with the former ones'. This ideology must be turned into 'a
complete political and legal system of the future Muslim state, from
state and national symbols to educational, social and economic institutions, and including the national government policy'. This means that
'no principle of Muslim ideology will be imposed on anyone by force,

---

[81] A. Jahić, 'Islam i nacionalitet'.

[82] A. Jahić, 'Krijeposna muslimanska država' [A sturdy Muslim state], *Zmaj od Bosne*
(September 27, 1993), reproduced in Fatimir Alispahić, *Krv boje benzina* [Petrol-
coloured blood], Tuzla: Radio Kameleon, 1996a, pp. 248–51.

[83] Adnan Jahić claims that he does nothing but reflect the personal choices of the SDA
leader Alija Izetbegović: '[the *Reis-ul-Ulema*] Mustafa Cerić has clearly confirmed to me
during a personal interview that the eternal dream of Alija Izetbegović, a "young
Muslim," has been, and still is, the creation of a Muslim state in Bosnia-Herzegovina;
his dream is now becoming a reality and this does not really disturb him'.

[84] Ibid.

according to the principle of *"la ikrahe fiddin"* ['no constraint in religion'], but that its spirit will be systematically promoted and infused in society . . . A complete equality of rights will be guaranteed to all citizens, yet the social achievement of each individual will depend not only on his own economical activity, but also on how much he will consciously accept and follow the principles and the spirit of the Muslim ideology'. Finally, Jahić points out that, 'during the first decades, it will be necessary to implement a centralised policy, to insist strictly on the enforcement and respect of the new laws, so that the state can as soon as possible stand on its own feet, and start promoting the content of Islamic ideology. Only after this can a large decentralisation and democratisation of the society take place.'[85] Adnan Jahić thus renders even more striking the similarities between the 'sturdy Muslim state' he is advocating and the former Communist party-state.

Conclusion: Bosnian peculiarities and 'European Islam'

The writings of Fikret Karčić, Enes Karić and Adnan Jahić show that the Bosnian Muslims and their religious institutions are also involved in the debates on Islam and Western modernity that affect the entire Muslim world, and contradict therefore the descriptions of Bosnian Islam as a homogeneous and *sui generis* reality. Certainly, their reflections take place under very specific circumstances: namely that of a post-Communist and post-Yugoslav Bosnia-Herzegovina. The imprint of the Communist past, for example, appears when Karčić considers the creation of a multiparty system as an opportunity to depoliticise religious institutions, or when Jahić intends to place Islam in the heart of a new kind of party-state. But these specific features, whose most surprising consequence is the fact that, in 1990, a secularised Bosnian Muslim population brought to power the representatives of a small pan-Islamist minority,[86] gives only a peculiar visibility or coloration to processes that can be met in many other places around the world.

This does not mean that the order of presentation of the three authors, or their personal careers, should be viewed as a summary of the recent evolutions of Bosnian Islam. Of course, it is not by chance that Enes Karić broke with the SDA at the end of the war, while Adnan Jahić became one of its leading figures. Yet, the internal factionalism of the

---

[85] Ibid.
[86] For an explanation of this paradox, see X. Bougarel, 'From "Young Muslims" to the party of democratic action'.

SDA, in power from November 1990 to November 2000,[87] does not reflect the state of Bosnian society, and certainly it does not suffice as an explanation of the changes and conflicts experienced by Bosnian Islam.

Without doubt, there was during the war an attempt by the SDA leaders to turn Islam into a discriminatory political ideology, and the writings of Adnan Jahić can thus be considered as the open expression of a political project that has remained implicit most of the time. But the resistances and paradoxes that thwarted this project have also resulted in the rediscovery of Islam as a common culture and individual faith. In their polemics with the SDA, non-nationalist parties and independent media sources have often resorted to these two conceptions of Islam. In a similar way, after the political instrumentalisation of the Islamic religious institutions resulted in their disrepute, some voices came to be heard within the *Islamska Zajednica*, pleading for a clearer separation between religion and politics. Finally, whilst Bosnian Muslims were accepting Islam as the base of their national identity, many of them used and reinterpreted it in order to contest the political hegemony of the SDA. From this point of view, the religious changes taking place in Bosnia-Herzegovina are reminiscent of those experienced by other Muslim countries, and often described with the generic term of 'post-Islamism'.[88]

At the same time, the Bosnian case is also a good illustration of another larger phenomenon: in the 1990s, European Muslims have become more and more politicised, and, everywhere in Europe, Islam has entered the public sphere.[89] This process, however, does not have the same origins in Western Europe and post-Communist Eastern Europe, and it often takes different forms. In Western Europe, the growing visibility of Islam is due to the rise of new generations of Muslims being born in Europe and enjoying the citizenship of their countries of residence. In Eastern Europe, this increased visibility is first of all a consequence of the restoration of

[87] In November 2000, the SDA was defeated by the Social Democratic Party (SDP), the Party for Bosnia-Herzegovina (SBiH) and other smaller parties gathered into an 'Alliance for Change', and found itself in the opposition for the first time since its creation in 1990.

[88] Expanding his analysis of the failure of political Islam in the 1980s, Olivier Roy defines post-Islamism as 'the appearance of a secular space in Muslim societies, not because of a decline in faith or practice, but because the religious field tends to dissociate itself from the political field. The individualisation of [religious] practices or their limitation to closed communities (sufi orders) tends to dissociate not only religious choices from political ones, but also the believer from the citizen, even if believers reformulate their political choice differently, for instance in terms of ethics or defence of moral values'. See O. Roy, 'Avant-propos: pourquoi le post-islamisme?' [Preface: why post-Islamism?], *Revue des mondes musulmans et de la Méditerranée*, nos. 85–6, 1999a, pp. 9–10.

[89] See e.g. Yasemin Soysal, 'Changing parameters of citizenship and claims making: organized Islam in European public spheres', *Theory and Society*, vol. 26, 1997, pp. 508–27.

religious freedom after the demise of the Communist regimes. In the first case, the waning of inherited ethnic and national identities facilitates the emergence of a new Muslim communitarianism, centred around religious institutions and demands. In the second case, the crystallisation of distinct ethnic identities goes hand in hand with the creation of separate political parties, the formulation of nationalist projects and, against this background, the 'nationalisation' of Islam and Islamic religious institutions.[90] Despite the fact that it has been initiated by the representatives of a pan-Islamist stream, the SDA, for example, hastened the break-up of the Yugoslav *Islamska Zajednica* in April 1993, in order to create new Islamic religious institutions limited solely to Bosnian Muslims. Five months later, it renounced the national designation of 'Muslim', and replaced it by a new one: 'Bosniac'.[91]

Finally, the debates that are dividing Bosnian Muslims and their religious institutions reflect some uncertainties common to all Muslim communities in Europe: in the Balkans, as well as in Russia and within the European Union, Muslims share a similar concern about the future of their presence in Europe, and have the same difficulty in defining their Muslim identity in a context where the state claims to be secular, but where the society is still, at least implicitly, permeated with Christian traditions. As shown by their reflection on their double Muslim and European identity, Fikret Karčić, Enes Karić and Adnan Jahić are obviously aware of the precarious geopolitical position of Bosnian Muslims, at the European margins of the *umma*. In the same way, their situation in a deeply secularised and individualised European cultural space explains why they focus so much on the issue of the relationship between Islam as a source of legal or moral norms, and the modern state defined as a secular and democratic one.

From this point of view, the debates that have taken place within the Bosnian Muslim community since 1878 constitute indeed an early attempt at formulating what it means to be Muslim in contemporary Europe. The political events of the 1990s, however, tend more and more to transform the Bosnian case into an exception, rather than a model for the other Muslim communities living in Europe. When, in the early 1990s, Fikret Karčić defines Islam as individual faith, he is also doing so

---

[90] On the recent evolutions of Islam in Europe, see e.g. Felice Dassetto, Brigitte Maréchal and Jorgen Nielsen (eds.), *Convergences musulmanes. Aspects contemporains de l'islam dans l'Europe élargie* [Muslim convergence. Contemporary aspects of Islam in an enlarged Europe], Paris: L'Harmattan, 2001; Felice Dassetto (dir.), *Paroles d'Islam. Individus, sociétés et discours dans l'Islam européen contemporain* [Islamic words. Individuals, societies and discourses in contemporary European Islam], Paris: Maisonneuve & Larose, 2000; X. Bougarel and N. Clayer (eds.), *Le nouvel Islam balkanique*.

[91] See note 1.

because he still places himself within a Yugoslav framework, with Muslims being only a minority among a majority of Christians. During the war, on the other hand, Enes Karić and Adnan Jahić adopted a narrower Bosnian perspective, in which majority Muslims had to choose between the preservation of a multiethnic state and the creation of their own nation-state. Despite their disagreements on the definition of Islam and the future of Bosnia-Herzegovina, both strive to restore Islam as the central reference around which the diversity of the Bosnian Muslim community should be organised.

Finally, Adnan Jahić formulates openly the geopolitical dream that motivates the founders of the SDA in 1990: the wish to bring back Bosnia-Herzegovina into the 'house of Islam' (*dar-al-islam*), from which it had been torn away in 1878. This implicit geopolitical utopia explains some speeches delivered by Alija Izetbegović to the fighters of the Bosnian army, reminding them for example that 'we have received Islam as *amanet* [legacy], and we have the duty to preserve it in this region, because this is the most Western part of Islam',[92] or claiming that 'Serbs and Croats will have in Bosnia-Herzegovina the same rights as Arabs in France'.[93] Moreover, this utopia explains at least in part some strategic moves of the SDA, a party that first intended to gather all the Yugoslav members of the *umma*, but ended up sacrificing their religious unity to the independence of Bosnia-Herzegovina, and then the territorial integrity of this country to the political sovereignty of the Bosnian Muslims.[94]

But, through this will to emancipate the Bosnian Muslims from their minority status, the SDA leaders shift away from the questions with which Muslim communities in Europe are concerned, and draw closer to those faced by the societies of the Muslim world. It is thus not surprising that the strong mobilisation of Western European Muslims in support of Bosnia-Herzegovina during the war was not followed by intense and regular exchanges at the religious level: the Islamic intellectuals of Western Europe still refer primarily to the debates of their countries of origin and countries of residence, whereas those in Bosnia–Herzegovina look for inspiration in the states of the Persian Gulf and South-East Asia. This observation also applies to the relations among Balkan Muslim intellectuals, despite their obvious geographical proximity and cultural closeness.

---

[92] Speech to the fighters of the 7th Muslim brigade of Zenica, held on 20 October 1994 and reproduced in the bulletin of the brigade (*El-Liva*, no. 16, November 1994, p. 4).

[93] Speech to the fighters of the 4th motorised brigade of Hrasnica, held in December 1993 and quoted by Ivo Komšić, former member of the Bosnian collective Presidency (*Svijet*, no. 29, August 15, 1996, p. 17).

[94] See X. Bougarel, 'Comment peut-on être Bochniaque?'.

With reference, then, to the case of Islam in the Bosnian context, we might conclude that there are many Islams in Europe, but that a 'European Islam' does not yet exist, in the sense that there is no shared religious and intellectual space to debate the issues that are common to all European Muslims.[95] This also means that the emergence of such an Islam does not imply the rediscovery of an Islam *sui generis*, but the invention of a new religious model, through the intensification of contacts among European Muslim communities, the confrontation of their uncertainties and the hybridisation of their practices. In this process, it is uncertain whether Bosnian Muslims will play the central part attributed to them by some of the representations of Bosnian Islam that appeared during the war. In fact, the cradle of this nascent 'European Islam' is probably not located in the Bosnian valleys, but in the larger European cities where various Muslim diasporas – including those originating from the Balkans[96] – meet one another, or in the hallways of the European Court of Human Rights, to which more and more Western European and Balkan Muslims turn when faced in their respective states with ethnic or religious discrimination.

Bibliography

Adelkah, Faribah and François Georgeon (eds.), *Ramadan et politique*, Paris: CNRS éditions, 2000.

Al-Ali, Nadja, 'Gender relations, transnational ties and rituals among Bosnian refugees', *Global Networks: A Journal of Transnational Affairs*, vol. 2, no. 3 (July), 2002, pp. 249–62.

Alispahić, Fatmir, *Krv boje benzina*, Tuzla: Radio Kameleon, 1996.

Bakic-Hayden, Milica, 'Nesting orientalisms. The case of former Yugoslavia', *Slavic Review*, vol. 65, no. 4 (Winter), 1995, pp. 917–31.

Bougarel, Xavier, 'From "Young Muslims" to the party of democratic action: the emergence of a pan-Islamist trend in Bosnia-Herzegovina', *Islamic Studies*, Islamabad, vol. 36, no. 2–3 (Summer–Autumn), 1997, pp. 533–49.

'L'Islam et la guerre en Bosnie-Herzégovine: l'impossible débat?', *L'Autre Europe*, no. 36–37 (Winter), 1998, pp. 106–16.

'Le ramadan, révélateur des évolutions de l'Islam en Bosnie-Herzégovine', in Faribah Adelkah and François Georgeon (eds.), *Ramadan et politique*, Paris: CNRS Editions, 2000, pp. 83–96.

[95] On the emergence of a 'European Islam', see, among others, J. Nielsen, *Towards a European Islam*, Basingstoke: Macmillan, 1999; O. Roy, *Vers un Islam européen* [Towards a European Islam], Paris: Esprit, 1999b.

[96] On the religious practices of Bosnian Muslims in Western Europe, see Marita Eastmond, 'Nationalist discourses and the construction of difference: Bosnian Muslim refugees in Sweden', *Journal of Refugee Studies*, vol. 11, no. 2, 1998, pp. 161–81; Nadja Al-Ali, 'Gender relations, transnational ties and rituals among Bosnian refugees', *Global Networks: A Journal of Transnational Affairs*, vol. 2, no. 3 (July), 2002, pp. 249–62.

'L'Islam bosniaque, entre identité culturelle et idéologie politique', in Xavier Bougarel and Nathalie Clayer (eds.), *Le nouvel Islam balkanique: les musulmans comme acteurs du post-communisme, 1990–2000*, Paris: Maisonneuve & Larose, 2001, p. 79–132.

'Comment peut-on être Bochniaque?', in Alain Dieckhoff and Riva Kastoryano (eds.), *Nationalismes en mutation en Méditerranée orientale*, Paris: CNRS Editions, 2002, pp. 173–93.

Bougarel, Xavier and Nathalie Clayer (eds.), *Le nouvel Islam balkanique: les musulmans comme acteurs du post-communisme, 1990–2000*, Paris: Maisonneuve and Larose, 2001.

Bringa, Tone, *Being Muslim the Bosnian way. Identity and community in a central Bosnian village* Princeton: Princeton University Press, 1995.

Burg, Steven and Paul Shoup, *The war in Bosnia-Herzegovina. Ethnic conflict and international intervention*, New York/London: Sharpe, 1999.

Čančar, Nusret and Enes Karić (eds.), *Islamski fundamentalizam. Šta je to?*, Sarajevo: Biblioteka 'Preporoda' i 'Islamske misli', 1990.

Dassetto, Felice (ed.), *Paroles d'Islam. Individus, sociétés et discours dans l'Islam européen contemporain*, Paris: Maisonneuve & Larose, 2000.

Dassetto, Felice, Marechal, Brigitte and Nielsen, Jorgen (eds.), *Convergences musulmanes. Aspects contemporains de l'Islam dans l'Europe élargie*, Paris: L'Harmattan, 2001.

Dieckhoff, Alain and Riva Kastoryano (eds.), *Nationalismes en mutation en Méditerranée orientale*, Paris: CNRS éditions, 2002.

Duhovna snaga odbrane, Sarajevo: Vojna biblioteka, no. 5, 1994.

Eastmond, Marita, 'Nationalist discourses and the construction of difference: Bosnian Muslim refugees in Sweden', *Journal of Refugee Studies*, vol. 11, no. 2, 1998, pp. 161–81.

Filandra, Šaćir, *Bošnjaci i moderna*, Sarajevo: Bosanski kulturni centar, 1996.

International Crisis Group, *Bin Laden and the Balkans: the politics of anti-terrorism*, Brussels: ICG, 2001.

Jahić, Adnan, 'Baqir As-Sadr i naša filozofija', *Hikmet*, vol. 8, no. 8/92, (August), 1995a, pp. 360–3.

'Bošnjaci i Zapad – principi budućih odnosa', *Hikmet*, vol. 8, no. 4/88 (April), 1995b, pp. 148–50.

'Islam i nacionalitet u svjetlu suvremenih prilika u islamskom svijetu', *Hikmet*, vol. 8, no. 10–11/94–95 (November), 1995c, pp. 448–52.

'Islam–pitanje zajednice', *Hikmet*, vol. 8, no. 9/93 (September), 1995d, pp. 390–1.

Muslimanske formacije tuzlanskog kraja u drugom svjetskom ratu, Tuzla: Bosnoljublje, 1995e.

'Neke opservacije o političkim perspektivama islamskog svijeta', *Hikmet*, vol. 8, no. 6/90 (June), 1995f, pp. 248–53.

'Znamo, a nećemo?!', *Hikmet*, vol. 8, no. 2/86 (February), 1995g, pp. 52–3.

'Krijeposna muslimanska država', *Zmaj od Bosne* (September 27, 1993), reproduced in Fatmir Alispahić, *Krv boje benzina*, Tuzla: Radio Kameleon, 1996a, pp. 248–51.

'Zavičajnost demokratije u islamskom političkom mišljenju', *Hikmet*, vol. 9, no. 9–12/105–108 (November), 1996b, pp. 247–54.

Karčić, Fikret, *Šeriatski sudovi u Jugoslaviji 1918–1941*, Sarajevo: Islamska Zajednica, 1986.

Društveno-pravni aspekti islamskog reformizma, Sarajevo: Islamski teološki fakultet, 1990a.

'Islamska Zajednica i reforma jugoslovenskog političkog sistema', *Glasnik Rijaseta IZ-e*, vol. 52, no. 1 (January–February), 1990b, pp. 7–13.

'O "islamskoj republici" u BiH', *Preporod*, vol. 21, no. 3 (February 1st), 1990c, p. 3.

'Razumijevanje islamskog vjerozakona (šeriata) u savremenom muslimanskom svijetu', in Nusret Čančar and Enes Karić (eds.), *Islamski fundamentalizam. Šta je to?*, Sarajevo: Biblioteka 'Preporoda' i 'Islamske misli', 1990d, pp. 37–43.

'Značenje i iskazivanje islama u svjetovnoj državi', in Enes Karić (ed.), *Suvremena ideologijska tumačenja Kur'ana i islama*, Zagreb: Kulturni radnik, 1990e, pp. 29–36.

'Distorted images of Islam: the case of former Yugoslavia', *Intellectual Discourse*, Kuala Lumpur, vol. 3, no. 2, 1995a, pp. 139–52.

'Ubijanje naroda u sjeni "sudara civilizacija" ', *Ljiljan*, vol. 4, no. 111 (March 1), 1995b, pp. 32–3.

'Islamic revival in the Balkans', *Islamic Studies*, Islamabad, vol. 36, no. 2–3 (Summer/Autumn), 1997, pp. 565–81.

Karić, Enes, 'Fundamentalizam Prokrustove postelje', in Nusret Čančar and Enes Karić, *Islamski fundamentalizam. Šta je to?*, Sarajevo: Biblioteka 'Preporoda' i 'Islamske misli', 1990a, pp. 89–93.

Hemeneutika Kur'ana, Zagreb: Biblioteka Filozofska istraživanja, 1990b.

'Dvosjekli mač vjeronauke u školi', *Muslimanski Glas*, vol. 2, no. 10 (June 28), 1991a, p. 15.

Kur'an u savremenom dobu, Sarajevo: Svjetlost, 1991b.

'Značenje i iskazivanje islama u budućoj Bosni i Hercegovini', in *Kongres bosansko-muslimanskih intelektualaca* (22 December 1992), Sarajevo: Bosnagraf, 1993, pp. 97–100.

'Agresija na Bosnu i Hercegovinu i pitanje džihada', in *Duhovna snaga odbrane*, Sarajevo: Vojna biblioteka, no. 5, 1994a, pp. 73–7.

'Bosna je bošnjački Bedr', *Ljiljan*, vol. 3, no. 58 (February 23), 1994b, p. 31.

'Bošnjaci su Ummetu osvjetlali obraz', *Ljiljan*, vol. 3, no. 61 (March 16), 1994c, p. 31.

'Suze, stepe i pustinje', *Ljiljan*, vol. 3, no. 100 (December 14), 1994d, p. 53.

Bosna sjete i zaborava, Zagreb: Durieux, 1997a.

'Islam u suvremenoj Bosni', in Enes Karić, *Bosna sjete i zaborava*, Zagreb: Durieux, 1997b, pp. 88–95.

'Naše bosanstvo i naše evropejstvo', *Ljiljan*, vol. 6, no. 263 (January), 1998a, p. 20.

'Naše bošnjastvo i naše muslimanstvo', *Ljiljan*, vol. 6, no. 264 (February 4), 1998b, pp. 20–2.

Karić, Enes (ed.), *Suvremena ideologijska tumačenja Kur'ana i islama*, Zagreb: Kulturni radnik, 1990c.

Kongres bosansko-muslimanskih intelektualaca (22 December 1992), Sarajevo: Bosnagraf.

Kur'an sa prijevodom na bosanski jezik, (translation: Enes Karić), Sarajevo: Bosanska knjiga, 1995.

Lockwood, William, *European Moslems. Economy and ethnicity in Western Bosnia*, New York, London: Academic Press, 1974.

Malcolm, Noel, *Bosnia: a short history*, London: Macmillan, 1994.

Mitri, Tarek, 'La Bosnie-Herzégovine et la solidarité du monde arabe et islamique', *Maghreb-Machrek*, no. 139 (January), 1993, pp. 123–36.

Nielsen, Jorgen, *Towards a European Islam*, Basingstoke: Macmillan, 1999.

Roy, Olivier, 'Avant-propos: pourquoi le post-islamisme?', *Revue des mondes musulmans et de la Méditerranée*, nos. 85–6, 1999a, pp. 9–10.

Vers un islam européen, Paris: Esprit, 1999b.

Sorabji, Cornelia, *Muslim identity and Islamic faith in socialist Sarajevo*, unpublished PhD dissertation, University of Cambridge, 1988.

Soysal, Yasemin, 'Changing parameters of citizenship and claims making: organized Islam in European public spheres', *Theory and Society*, vol. 26, 1997, pp. 508–27.

Bérengère Massignon

Researchers have usually dealt with the Europeanisation of Islam at the *grass-roots level* (recomposition of religious beliefs, trends in interethnic and cross-border marriages, mixed couples, internet-based Muslim networks, large-scale European gatherings, and the role of religious leaders influential in Europe such as Tariq Ramadan).[1] In this chapter, this process of Europeanisation will be considered *at the institutional level* with a focus on transnational Muslim organisations in relation to the European institutions.[2] A twofold movement has taken place simultaneously. On the one hand, European Muslims have actively sought the opportunity to become actors in the European integration process. On the other hand, since the Delors presidency, the European Commission has developed tools in order to facilitate dialogue with religious and humanistic bodies through the Forward Studies Unit (FSU), a 'think tank' attached to the Presidency of

---

[1] Amongst many works, let us mention: Felice Dassetto, *La construction d'un Islam européen*, Paris, L'Harmattan, 1996; Chantal Saint-Blancat, *L'Islam de la diaspora*, Paris: Bayard, 1997; Felice Dassetto, Brigitte Maréchal and Jorgen Nielsen (eds.), *Convergences musulmanes. Aspects contemporains de l'Islam dans une Europe élargie*, Paris: L'Harmattan, 2001; Olivier Roy, *Vers un Islam européen*, Paris, Editions Esprit, 1999; Jocelyne Cesari, *L'Islam à l'épreuve de l'Occident*, Paris: La Découverte, 2004; and Stefano Allievi and Jorgen Nielsen (eds.), *Muslim networks and transnational communities in and across Europe*, Leiden: Koninklijke Brill NV, 2003. Tariq Ramadan, professor of Islamology and grandson of Hassan El Banna, the founding father of the Muslim Brotherhood, has developed a reflection on the situation of Muslims in the West in numerous books, particularly: *Etre Musulman européen. Etudes des sources islamiques à la lumière du contexte européen*, Lyon: Tawhid, 1999, and *Musulmans d'Occident. Construire et contribuer*, Lyon: Tawhid, 2002. He chairs a travelling seminar in Nîmes, Paris, Lyon, Strasbourg, Toulouse, Nantes, Geneva, and Brussels. A platform called 'Présence musulmane' (Muslim presence) brings together local youth associations, and provides organisational support to this travelling training. See Jocelyne Cesari, *L'Islam à l'épreuve de l'Occident*, pp. 221–4, and especially p. 222.

[2] As the transnational structuring of Islam on the European level is a new field of study, I have turned to various experts for their insight (including Felice Dassetto from Louvain-la-Neuve University, and Father Maurice Borrmans from PISAI in Rome). I wish to thank them for their kind cooperation.

the Commission, which was replaced in 2001 by the Group of Policy Advisers (GOPA). The following analysis will focus on this particular level of the European institutions, as it is both transversal and political. Very early the Commission wished to engage Muslims in this dialogue, but it faced difficulties finding representative interlocutors on a European level.

Following the signing of the Single European Act in 1986, and in the prospect of the European Single Market in 1992, a growing number of pressure groups opened liaison offices in Brussels. Religious organisations, mostly Christians, were part of this trend. At that time, both Catholics and Protestants increased their presence in Brussels through COMECE and EECCS respectively.[3] Meanwhile, Muslims were becoming organised at local and national levels in order to be in a position to negotiate advantages comparable to those granted to the Christian groups. Until then, Islam had been treated, from within European Union institutions, as an issue of migration, through a socio-economic approach and irrespective of the religious dimension.[4] However, EU migration policies inevitably gave rise to a first articulation of Muslim interests on the EU level. In the early 1990s, the 'Migreurope' network was established and became a forum recognised by the EU Directorate-General for Social Affairs. It was founded on the initiative of NGOs active in lobbying in the field of European migratory policies, especially Christian organisations such as the Catholic European Study and Information Centre, OCIPE (a Brussels-based Jesuit-owned office that works in connection with the *Jesuit Refugees Service*).[5] As representatives of the migrants, Muslims took part in that network. Each European country had a representation, but conflicts between Turkish and Arab Muslims eventually undermined the network. Moreover, at

---

[3] COMECE, or the Commission of the National Bishops' Conferences of the European Union, is the main Catholic organisation in Brussels and was established in 1980. It includes representatives from bishops' conferences of the EU Member States. EECCS, or the European Ecumenical Commission for Church and Society, is the main European Protestant organisation and was established in 1973. After the fall of the Berlin Wall and in the prospect of enlargement, it became part of the Conference of European Churches (CEC) as its Church and Society Commission. The CEC is a pan-European body, set up in 1959, that includes members of the Anglican, Protestant and Orthodox churches.

[4] Riva Kastoryano, 'Participation transnationale et citoyenneté: les immigrés dans l'Union européenne', in *Cultures et Conflits*, no. 28 (Winter) 1997, pp. 59–74.

[5] Claire de Galembert has highlighted the role the Catholic Church played in the 1980s as a mediator between Muslims and public authorities in France and Germany. On the European level, and at the initiative of Christian churches, Muslims have been partners in the inter-religious dialogue, within a joint committee on Islam set up in 1974 by the Conference of European Churches (CEC, Protestant and Orthodox) and the Council of European Bishops' Conferences (CCEE, Catholic).

the beginning of the Prodi presidency, a tightening of the Commission's financial procedures led to cuts in funding available for all European civil society forums, including Migreurope. The Migreurope network finally dissolved in the wake of the collapse of the Santer Commission. But at that time the relationship between the Commission and religious Muslim organisations as such had been organised at a different institutional level (FSU, and subsequently GOPA). The following analysis focuses on this institutional level, as it is the only mechanism within the European Commission which deals explicitly with religion.

The place of Muslims in the system of relations between the Commission and religions is symptomatic of the degree of pluralism of the European model of regulation of religion. I would like to take a close examination of this place occupied by Muslims by addressing the following questions. When and how did Muslims become part of this system of relations and are the Muslim organisations selected representative of European Islam? What action framework did the advisers to the President of the Commission institute with regard to Muslims, and why? To what extent have the events of 11 September 2001 impacted on the initiatives that were developed in relation to the Muslim community by the Group of Policy Advisers (GOPA, the body that succeeded the FSU under the Prodi presidency)?[6] How have Muslim organisations and leaders developed a vision of Europe as a result of their will to be part of the European integration process? These questions will form the structure of the pages which follow.

Religions and EU institutions: a late and symbolic Muslim presence

The relations between the European Union and religious actors are recent. Their symbolic birth traces back to the speech Jacques Delors delivered in 1992 before the representatives of the Evangelical Church of Germany (EKD): 'If in the next ten years we haven't managed to give a Soul to Europe, to give it spirituality and meaning, the game will be up'. This speech was delivered in a context where the nature of European integration was changing. The project was no longer merely economic and technical, but would involve political, social and ethical concerns related to the achievement of the Single Market and the ratification of the Treaty of Maastricht. As a result of this evolution, the issue of European identity and the meaning of the European project rose

---

[6] See http://europa.eu.int/comm/dgs/policy_advisers/activities/dialogue_religions_humanisms/index_en.htm for general information on GOPA.

to the fore, together with the question of how to define a political Europe that would be capable of mobilising its citizens. In this context, both religious representatives and Humanists are invited to foster Europhile sentiment in the member states as well as in the candidate countries.

The first formal relations between the European Commission and religions began under Jacques Delors' second term of office against a background of presidentialisation of the Presidency of the European Commission.[7] Key features of Delors' leadership included the development of new forms of consultation with social partners; in his previous posts, first as the Commissioner of the French planning office, then as a minister in the Chaban–Delmas and Mauroy governments, Jacques Delors was always a strong advocate of such processes. Therefore we must put the relations with religious representatives in this wider context: that is, as a will to consult with civil society, beyond the democratic representative legitimacy represented only by the member states (the Council) and the European Parliament. The invitation made to religious leaders was part of an attempt at further legitimising a European Commission often labelled a soulless technocracy and deemed a symbol of Europe's democratic deficit.

The Muslims were not present at the inception of the relationship between the European Commission and religious leaders (1982–94). It was only when a number of tools for dialogue were developed, and when links became more formal, that the Muslim presence turned into a reality. Thus, the presence of Islam corresponded to a stage where the institutionalisation of the relationship between the EU and religions required, in terms of legitimacy, a certain degree of pluralism. However, Muslim participation initially remained a symbolic one, for there were no adequate Europe-wide Muslim organisations. The Muslim participation was structurally different from the other religious and humanist partners that were already organised in institutions at the European level and involved in the European integration process. On 20 December 1994, at

---

[7] Helen Drake, *Jacques Delors en Europe, histoire et sociologie d'un leadership improbable*, Strasbourg: Presses Universitaires de Strasbourg, 2002. Although the European Commission has a primary responsibility in terms of proposal-making, the President of the Commission does not necessarily carry out a leadership function with regard to European integration, in a multi-level organisation which functions as a college (the college of the EU Commissioners), and vis-à-vis the decision-making power retained by the heads of government of each member state. Nonetheless Jacques Delors managed to personify European integration thanks to crucial circumstances (the 1992 Objective and the completion of the European Single Market, the fall of the Berlin Wall and geopolitical transformations in the East). Thanks to his own assets (expertise, resourcefulness, networking, methods of government), he injected unprecedented, and so far unparalleled, power in the Presidency of the EU.

the end of his second term in office, Jacques Delors invited Catholic, Protestant and Jewish representatives to an inter-faith meeting. The presence of Humanist and Muslim leaders was considered at the last minute only. For lack of a Muslim Europe-wide structured representation similar to that in other major religious and philosophical European traditions, a Muslim intellectual, Mohammed Arkoun, was invited. While he was a frequent guest in meetings of international forums (UNESCO, Council of Europe), he did not represent any Muslim organisation. The invitation was also extended to a community leader from one of the EU countries: Mehmet Yildrim, Secretary-General of the Turkish-Muslim Union of Germany. This Union is however, under the auspices of the Turkish government body, *DIYANET*,[8] and Yildrim's statements revealed that he regarded himself more as a representative of the Turkish government than as a spokesperson of the Muslim immigrants in Europe. This first attempt to include Muslims alongside other European religious leaders was not successful since neither invitee could claim to represent a 'European Islam', nor meant to do so.

Subsequently a twofold process has developed. Firstly, a Muslim discourse on European Islam, targeting second-generation immigrants, has brought about the creation of ad hoc European-wide Muslim collectivities, though it is difficult to assess their degree of organisation at the European level. Secondly, a growing awareness of Muslim reality in Europe has led European officials to seek representative interlocutors. Two Muslim organisations specialising in European matters are invited to the briefing conferences organised by the Counsellor for Religious Affairs of the European Commission: the Muslim Council of Cooperation in Europe (CMCE), created in 1996 and invited since 1997, and the Forum of European Muslim Youth and Student Organisations (FEMYSO), created in 1995 and invited since 2003.

The CMCE is a heterogeneous structure of Muslim groups that have gathered around leaders in efforts to establish local legitimacy. It is composed of organisations which are, for the most part, not the predominant ones in each European member state.[9] It benefits from the

---

[8] The administrative body in charge of Islam in the Turkish government.
[9] The CMCE was founded in 1996, in Strasbourg and became, on 10 January 2003, an organisation registered under Belgian law. According to the analyses made by Felice Dassetto and Father Maurice Borrmans, it was at that time, when the future European constitution was under discussion that it got in a position to act on the European scene. The CMCE includes minority organisations such as two large French mosques that are not linked to the large Federations (Union des Organisations Islamiques de France, Fédération Nationale des Musulmans de France): (a social and cultural centre – the Add'awa mosque and the mosque of Strasbourg) as well as a small youth association (the Association of Islamic Students in France, AIEF). In Italy, *Comunità Religiosa*

desire of the European institutions to have *moderate Muslim partners*. In fact, there are other Muslim organisations, structured on the European level, that represent an Islam often closer to the Muslim Brotherhood, such as: the European Fatwa and Research Council,[10] the Federation of Islamic Organisations in Europe (FIOE),[11] or the Union of Islamic Organisations in Europe (UIOE). The *Milli Görüş* also opened a European branch in 1973 (its headquarters are in Cologne). It represents the Turkish immigrant community's (Islamic) organisation, linked to the Virtue Party (active at that time in Turkish politics). It seems that, under Romano Prodi's presidency, there was an easier access to the forum of dialogue with religious organisations established by the Commission: at the end of 2003, the Church of Scientology and a Hindu group, the Vaishnava Institute, were invited to GOPA meetings. A greater variety of European Jewish Organisations were also invited. It was at also at that time that the invitation was extended to FEMYSO, an organisation that represents Islam akin to the Muslim Brotherhood.[12]

Islamica (CO.RE.IS) is a minority organisation of converts while the *Unione delle Comunità ed Organizzazioni Islamische in Italia* (UCOII) has been busy trying to reach an agreement with the State. Similar contrast can be found in the Netherlands between a minority organisation, Vereening Imam's Nederland (Nederland), and the platform of three major federations, the Islamic Council of the Netherlands (IRN). However, the Central Council for Muslims in Germany (*Zentralrat der Muslim in Deutschland*, ZMD) is an important alliance along with *Islamrat für die Bundesrepublik Deutschland*. It includes very diverse organisations (*Diyanet Isreli Türk Islam Birligi* (DİTİB), which represents Turkish official Islam, the *Suleymancı* community, and very active student organisations). In Spain, the *Union de Comunidades Islámicas de España* includes Muslims from the Middle East. It is a member organisation of the Islamic Commission of Spain along with the Federation of Islamic Religious Entities, the latter being an initiative of converts. The following movements can be mentioned as well: Conseil *Supérieur des Musulmans de Belgique*; Northern Ireland Muslim Family Association; Union of Muslim Organisations of UK and Ireland; Hungarian Islamic Community; and *Den Islamiske Forening* (Denmark).

[10] This council 'represents two fields of action of the Muslim Brotherhood: a theological thought based upon *itjihad*, and an intellectual production . . . Their fatwas are answers to questions posed by believers across Europe'. Founded in 1997 in London, on the initiative of the Federation of Islamic Organisations in Europe (FIOE), it is made up of thirty-five members, who represent most Western European countries. It is chaired by Sheikh Qardai, sponsor of the *Union des Organisations Islamiques de France* and the *Union des Organisations Islamiques d'Europe*. His book *Le licite et l'illicite* reflects his moderate positions on the interpretation of law. 'All decisions tend to combine the demands of Islam with secular life, which results in a certain rigour in private life and a commitment to civic and political life'. See Jocelyne Cesari, *L'Islam à l'épreuve de l'Occident*, p. 212.

[11] It was founded in 1989 and includes twenty-six national associations in as many European countries.

[12] FEMYSO was founded in 1995 further to a meeting between the *Sveriges Unga Muslimer* (Sweden) and the Swedish government. Its founding members are: the Young Muslims (UK); *Sveriges Unga Muslimer* (Sweden); *Jeunes Musulmans de France* (JMF); Federation of Islamic Organisations in Europe (FIOE), close to the Muslim Brotherhood (see note 10 above), and the Islamic Foundation (Leicester). The latter

Why have certain Muslim organisations or intellectuals been invited by the Presidency of the European Commission rather than others? The links between the Commission and Muslim institutions may be the result of a pragmatic approach due to fortuitous connections with other European Institutions (the European Parliament, a specific General Directorate of the European Commission or the Council of Europe). In reality, the institutions of the European Union and the Council of Europe are not rigidly compartmentalised, and the same experts move from one to another. In 1991 Mohammed Arkoun prepared a report for the Council of Europe on 'the contribution of Islamic civilisation to European culture'. This could be the reason why Jacques Delors invited Mohammed Arkoun to attend the inter-religious conference that was held at the end of his second term as President of the Commission. In the case of CMCE a local mobilisation led to a relationship with European institutions. The founder of the CMCE, Mohammed Boussouf, rallied the project of a central mosque in Strasbourg. Initially those behind the project had intended – in a symbolic move – to locate the building in front of the European Parliament. In the context of a local mobilisation, relations were established with the European Parliament, which facilitated contacts with the Commission. On 26–27 November 1996, in Strasbourg, the local representation of the Association of Islamic Students in France, which had been very involved in the central mosque project, organised a seminar at the European Parliament on the subject of 'Islam and Muslims in Europe'. It was on that occasion that the idea of a 'Muslim Council for Cooperation in Europe' was first proposed.[13] European networking strengthens the legitimacy of a local leader, Mohamed Boussouf, in a context of competition between Muslim leaders at a local level. Links with the European Parliament, a wide-open forum for civil society groups, also led to inclusion of FEMYSO in the GOPA's listing of invited religious organisations. On 15 September 2003, FEMYSO was also invited to a conference on 'Muslim Youth – Enrichment of Society?' organised by European deputies at the European Parliament, alongside other groups including the European Youth Forum and such Christian confessional organisations as the Ecumenical Youth Council in Europe, the World Student Christian Federation, and Pax Christi International.

was founded in 1973. It is sponsored by Ahmad Kurshid from *Jamaat Islamiyya* (Pakistan), and has made a name for itself as a research centre on Islam-related issues in the European context.

[13] Franck Frégosi, 'L'Islam à Strasbourg', *Annuaire de l'Afrique du Nord*, vol. 34, 1995, p. 970, and Franck Frégosi, '"Droit de cité" de l'Islam et politiques municipales: analyse comparative entre Strasbourg et Mulhouse', in Franck Williame Frégosi (ed.), *Le religieux dans la commune*, Genève: Labor et Fides, 2001, p. 123.

The organiser, MEP Roy Perry, planned on creating a group of 'Friends of Islam' within the Parliament in order to enable the participation of young Muslims in European integration. Then, in conjunction with the Directorate-General of Youth and Sports of the Council of Europe, FEMYSO organised a conference on 'the contribution of European Muslims' on 20–27 October 2003 at the European Youth Centre in Budapest.[14] It is in that respect that FEMYSO became well known to European Commission officials and was subsequently invited by the GOPA.

Nevertheless these Muslim organisations do not carry the same weight as the major Christian organisations. Because the relations between religious groups and European institutions have not yet been formalised, the development of strategies for lobbying in the European decision-making process, and the mere monitoring of the developments of European integration, require significant human, organisational, relational and financial resources. The fact that the European Commission does not have a system of accreditation, which would make it more open to organisations regardless of their size and strength (as is the case for the Council of Europe) accounts for the difficulties experienced by the Muslims in getting mobilised on the European scene. It further explains why they are more involved with the Council of Europe and the European Parliament, as both institutions offer a variety of forums and initiatives related to civil society.

Furthermore, the number of persons working in the Brussels-based offices of religious entities shows an inequality in terms of human resources. For instance, there is a secretariat of eight full-time employees at the Commission of the National Bishops' Conferences (COMECE, a Roman Catholic organisation), and six at the Church and Society Commission of the European Conference of Churches (CEC, of the Protestant and Orthodox churches). By contrast, the CMCE representative in Brussels, Mohammed Laroussi, does not act as a full-time representative as he also works on the local organisation of Muslim worship. When Mohammed Boussouf (the founder of the CMCE) represented the CMCE, he often failed to attend the meetings with the Commission. He was more absorbed in local issues raised by the building of a central mosque in Strasbourg.

Thus, unlike their Christian counterparts who have expertise on European matters and are busy lobbying, Muslim organisations in Brussels do not have the resources to deal actively with the European institutions. The Muslim presence is rather a symbolic one: they represent an element

[14] For the report on the study session, see the FEMYSO website: http://www.femyso.org

of religious diversity in the inter-faith meetings hosted by the Commission. Three such examples are the inter-religious meeting in Toledo, which was planned in November 1995 as a fringe event of the Euro-Mediterranean Conference in Barcelona and which took place in the presence of President Jacques Santer; the inter-religious meeting organised in November 2001 by the Ecumenical Patriarchate of Constantinople, under Romano Prodi's sponsorship; and the seminar on inter-cultural dialogue organised by the Directorate-General for Education and Culture in March 2002.

What place do Muslims occupy in the system that the Commission has developed in order to conduct dialogue with the religious groups represented in Europe? I now turn to a more in-depth analysis of the particular institutional mechanisms established by the Commission. The informal yet structured dialogue between the European Commission, religions and Humanists is based upon *two major initiatives*. Both reflect different levels of representation of religious and philosophical pluralism, and in both cases, Muslim representatives have been invited to participate.

First and foremost, the initiative *'A Soul for Europe'*,[15] founded at the end of 1994, provides funding for ecumenical or inter-religious seminars for the discussion of the meaning of European integration. Until 1999, this specific initiative was coordinated by an unofficial screening committee in charge of giving expert advice on the selection of projects that were likely to obtain European funding. It comprised two representatives from each of the following religions and philosophical trends: Catholicism, Protestantism, Judaism and Humanism. A Muslim participation was contemplated as early as 1994, but it became a reality only in September 1997 through the CMCE. A humanist chaired the screening committee from its inception until 2004 (succeeded by a Catholic member), and the responsibility of its secretariat lay with the Protestants of the European Ecumenical Commission for Church and Society (EECCS).[16] This arrangement demonstrates a willingness to represent minority groups in Europe. The idea is to ensure not an arithmetical representation based upon the numerical weight of each faith, but rather to exhibit a will to represent the major faiths as well as

---

[15] For more information and links to the member organisations, see GOPA's website: http://europa.eu.int/comm/dgs/policy_advisers/activities/dialogue_religions_humanisms/ issues/soul_for_europe/index_en.htm

[16] The EECCS's name has been changed to 'the Church and Society Commission of the Conference of European Churches'. This 'screening committee' mechanism was discontinued in February of 2005, following the decision of Special General Assembly of the Initiative 'A Soul for Europe' on 23rd November 2004.

Humanism on an equal footing, all of which are at the root of the European religious and philosophical heritage.

Second, there are *biannual briefing sessions* held by GOPA after the European Summits. This forum, instituted by Jacques Santer, is characterised by a higher degree of pluralism. In September 2004, it included forty-nine religious and humanistic organisations: religion representatives, faith-based NGOs, as well as the European liaison offices of religious groups. Unlike the initiative 'A Soul for Europe', there is also participation by Buddhists, Hindus, the Church of Scientology and Christian Scientists, as well as a more comprehensive representation of Protestant diversity with Evangelicals, Pentecostals and Quakers, as well as a wide array of Jewish and Muslim organisations (including CMCE and FEMYSO).

The pluralistic character of EU inter-religion relations stems from structural and conjectural factors related to the intermediation of interests on the European scene. The motivation of Muslims to be active on the European scene is to be understood against this background.

In the first place, the consultation process with religious groups which began under the Delors presidency was a stimulus and prompted religious groups to open liaison offices in Brussels.[17] This occurred in a context marked by competition, a major feature of the pluralistic system: the first reason to open an office in Brussels was the success of one's competitors.[18] Thus the humanists, after having learned about consultations between the European Commission and the Catholics and Protestants in 1990, expressed their displeasure. They were advised by an EU Commission official to become organised as a European movement. The result was the creation of the European Humanistic Federation in 1991 and the invitation of its president to the inter-faith meeting of December 1994. As regards Islam, the development of funding possibilities with the initiative 'A Soul for Europe', as well as the wish of the European institutions to find a moderate Muslim partner, opened a window of opportunity for a little-known organisation (CMCE) whose Strasbourg-based founder was already maintaining relations with the European Parliament.

Furthermore, the opening of liaison offices in Brussels can be conceived as *a defensive act* to monitor vigilantly the inflation of EU regulations that

---

[17] Justin Greenwood and Mark Aspinwall, 'Conceptualizing collective actors in the EU. An introduction', in *Collective action in the European Union. Interests and politics of associability*, New York, London: Routledge, 1998, pp. 1–30.

[18] Pascaline Winand and Isabelle Smets, 'A la recherche d'un modèle européen de représentation des intérêts', in Paul Magnette and Eric Remacle (eds.), *Le nouveau modèle européen*, VI *Institutions et gouvernance*, Bruxelles: Institut d'Études Européennes, 2000, p. 141.

could indirectly affect the positions and privileges of the main religions in the member states.[19] This is what drove national *churches* to open an office in the capital of the Union along with European religious organisations. Let us mention for instance the case of the Evangelical Church of Germany (EKD) at the beginning of the 1990s, or the Orthodox Church of Greece in 1998. The Greek Church opened an office in Brussels, among other reasons, in reaction to European pressures on Greek religious legislation, in particular with regard to the mention of religion on the national identity card.[20] Conversely, Muslim groups may very well conceive of their presence on the European scene in terms of an *offensive approach*, in pursuit of a European norm ensuring a high degree of integration of Islam in the legal systems of the member states. A good illustration of this process of transnational mobilisation is the 'Muslim Charter' published by the CMCE, which in fact has its source in the Charter that the Central Council for Muslims in Germany (ZMD) drew up on 20 February 2002.[21] The CMCE document sets forth a list of ambitious demands in favour of European Muslims in terms of recognition, both symbolic and financial. These demands aim at an equality with the historic religions as well as a recognition of the specificity of Islam.

On the basis of this text, it appears that the logic of Europeanisation advocated by the CMCE does not fit in with a *strategy of assimilation* but with one of *assertion of identity* in a context of sedentarisation of the European Muslims and their access to national, and therefore European, citizenship. The Muslim intellectuals whom Romano Prodi invited to write a report on the future of the Euro-Mediterranean Partnership are hoping that the integration of Orthodox countries will change the terms of the debate on the Muslim integration, especially the principle of separation of the public and private spheres:[22]

---

[19] Pascaline Winand and Isabelle Smets (2000) have remarked that the establishment of liaison offices to the European Union is of a reactive, and not proactive, nature.

[20] The factor of competition may also be seen to play a role in the case of the establishment of a liaison office by the Orthodox Church of Greece, but in this case in competition with the Ecumenical Patriarchate, which had established an office to represent all of Orthodox Christianity in 1995.

[21] The author has been given a copy of the Islamic Charter of the ZMD by Mohammed Laroussi. For the Muslim Charter of the CMCE, see their website: http://www.cmce-europe.net

[22] The 'Report by the High-Level Advisory Group on the dialogue between peoples and cultures' is the outcome of a collaboration between European and Muslim intellectuals, including personalities representative of a wide spectrum of opinions, such as Tariq Ramadan, Malek Chebel and Fatima Mernissi. This report was submitted to Romano Prodi in autumn 2003.

the enlarged EU will move beyond the traditional relationship between Western Judeo-Christian culture and Islam by incorporating people of Orthodox religion and culture: in addition to strengthening the role of Orthodoxy within the EU and beyond, this incorporation will transform the dialogue into a 'trialogue'. Furthermore, Orthodoxy sometimes leads to behaviour which is surprisingly similar to that of Islam – particularly in relation to secularisation – which will have a major impact on, even radically change, the relationship between the enlarged Union and the Arab-Muslim world, and more broadly the Euro-Mediterranean dialogue. Such similarities could raise awareness of their long history and common destiny, while helping to relativise and then transcend differences.[23]

The idea that the Union may be a place where high standards of recognition of Muslim legal or religious specificities could translate into national legislations appears to be an illusion insofar as religious matters remain within the area of competence of the member states (see declaration No. 11 of the Treaty of Amsterdam, and Article I-52.1 of the European Constitution). However, a certain convergence of the European models of state-religions relations could be favoured at the European level. On 20 September 2000, the Forward Studies Unit organised a meeting of European decision-makers in charge of religious matters. The purpose of this meeting was to exchange views on common problems (amongst which was the integration of Islam), but not to draw up a common policy. Though, there has been no follow-up, and no 'lessons learnt', a process has been initiated at the European level in order to reach a common understanding of problems and solutions as regards religious matters.

There is a third reason behind the opening of the European Union to religious groups. The European administration is undersized and lacks both staff and resources. This explains its *search for information and expertise from outside groups*, a large opening vis-à-vis interest groups, combined with a search for legitimacy through direct contact with European civil society organisations.[24] Thus, the first contacts between the European Commission and the churches have entailed requests for expertise as well as meetings on technical issues related to European integration (agriculture, employment, environment, Lomé Agreements). Churches were invited to 'dialogue seminars' in order to contribute an ethical dimension. However, to have a minimum of legitimacy before European high-level functionaries implied a representation by

---

[23] Report by the High-Level Advisory Group established at the initiative of the President of the European Commission, 'Dialogue between peoples and cultures in the Euro-Mediterranean area', 8 September 2003, p. 10. See http://europa.eu.int/comm/dgs/policy_advisers/experts_groups/docs/rapport_complet_en.pdf

[24] Pascaline Winand and Isabelle Smets, 2000, p. 145.

experts equipped with the appropriate knowledge and whom the churches would select within their Europe-wide network. Muslim organisations, however, do not generally have at their disposal experts who are knowledgeable on European issues. Besides, there is no Muslim equivalent of the Social Doctrine of the Church, consistent with the European ethos. No Muslim (or Orthodox) organisation had been invited to the 'Dialogue Seminars' that brought together a limited number of actors designated by EECCS (Protestants) and the Commission of the National Bishops' Conferences of the European Union (COMECE, Catholics).[25] These seminars comprise the oldest and most efficient mechanism since they form a space where religious leaders discuss about specific European issues and policies with top European officials. EECCS and COMECE are the only European religious organisations that are invited since they are the only ones able to provide accurate expertise built among their specialised working groups.[26]

Recently, however, the *prospect of enlargement*, as well as the entry of new members into the EU, has increased the potential number of religious actors. For example, the Austrian Bishops' Conference, which worked a great deal in favour of Austria's entry into the EU, set up an office in Brussels after Austria joined the Union. Similarly, the prospect of the enlargement expanding eastwards accounts for a growing mobilisation of the Orthodox community, as shown by the creation of the Inter-Parliamentary Assembly on Orthodoxy, founded in 1993 on the initiative of Greece (a country that comes forward as the leader of Orthodoxy in the European Union). Orthodox churches have multiplied contacts with the Presidency of the Commission, in particular with visits by the Orthodox Churches of Russia and Byelorussia in 1999, and the opening of a liaison office of the Russian Orthodox Church in Brussels in 1999. In 2003, a liaison office of the Catholic Church of Ukraine opened its doors in Brussels and the chaplain of the Serbian Orthodox community in Brussels was invited to briefing sessions. In addition, the possibility of Turkey and Albania joining the EU has been instrumental in terms of

---

[25] These dialogue seminars were discontinued during most of Prodi's Presidency.

[26] In 1999, the COMECE had six working groups: Judicial Affairs, Bioethics, Social Affairs, Media, Islam in Europe, and Migration). To that list one must add an ad hoc group working on 'Global governance' and chaired by Michel Camdessus, former Chairman of the World Bank, and another ad hoc group established to follow the Convention on the Future of Europe. At the same time, the CES of the CEC (previously named EECCS) had nine working groups: Bioethics and Biotechnologies, Economics, Environmental and Social Issues, North–South issues, Economic and Political Union, European Legislation, Human Rights Issues at the European level (EU, Council of Europe and OSCE), a theological commission thinking about general European issues, and a European Christian network on environment, employment and social affairs.

Muslims developing a European consciousness. Characteristically, some Muslims add the number of European Muslim immigrants to the population of those Muslim-majority countries that may join the Union, in order to highlight the weight of Islam in Europe. The Report by the High-Level Advisory Group argues that

enlargement in the longer term to Bulgaria (where 10% of the population is Muslim), and then to the Balkans (including Bosnia-Herzegovina, which has a Muslim majority), and finally to Turkey (combining a secular political regime with the Muslim religion, with 80 million inhabitants at present), will lead to the inclusion of a 'historically' European Islam. This, combined with the presence in Germany and Austria of populations of Turkish rather than North African origin, will contribute to the diversification of Islam in Europe.[27]

Islam in the action framework of the European Commission: addressing a European Islam or managing geopolitics?

The Muslim presence in the consultation forums between the Commission and religious representatives has become possible thanks to an action framework through which their inclusion has been made both desirable and necessary. However, an ambiguity is showing through the various initiatives undertaken by the European Commission at the level of FSU (then GOPA): Islam seems to be considered mainly as an external geopolitical issue, rather than as an internal reality.

One feature of the action framework that guides the relations between the European Commission and Islam is a rejection of Huntington's theory of a 'clash of civilisations'. Against the notion that civilisational divides (to a large extent based on the geographical areas of the major world faiths) would be the key factor of explanation of international conflicts, the report produced by the FSU opposes an argument whereby each religion is divided between pre-modernists, modernists, and post-modernists.[28] This proposition makes it possible to have alliances in favour of the common good between the major religious traditions. According to Marc Luyckx, author of the report,

---

[27] Report by the High-Level Advisory Group established at the initiative of the President of the European Commission, 'Dialogue between peoples and cultures in the Euro-Mediterranean Area', 8 September 2003, p. 10.

[28] The report was prepared by Marc Luyckx, who was in charge of the relations with religions during the Delors presidency. Under the auspices of the Forecasting and Assessment in Science and Technology programme (FAST), Marc Luyckx launched a broad consultation, the outcome of which was a report released in November 1991: *Les religions face à la science et la technologie, églises et éthiques après prométhée, rapport exploratoire*, European Commission: FAST.

we are undergoing a profound cultural change, which means that our cosmology, our Weltanschauung, our worldview is changing. Religions are going through these changes and one will find religious actors in the three categories (pre-modern, modern, and post-modern). There is a need for a strategy that would help the constitution of a European Islam open to the changes in the post-industrial era. It seems ineffective to propose a modern cosmology (secularisation) to European Muslims now that is under discussion.[29]

The question of the presence of millions of Muslims on European soil arose belatedly in the debates of the Forward Studies Unit. On 20 December 1994, during the inter-religious conference with Jacques Delors, the two Muslim participants did not raise the issue of the Muslim presence in Europe. The representative of the Turkish community in Germany advocated the cause of his country by inquiring about the chances of Turkey joining the Union. Meanwhile, the focus of Mohammed Arkoun's speech was a request for more intense links between academics and intellectuals on both sides of the Mediterranean for, according to him, 'only Europe is capable of providing an environment that is sufficiently free from an intellectual standpoint, yet rich with its knowledge of the historic tradition, so that a reflection on Muslim history and theology can take place, sheltered from pressures, wherever they come from'.[30]

Islam in Europe first became a subject of reflection and study for the Commission as part of an effort to acquire knowledge *and* control of a new population (knowledge is power, as Michel Foucault emphasised). The first study of Europe's Muslim community, for which Louvain-la-Neuve University's Felice Dassetto was commissioned by the Forward Studies Unit in 1999, found its justification in the need to carry out a Europe-wide comparative assessment, upon the recommendations of the European Parliament.[31] The purpose of this study was to gain an understanding of socio-cultural changes in Europe (cognitive aspect) in order to enhance the legitimacy of the European institutions (normative

---

[29] Marc Luyckx, Note to President Delors, 22 December 1992, fourth quarterly report on religions. Dossier Marc Luyckx, no. 32, 'Note de réflexion'.

[30] Marc Luyckx, Note de dossier, 10 January 1995, Report on the meeting between President Delors and representatives of the major European religious traditions and philosophical traditions, held on 20 December 1994, Archives of the Forward Studies Unit, Dossier Marc Luyckx, 'Rencontres avec le Président 1990–1994'. Author's translation.

[31] Felice Dassetto had maintained contacts with the Commission since 1991, and had proposed a study of Islam in Europe as early as 1993. This study was the basis for a book edited by Felice Dassetto, Brigitte Maréchal and Jorgen Nielsen (eds.), *Convergences musulmanes*, then under the direction of B. Maréchal, S. Allievi, F. Dassetto and F. Nielsen (eds.), *Muslims in the enlarged Europe*, Boston/Leiden: Brill, 2003.

aspect): 'in order to legitimise the existing European order and institutions, it is essential to guarantee integration or co-existence of diverse ethnicities and cultures in Europe'.[32]

We see an element of ambiguity arising in this regard, because in terms of EU activity and policy development, the relations between the institutions of the European Union and Islam arose first as a geopolitical issue, i.e. EU relationships with the outside environment. The informal meeting which took place in Toledo in November 1995 was in this regard revealing. It was held as a fringe event of the Barcelona Summit, which in turn launched the Euro-Mediterranean Partnership (EMP). The final document of the Barcelona Conference included inter-religious dialogue as part of the cultural component of the EMP and as one of the tools for a closer relationship that would facilitate a wider cooperation:

A greater understanding among the major religions present in the Euro-Mediterranean region will facilitate greater mutual tolerance and cooperation. Support will be given to periodic meetings of representatives of religions and religious institutions as well as theologians, academics and others, with the aim of breaking down prejudice, ignorance and fanaticism, and fostering cooperation at grass-roots level.[33]

Despite the support of all heads of state and governments, the results of the Toledo meeting were limited because of internal opposition within the Commission: an opposition as a matter of principle in the name of the secular character of the European institutions, and an administrative rivalry between the Forward Studies Unit and the Directorate-General for External Relations. Other initiatives included a conference in Copenhagen on 16–18 June 1996, 'Islam in a changing world', and the second Euro-Islam Conference, organised by the Swedish government in partnership with the European Commission and the Jordanian government in Al al-Bayt on 10–13 June 1996. However, the Middle East context, dominated by the Israel–Palestine conflict, weighed so much on such events that the meetings differed greatly, in content and in spirit, from that held in Toledo, and neither Jews nor humanists were invited.

The documents of the Forward Studies Unit constantly make a connection between Orthodoxy and Islam. According to these, for Europe the point is to offer a democratic model to its neighbours.

---

[32] *Carrefours Newsletters*, no. 11, October 1999, p. 6.
[33] Commission européenne, *Les religions méditerranéennes: Islam, Judaïsme et Christianisme. Un dialogue en marche*, Les cahiers de la Cellule de Prospective, Luxembourg: Editions Apogée, Office for Official Publications of the European Communities, p. 59.

Beyond the relationships between the European Commission and Muslims' organisations, the European People's Party (EPP) also invites Muslims to attend the yearly meetings it organises in conjunction with the Ecumenical Patriarchate of Constantinople to promote a model of Christian democracy in Orthodox countries in democratic transition. In 1994, Stephen Biller, adviser to the EPP President, considered supporting the democratic movement in Turkmenistan which aimed to develop on the model of the Christian Democratic Parties. On 22 April 1993 in Moscow, and on 24 January 1993 in Paris, the international branch of the EPP (Christian Democratic International) organised meetings with representatives of the World Islamic League (under the influence of Saudi Arabia). In other words, the relations between Islam and the European institutions can be seen as part of a broad web of foreign policy concerns.

After September 11: an internationalisation of the framework for action

The attacks on 11 September led to a revival of the Euro-Mediterranean Partnership: numerous statements by European officials called for a strengthening of the 'dialogue of cultures and civilisations' to prevent a 'clash of civilisations'. The Ghent European Council, on 19 October 2001, decided to foster cross-cultural dialogue with a general aim of encouraging 'a dialogue of equals between our civilisations . . . both at international level and within [EU] societies', and with a specific aim of giving 'concrete priority to the dialogue between cultures', especially under the Barcelona process and to 'avoid any equating of terrorism with the Arab and Muslim world'. On 21–22 March 2002, during a seminar on inter-cultural dialogue organised by the Directorate-General for Education and Culture, Pat Cox, the then President of the European Parliament, stated: 'the events of 11 September 2001 created a keen awareness that we need to avoid the trap of a clash of civilisations that could lead to an apocalyptic confrontation'.[34] International thinking influences the public action framework of the Commission on religions: this is an effect of globalisation on Commission–religion relationships. Consequently, it was decided to establish a Euro-Mediterranean Foundation for cultural cooperation, and contacts were made with UNESCO so as to define a common analytical framework.

In this new policy, the religious factor tends to be subsumed under culture, and the emphasis is laid on common secular values (human

[34] http://europa.eu.int

rights, tolerance, respect of diversity, etc.). The Conference on inter-cultural dialogue, held on 20–21 March 2002, aimed toward the revival of the Euro-Mediterranean Partnership, included inter-faith dialogue in its third session. Nevertheless the final statement simply mentions the necessity to take the 'the religious factor' into account in the inter-cultural dialogue policy of the EU. However, the emphasis is placed on human-rights education. In early 2003, Romano Prodi created the 'High-Level Advisory Group on the dialogue between peoples and cultures' for a rethinking of the whole question of cross-cultural dialogue between the two sides of the Mediterranean. Rather than choosing religious representatives, as had been the case in Toledo in 1995, he preferred to turn to European and Muslim intellectuals.[35] This development represents a deinstitutionalisation of the relations between the Commission and the religions. The High-Level Advisory Group identified three 'operational' guidelines in order to promote inter-cultural dialogue through initiatives in the realms of education, mobility, and the media. Amongst these, with regard to inter-cultural education, there is mention of a comparative teaching of religions. This comparative element will, according to the Advisory Group, 'contribute to the expression of freedom of conscience and the construction of imaginary worlds and cultures in all their geographical diversity'.[36] Such teaching is distinct from religious teaching per se. It implies the training of teachers from both primary and secondary schools in the field of comparative analysis, through the constitution of a network of academic institutions on both sides of the Mediterranean.[37]

A will to fulfil the objectives of the Euro-Mediterranean Partnership and to take into account Muslim migrants became more apparent in the wake of 9/11. Muslim immigrants are now viewed by the GOPA as bridges between two worlds:

The integration of immigrant populations who have legally settled can be seen as the result of these two dynamics, both internal and external. There are two-way issues here: at the same time as creating a sense of belonging to the Union and to

---

[35] The members are: Assia Bensalah-Alaoui, Fatima Mernissi, Simone Susskind-Weinberger and Tullia Zevi as well as Jean Daniel, Malek Chebel, Juan Diaz Nicolas, Umberto Eco, Shmuel N. Eisenstadt, George Joffré, Ahmed Kamal Aboumagd, Bichara Kahder, Adnan Wafic Kassar, Pedrag Matvejevic, Rostane Mehdi, Tariq Ramadan, Faruk Sen, and Faouzi Skali.

[36] Report by the High-Level Advisory Group established at the initiative of the President of the European Commission, 'Dialogue between peoples and cultures in the Euro-Mediterranean Area', 8 September 2003, p. 29.

[37] Braudel-Ibn Khaldoun network project on the model of the Jean Monnet chair; extension of existing programmes like MED TEMPUS.[0].

each host Member State, there is a bridging role to be played with the countries and civil societies of origin, all the while upholding respect for the different identities.[38]

However, this discussion amongst European and Muslim intellectual elites, on the GOPA level, does not include a review of the migration policies that are emerging in the EU. It does take into account the religious dimension of racism, as is the case in the international reports of the UN Human Rights Commission and the Council of Europe. From the EU side, the European Monitoring Centre on Racism and Xenophobia (EUMC) has published several reports,[39] including a synthesis report released on 20 November 2001, on 'Anti-Islamic reactions within the European Union after the acts of terror against the USA'; a study (also in November 2001) on 'The situation of Islamic communities in five European cities'; and a report published in May 2002 on 'Islamophobia in the EU after 11 September 2001'. In addition, the founder of the 'Network of Comparative Research on Islam and Muslims in Europe' (NOCRIME), Jocelyne Cesari, was commissioned by the Directorate-General for Research to conduct a new study on Islam in Europe. All of the above can be considered special efforts which developed in the light of the events of 11 September 2001.

Muslim endeavours to place Islamic culture in the European heritage

When looking at the policies developed first by the Forward Studies Unit, and later by GOPA, Islam seems to be approached as an external and internal border in Europe. Meanwhile, the presence of Muslims within the Union as well as the issue of Turkey's entry into the EU raise the question of an inclusive or exclusive definition of European identity, in terms of civilisational heritage based upon Christian values or areligious norms (human rights, democracy, rule of law). A debate on this question took place during the discussions on the preamble of the Charter of Fundamental Rights (religious or spiritual legacy) and on the preamble of the Constitutional Treaty (religious or Christian legacy). Within this context, Muslims mobilised and approached the European institutions in order to have the place of Islamic culture taken into account in the European heritage.

---

[38] 'From the future of the European Union to a dialogue between societies in the Euro-Mediterranean area: role and aims of this dialogue. Issue paper'. See GOPA's website.
[39] To peruse these reports, see the website of the European Monitoring Center: http://www.eumc.org

One such attempt was made earlier by a Spanish Muslim MEP, Abdelkader Mohamed Ali, who in 1996 proposed a European 'Averroes[40] Day' at the European Parliament to highlight the 800th anniversary of Averroes' death. He argued that the value of this would be both cultural and symbolic:

From a cultural standpoint, it recalls the contribution made by Islamic civilisation to European culture, above all via Al-Andalus, the place of Ibn Sina in this civilisation and the influence of Averroes on the culture of the Christian Middle Ages. . .From a symbolic standpoint, [it] could provide an opportunity to highlight the modernity of Averroes' thinking, in seminars and other public events, and take up the challenge of fighting against exclusion and xenophobia – the fruit of obscurantism, ignorance and prejudice – on the eve of the third millennium, within the European Community itself, for all that it is imbued with democracy, pluralism and respect for human rights.[41]

According to Abdelkader Mohamed Ali, such a celebration in the form of an 'Averroes Day' could serve to stimulate hard thinking about how to address questions surrounding the cultural identity of millions of Muslims who live here and the future of Islam in Europe. Such thinking, he argues, should not be inhibited by considerations such as the political situations in Islamic countries.[42] Although the idea of a seminar was given the green light by the European Parliament in 1998, the 'Averroes Day' did not take place.

[40] Arabian philosopher, astronomer, doctor, and writer on jurisprudence; born at Cordova, 1126; died in Morocco, 1198. Ibn Roschd, or Averroes, was educated in his native city, where his father and grandfather had held the office of *cadi* (judge in civil affairs). Under the Califs Abu Jacub Jusuf and his son, Jacub Al Mansur, he enjoyed extraordinary favour at court and was entrusted with several important civil offices in Morocco, Seville, and Cordoba. Later he fell into disfavour and was banished with other representatives of learning, under the pressure of malekites lawyers. Shortly before his death, the edict against philosophers was recalled. A common theme throughout his writings is that there is no incompatibility between religion and philosophy when both are properly understood. His contributions to philosophy took many forms, ranging from his detailed commentaries on Aristotle, his defence of philosophy against the attacks of those who condemned it as contrary to Islam and his construction of a form of Aristotelianism which cleansed it, as far as was possible at the time, of Neoplatonic influences. In the Western world, he was recognised, as early as the thirteenth century, as the commentator of Aristotle, contributing thereby to the rediscovery of the Master, after centuries of near-total oblivion in Western Europe. That discovery was instrumental in launching Latin scholasticism.

[41] Report on Islam and European Averroes Day, Committee on Culture, Youth, Education and the Media, Rapporteur: Mr Abdelkader Mohamed Ali, A4-0167/98, PE 221.802/fin., 29 April 1998, p. 11. The same MEP submitted a working document on 9 October 1996, PE 219.405 Or.es.

[42] Report on Islam and European Averroes Day, Committee on Culture, Youth, Education and the Media, Rapporteur: Mr Abdelkader Mohamed Ali, A4-0167/98, PE 221.802/fin., 29 April 1998, p. 11.

During the debates on the future European Constitution, the CMCE brought forth its own contribution. The argument developed at that time by CMCE was ambiguous. The group claimed that the sources which Europeans viewed as a foundation of their civilisation actually originated from the margins of the geographical Europe ('the Greco-Roman source which did not spring from the heart, but from the periphery of Europe'[43]), or they were extra-European ('the Judeo-Christian source which was but a pure gift from the immaculate heavens of the Orient'). The CMCE argued that Europe does not possess any heritage of its own; everything has come from the outside, and it made no comment on the contribution made by the Enlightenment, the key element in the invention of Western modernity. On the other hand, Islam is regarded as the only legacy to have shaped the Orient whereas the many previous legacies are ignored ('the Islamic source whose radiant theology and culture dispelled the darkness of the Middle East without arrogance or paternalism'). As such, Islam can regenerate a Western civilisation that is running out of steam:

Crushed by nihilism, weakened by declining convictions, asphyxiated by an oppressively dazzling atmosphere, our world is in distress, in distress for not being able to believe, in decay because of the madness of living without believing. Transcendence, God and religion will be our compass. They will enable us to harmonise our relationships, to give meaning to our existence, and to act as a stimulus for enhancing our citizenship through duties to accomplish and rights to deserve.

Typically, the evocation of Andalusian Islam is used to justify the desire to contribute to 'the cultural symbiosis and social harmony of our common home: Europe'.[44] In short, the Muslim activities towards the European Union institutions, seeking to place Islamic culture in the European heritage, have been relatively limited in terms of impact, scope and content.

---

[43] Letter addressed to the President of the Convention, Valery Giscard d'Estaing, submitted by Mohammed Laroussi, President of the CMCE. Author's translation. The quotations which follow in this paragraph are from the same source.

[44] A comparison can be made with Article 14 of the Islamic Charter of the Central Council for Muslims in Germany: 'European culture resulted from the classical Hellenistic-Roman heritage, the Judeo-Christian–Islamic one, and the Enlightenment. In fact, European culture has been heavily influenced by Islamic philosophy and civilisation. Also during the current transition from modernity to post-modernity Muslims are ready to contribute decisively to the overcoming of contemporary crises. This includes their Qur'anically demanded commitment to religious pluralism, their unconditional rejection of racism and chauvinism, as well as their wholesome way of life that shuns any form of addiction.' See http://www.islam.de/?site=sonstiges/events/charta&di=en.

Conclusions

The model of relations between the EU, religions and humanists is in constant flux. Though the system of interest intermediation in Brussels entails certain limitations on pluralism, this should not conceal the fact that religion–state relations in each member state are far less pluralistic. Indeed, at the level of the nation-state, long traditions of relationships between the state and the major faiths define the scope of centuries-old agreements with the historic religions. As a result, the national systems of church–state relations have difficulty opening up to the growing pluralism and deregulation of the European religious scene. The European Union has the advantage of being a new political struc-ture whose institutional arrangements are yet to be fully determined. Therefore, for religious groups and humanists, the EU constitutes a laboratory for new kinds of links with the political and administrative institutions. This is especially the case for Muslims. Thus, from the scholar Mohammed Arkoun (1994), to the local Muslim leader Imam Boussouf (1997) and the European-wide Muslim Youth organisation, FEMYSO (2003), there is an institutionalisation combined with an increasing pluralism of the Muslim presence vis-à-vis the Forward Studies Unit/GOPA.

The initiatives undertaken in the framework of the Commission–Islam dialogue, at the level of the Forward Studies Unit, may appear to be timid (considering the limited results of the inter-faith meeting in Toledo, the biannual briefing sessions of little effectiveness, and the dilution of the religious factor to that of culture in the context of the dialogue between cultures and civilisations). Nevertheless, one must be mindful of the constraints on the dialogue between the Commission and the religions in general. As they are not mentioned in the treaties, these links can only remain of an informal nature as long as the Constitution is not ratified (its Article 51.3 would permit the officialisation of these relations). The Constitution includes the European Union Charter of Fundamental Rights that sets out legal provisions to defend religious freedom. Article 13 of the Amsterdam Treaty on non-discrimination already includes proscription against racism related to religion (anti-Semitism, Islamophobia). Moreover, the functions of the European institutions should not be misunderstood. These institutions possess certain tools thanks to public policies and the definition of EU norms, but they are also transnational forums where actors of all opinions and from all member states convene. A learning process is taking place through the pursuit of the European ideals. A common vision of problems and objectives is emerging, which results in a convergence in the ways of doing and thinking that goes beyond national borders.[45] In fact the European Union is functioning as a cognitive and normative constraint for member states. Access to these forums entails an opportunity for Muslims to place their local and national endeavours in a wider environment. The variety of Muslim actors who are invited to attend these forums can lead to confrontations between the champions of the various Islamic trends, who otherwise would not have the opportunity to meet. Therefore, more than a role of legal regulation, the European commission is playing, for the time being, the role of a mediator which facilitates interfaith and inter-religious meetings.

Bibliography

Allievi, Stefano and Jorgen Nielsen (eds.), *Muslim networks and transnational communities in and across Europe*, Leiden: Koninklijke Brill NV, 2003.

Cesari, Jocelyne, *L'Islam à l'épreuve de l'Occident*, Paris: La Découverte, 2004.

Commission Européenne, *Les religions méditerranéennes: islam, judaïsme et christianisme. Un dialogue en marche*, Les cahiers de la Cellule de Prospective, Luxembourg, Editions Apogée, Office for Official Publications of the European Communities.

Dassetto, Felice, *La construction d'un Islam Européen*, Paris: L'Harmattan, 1996.

Dassetto, Felice, Brigitte Maréchal and Jorgen Nielsen (eds.), *Convergences musulmanes. Aspects contemporains de l'Islam dans une Europe élargie*, Paris: L'Harmattan, 2001.

Drake, Helen, *Jacques Delors en Europe, histoire et sociologie d'un leadership improbable*, Strasbourg: Presses Universitaires de Strasbourg, 2002.

European Monitoring Center: http://www.eumc.org

Frégosi, Franck, 'L'Islam à Strasbourg', *Annuaire de l'Afrique du Nord*, vol. 34, 1995, pp. 949–70.

Frégosi, Franck, '"Droit de cité" de l'Islam et politiques municipales: analyse comparative entre Strasbourg et Mulhouse', in Franck Frégosi (ed.), *Le religieux dans la commune*, Genève: Labor et Fides, 2001, pp. 92–137.

---

[45] Numerous approaches to public policies have underlined the learning aspect that comes with belonging to a 'policy community'. For example, Jenkins-Smith and P. Sabatier, *Policy change and learning. An advocacy coalition approach*, Boulder: Westview Press, 1993, and 'The advocacy coalition framework: an assessment', in Paul Sabatier (ed.), *Theories of the political process*, Boulder: Westview Press, 1999, pp. 117–68. Yves Surel points out that the European integration process can be studied as an information-integration process in the context of a multi-level governance. The idea is to show how European public policies generate common cognitive resources. He mentions policy learning devices at the European level such as the role of the European agencies that institutionalises integration and information dynamics, as well as the role of European law as a common cognitive framework for all European agents, especially economic ones. See Yves Surel, 'Logiques du pouvoir et récits dans les politiques publiques de l'Union européenne', *RFSP*, vol. 50, no. 2, April 2000, pp. 235–54.

Grant, Charles, *Delors, inside the house that Jacques built*, London: Nicolas Brealey Publishing, 1994.

Greenwood, Justin, and Mark Aspinwall, 'Conceptualizing collective actors in the EU. An introduction', in *Collective action in the European Union. Interests and politics of associability*, New York, London: Routledge, 1998, pp. 1–30.

Islamic Charter of the Central Council for Muslims in Germany, available online at: http://www.islam.de

Jenkins-Smith, F., and P. Sabatier, *Policy change and learning. An advocacy coalition approach*, Boulder, Westview Press, 1993, and 'The advocacy coalition framework: an assessment', in Riva Kastoryano, 'Participation transnationale et citoyenneté: les immigrés dans l'Union européenne', in *Cultures et Conflits*, no. 28, Winter 1997, pp. 59–74.

Luyckx, Marc, *Les religions face à la science et la technologie, églises et éthiques après prométhée, rapport exploratoire*, European Commission: FAST, November 1991.

Note au President Delors, 22 December 1992, Fourth quarterly report on religions. Dossier Marc Luyckx, no. 32, 'Note de réflexion'.

Note de dossier, 10 January 1995, Report on the meeting between President Delors with representatives of the Major European Religious Traditions and Philosophical Traditions, held on 20 December 1994, Archives of the Forward Studies Unit, Dossier Marc Luyckx, 'Rencontres avec le Président 1990–1994'.

Maréchal, B., S. Allievi, F. Dassetto and F. Nielsen (eds.), *Muslims in the enlarged Europe*, Boston/Leiden: Brill, 2003.

Ramadan, Tariq, *Etre Musulman européen. Etudes des sources Islamiques à la lumière du contexte Européen*, Lyon: Tawhid, 1999.

Musulmans d'Occident. Construire et contribuer, Lyon: Tawhid, 2002.

Report by the High-Level Advisory Group established at the initiative of the President of the European Commission, 'Dialogue between peoples and cultures in the Euro-Mediterranean area', 8 September 2003, available online at: http://www.euromedalex.org/En/Files/rapport_complet_en.pdf

Report on Islam and European Averroes Day, Committee on Culture, Youth, Education and the Media, Rapporteur: Mr Abdelkader Mohamed Ali, A4-0167/98, PE 221.802/fin., 29 April 1998. Available online at: http://www.europarl.europa.eu/omk/sipade3

Riva Kastoryano, 'Participation transnationale et citoyenneté: les immigrés dans l'Union européenne', in *Cultures et Conflits*, no. 28, Winter 1997, pp. 59–74.

Roy, Olivier, *Vers un Islam Européen*, Paris: Editions Esprit, 1999.

Sabatier, Paul (ed.), *Theories of the political process*, Boulder: Westview Press, 1999.

Saint-Blancat, Chantal, *L'Islam de la diaspora*, Paris: Bayard, 1997.

Surel, Yves, 'Logiques du pouvoir et récits dans les politiques publiques de l'Union Européenne', *RFSP*, vol. 50, no. 2, April 2000, p. 235–54.

Winand, Pascaline, and Isabelle Smets, 'A la recherche d'un modèle Européen de représentation des intérêts', in Paul Magnette, Eric Remacle (eds.), *Le nouveau modèle Européen*, V.I. Institutions et gouvernance, Bruxelles, Institut d'études Européennes, 2000.

8 Development, discrimination and reverse discrimination: effects of EU integration and regional change on the Muslims of Southeast Europe

Dia Anagnostou

In the past fifteen years, European integration has been characterised by two seemingly contradictory but arguably interrelated phenomena of supranational market integration on the one hand, and growing minority mobilisation at the local and subnational level, on the other. The former is driven by economic imperatives to redefine the structures of national and regional political economy in order to enhance their production and administrative capacity, as well as their ability to compete in and converge with the European common market. A growing literature on the 'new regionalism' and regionalisation describes the emergence and construction of sub-state regions and institutional–administrative structures along such lines.[1] Meanwhile, territorially concentrated minorities assert a strong sense of cultural distinctiveness, and advance demands for political self-determination, either in some form of self-government, autonomy or occasionally secession. Such politicisation is driven by a different logic that draws upon historically specific patterns of cultural affinity, collective solidarity and membership in a national or ethnic community. The upsurge of minority nationalisms in the 1980s and 1990s, in Catalonia, the Basque Country, Scotland and Wales, was arguably inseparably linked to EU integration and the processes of regionalisation. Together with the growing significance of sub-state regions in the EU, these were central factors driving the minority nationalisms.[2] At the intersection of

---

[1] Michael Keating, *The new regionalism in western Europe*, Cheltenham: Edward Elgar, 1998.

[2] Peter Lynch, *Minority nationalism and European integration*, Cardiff: University of Wales Press, 1996; James Mitchell and Michael Cavanagh, 'Context and contingency: constitutional nationalists and Europe', in Michael Keating and John McGarry (eds.), *Minority nationalism and the changing international order*, Oxford: Oxford University Press, 2001.

these two sets of processes – market integration and minority mobilisation – this chapter explores the regional changes occurring within the frame of European integration and enlargement. By focusing specifically on the Muslim communities of Southeast Europe, it examines the ways in which minorities mobilise in response to these changes.

The Muslims of Southeast Europe are autochthonous and territorially concentrated historical minorities, largely comprising farming communities that inhabit mountainous, agricultural and less developed areas often lying along state borders. Their sizeable presence is a legacy of the *millet* system in the predominantly Christian Orthodox states of the region, where they remained after national independence despite large-scale immigration to the rump Ottoman Empire and subsequently to Turkey. In shaping a distinct cultural identity, their Muslim identity rendered difficult their assimilation into Christian Orthodox states such as Bulgaria and Greece, as well as in Albania and the Yugoslav lands (notably Bosnia-Herzegovina, Serbia and Montenegro). Insofar as Islam has been a bridge facilitating their incorporation into Turkish national identity, Muslim communities have been viewed as a threat to Southeast European states engaged in nation-building processes, becoming a bone of contention between them.[3] In the post-World War II period, Muslims in countries like Greece and Bulgaria gradually acquired an ethnic Turkish consciousness, on the basis of which they have politically asserted themselves. Their politicisation became particularly pronounced in the post-1989 period, in some cases coinciding with the intensification of EU integration, as in Greece, and in other cases like Bulgaria, following transition from communism to democracy and subsequently the onset of EU enlargement processes.

Border areas, together with the frontiers that delimit them, comprise institutions and processes that have played a significant role in the formation of contemporary national states.[4] Rarely remaining impermeable to external influences, they are sites where political loyalties and national–ethnic identities have been strongly pronounced but also most sharply contested. Diverse ethnic and religious communities have often resisted assimilation into the dominant nation. In Southeast Europe many minority communities have retained and even cultivated their political allegiances and cultural affinities to a national homeland outside or across the state border. In view of this, as expounded in Malcolm

---

[3] Dia Anagnostou, 'National interpretations in Bulgarian writings on the Pomaks from the communist period through the present', *Journal of Southern Europe and the Balkans*, vol. 7, no. 1, April 2005, p. 57.

[4] Malcolm Anderson, *Frontiers – territory and state formation in the modern world*, Cambridge: Polity Press, 1996.

Anderson's important study, border regions have historically been a target of specific state policies and government attempts aimed at securing state frontier and territorial integrity, as well as consolidating central national authority over diverse ethnic–religious communities.[5] In the context of the 'new Europe', however (both within the EU but also in candidate states), central government capacity to interfere in this regard in border regions, although still salient for national interests and identities, arguably tends to diminish.[6]

Often lying near or across state borders, Muslim-inhabited areas in Southeast Europe comprise enclave, interface or external peripheries, zones historically characterised by conflict and highly sensitive for state sovereignty. While national consciousness has rarely been uniform in these areas, aspiration of the central state to instil homogeneity has been strongest, rendering these areas sites of competing ethno-national claims. The position of Muslims after World War II has not been defined solely by international treaty commitments, inter-state relations and political priorities. Whether under state socialism or under a liberal market economy, and similarly to states elsewhere in Europe, national governments have employed state structures and regional policies to pursue assimilation of territorially concentrated minorities, to marginalise, or conversely, to devise various mechanisms for accommodating them.[7] In minority regions, the territorial distribution of power between central and local levels, and the formation of administrative structures and government institutions, have been of cardinal importance. They have been instrumental for the demarcation of state boundaries and often highly contested with regard to the ability of the centre to establish control over national territory. In this sense, historical processes of nation-state building form legacies that thoroughly permeate contemporary territorial and administrative structures. At the same time, they bear a strong imprint on the workings and culture of local economy and regional government of border regions.

Over the 1990s, post-communist restructuring and European integration have reinforced a series of economic and institutional changes at the subnational level that are transforming the nature of border and minority-inhabited areas, as well as the interests and identities of the communities inhabiting them. Driven largely by functional and economic imperatives, such changes are far from uniform or unidirectional. Yet, broadly speaking, a process of regionalisation, in terms of growing significance of

[5] Anderson, Frontiers, pp. 1–2.
[6] Anderson, Frontiers, p. 4.
[7] Stein Rokkan and Derek W. Urwin, 'Introduction' and 'Conclusion' in Stein Rokkan and Derek W. Urwin (eds.), Politics of territorial identity, London: Sage 1982.

regional economies and of subnational political and administrative institutions, seems to be underway throughout the EU and in candidate states. Regionally specific policies and administrative–territorial reforms were already in vogue in the 1960s in Western Europe.[8] These, however, were largely a component of central economic management and a mechanism for consolidating the nation-state.[9] In the context of European integration such policies and reforms are seen to have gone hand-in-hand with greater regional assertion and economic mobilisation. In some cases, they have arguably reinforced a revival of ethno-cultural identities in areas inhabited by historical minority nations and communities.[10]

In the context of economic restructuring, market integration and EU enlargement from the late 1980s onwards, states in Central-East and Southeast Europe have also instituted a series of regional reforms and related policies. Post-communist restructuring and the creation of a European single market made more acute the deep socio-economic disparities of the less developed areas. Redistributive policies and measures on the part of national governments to redress these disparities have been limited due to macroeconomic constraints made imperative by convergence with the Common Market. In part, however, redressing such disparities has been incorporated as a goal in the EU's cohesion policy. Already in the late 1980s following the Mediterranean enlargement, the EU undertook redistribution of development funds to deal with the large regional disparities of the less developed states of south Europe.[11] Upholding the post-war model of social democracy and the principle of social cohesion, structural funds were a compensation for those regions and populations likely to be placed at a disadvantage in the competitive European Common Market.[12]

Through assistance to disadvantaged regions to help them develop economically and converge with the European economy, cohesion policy was intended to contribute to stabilisation and political normalisation in the newly democratised states of Southern Europe. Besides being a social counterpart to the European liberal project of economic deregulation and market integration, the underlying philosophy had analogies with the historical underpinnings of the EU as a whole: economic development and integration can challenge both physical borders

---

[8] Anderson, *Frontiers*, pp. 113–14.
[9] Keating, *The new regionalism*, pp. 46–7.
[10] Keating, *The new regionalism*, p. 75.
[11] Loukas Tsoukalis, *The new European economy – the politics and economics of integration*, Oxford: Oxford University Press, 1991, p. 206.
[12] Liesbet Hooghe, 'Reconciling EU-wide policy and national diversity', in Liesbet Hooghe (ed.), *Cohesion policy and European integration*, Oxford: University Press, 1996, p. 5.

and national boundaries that have historically been loci of national and ethnic antagonisms. From the second half of the 1990s onwards, cohesion policy in the form of pre-accession funds has increasingly been directed to the Associate Candidate Countries (ACC) and to the new EU member states of Central-East and Southeast Europe (CESE). Being largely pervaded by functional economic priorities, structural funds seek to enhance administrative efficiency and regional competencies with the goal of promoting production, development and market competitiveness. While by no means specifically aimed at territorially concentrated minorities, they have had indirect and largely unintended effects, potentially influencing the workings of subnational structures, as well as patterns of political participation and interest representation in border regions.

A second set of regional changes evidenced across the EU and the ACC is the establishment or reform of regional–subnational institutions, reconfiguring in varying ways state territorial and administrative structures. In the ex-communist countries such reforms were in part a reaction to the legacy of entrenched centralisation under the former regime and a response to the call for democratising state structures by restoring powers and functions to local–regional levels of government.[13] Besides this, a strong impetus for subnational reform has come from the EU regional policy. The latter has introduced pressures for the establishment of regional-level institutions capable of effectively managing structural funds in member states, as well as in the course of enlargement to the East.[14] As beneficiaries of pre-accession funds such as PHARE, the candidate states of CESE have engaged in regional reforms to enhance planning and programming competencies of their subnational structures, largely in preparation for implementation of EU structural funds.[15]

To be sure, the EU does not promote a specific model of regionalisation, let alone political decentralisation of sub-state structures. The political connotations of the infamous principles of partnership and subsidiarity have receded in the scholarly literature. Premised on the

---

[13] Andrew Coulson, 'From democratic centralism to local democracy', in Andrew Coulson (ed.), *Local government in Eastern Europe*, Brookfield, VT: Edward Elgar, 1995, p. 16; Judy Batt, 'Introduction', in Judy Batt and Kataryna Wolczuk (eds.), *Region, state and identity in Central and Eastern Europe*, London: Frank Cass, 2002, p. 8.

[14] John Bachtler, Ruth Downes and Grzegorz Gorzelak, 'Introduction: challenges of transition for regional development', in John Bachtler et al. (eds.) *Transition, cohesion and regional policy in Central and Eastern Europe*, Aldershot: Ashgate, 2000, p. 6.

[15] Michael Keating, 'Territorial restructuring and European integration', in Michael Keating and James Hughes (eds.) *The regional challenge in Central and Eastern Europe*, Brussels: PIE- Peter Lang, 2003, p. 16.

involvement of subnational actors along with national authorities and the Commission, such principles were understood to imply a transfer of power from central to local–regional government.[16] In fact, in the context of enlargement to CESE, the EU approach has tended to underscore the need for speedy and efficient absorption of funds, placing now the emphasis on expanding regional administrative capacity rather than decentralisation.[17] In this way, it is argued, it effectively promotes centralisation and the concentration of management responsibility in the hands of central government, at the expense of local–regional authorities.[18]

Irrespective of the intent and approach of EU authorities, however, case studies show that structural policy has become an important frame in which national political actors have anchored regional reform initiatives, and in reference to which debates about regionalisation and decentralisation have taken place.[19] Domestic actors widely perceive the EU to be closely associated with partnership and subsidiarity.[20] Some attribute to the latter a reform imperative in the direction of self-government and devolution of power, while others depict such principles through the lens of administrative decentralisation.[21] National regional reforms have faced greatest controversy in minority-inhabited areas. In some cases domestic actors put forth a functional and efficiency-driven form of regional reform, while others advocate ethnic regionalisation that takes into account historical divisions and ethnic–cultural faultlines existing within a state.[22] In any case, it becomes

---

[16] Raffaella Y. Nanetti, 'EU cohesion and territorial restructuring in the member states', in Liesbet Hooghe (ed.), *Cohesion policy and European integration*, Oxford: University Press, 1996.

[17] James Hughes, Gwendolyn Sasse and Claire Gordon, *Europeanization and regionalization in the EU's enlargement to Central and Eastern Europe*, New York: Palgrave Macmillan, 2004, p. 139.

[18] Keating, 'Territorial restructuring', p. 21; James Hughes, Gwendolyn Sasse and Claire Gordon, 'EU enlargement, Europeanisation and the dynamics of regionalisation in the CEECs', in Michael Keating and James Hughes (eds.), *The regional challenge in Central and Eastern Europe*, Brussels: PIE–Peter Lang, 2003, p. 77.

[19] Kataryna Wolczuk, 'Conclusion: Identities, regions and Europe', in Judy Batt and Kataryna Wolczuk (eds.), *Region, state and identity in Central and Eastern Europe*, London: Frank Cass, 2002, p. 204.

[20] Hughes et al., 'EU enlargement', p. 81.

[21] Brigid Fowler, 'Hungary: patterns of political conflict over territorial–administrative reform', in Judy Batt and Kataryna Wolczuk (eds.), *Region, state and identity in Central and Eastern Europe*, London: Frank Cass, 2002, pp. 25–30; Martin Brusis, 'Regionalisation in the Czech and Slovak Republics: comparing the influence of the European Union', in Michael Keating and James Hughes (eds.), *The regional challenge in Central and Eastern Europe*, Brussels: PIE–Peter Lang, 2003, p. 107.

[22] Jan Bucek, 'Balancing functional and ethnic regionalisation: lessons from Slovakia', in M. Keating and J. Hughes (eds.), *The regional challenge in Central and Eastern Europe*, Brussels: PIE–Peter Lang, 2003.

apparent that the on-going and pending nature of regional reforms potentially set the stage for local and minority actors to mobilise in order to contest and influence outcomes.

This chapter examines the direct and indirect effects of EU integration on minority communities in Southeast Europe, by focusing on two specific contexts. More specifically, it explores domestic, regional economic and institutional changes in Greece, a long-standing member of the EU since 1981, and in ex-communist Bulgaria, an ACC since 1999. Through this exploration, it seeks to understand the consequences of such changes for the interests and identities of Turkish-Muslim minorities in border regions. The first part begins with an overview of the legacies of regional policies and territorial structures and their entanglement with nation-building processes in the Muslim-inhabited areas under study. The second and third parts describe the regional reforms and economic changes that have taken place in the 1990s in the two country-cases in the frame of post-communist democratisation, market restructuring, EU integration and enlargement. Furthermore, these sections explore changing patterns of minority participation at the local level, and their divergent perceptions of ethnic–national identity and citizenship in a united Europe. In the frame of regional institutional and economic change, regional and minority actors mobilise diverse understandings of 'Europe' and perceptions of the EU with regard to national and ethnic identity.[23] By understanding domestic regional changes and the politics of identity that they spark, we gain insight into nation-states' processes of internal restructuring, as well as patterns of minority mobilisation within the frame of European integration.

Central state, regions and the Muslim communities of Greece and Bulgaria

The border region of Western Thrace in the northeastern part of Greece is home to a small but politically significant population of about 120,000 Muslims, who inhabit the region together with a Greek-Christian majority.[24] Comprising individuals of Turkish origin, Gypsies (Roma), and Slav-speaking Pomaks, the Muslims of Thrace had been exempt

---

[23] Batt, 'Introduction', p. 10.
[24] The overall population of Thrace is 340,000. The precise size of the Turkish-Muslim population is a matter of dispute due to their large-scale immigration over the years and the lack of an official census since the 1950s. Estimates range from 90,000 to over 120,000, while official accounts put it between 110,000 and 135,000. Alexandris estimated the minority in 1981 to be about 120,000, with 45% Turkish-speaking, 36% Pomaks and 18% Roma. See Alexis Alexandris, 'To mionotiko zitima 1954–1987', *Oi ellinotourkikes scheseis 1923–1987*, Athens: Gnosi & ELIAMEP, 1988, p. 524.

from the population exchange between Greece and Turkey in the 1920s (together with the Greeks of Istanbul). Prior to World War II, they coexisted largely as a religious community characteristic of the Ottoman *millet* system, without joint bonds of political solidarity. Since the 1950s however (as explained below), they have transformed into an ethnic minority and have mobilised to claim a common Turkish identity. With its strategic location between three states and two continents, the Muslim community of Western Thrace marks a particular kind of geographical and cultural–historical boundary between East and West. In Europe's southernmost corner, the region of Thrace borders with Turkey to the east and Bulgaria to the north. Thrace is part of the administrative region of East Macedonia and Thrace (*Perifereia Anatolikis Makedonias & Thrakis*),[25] and consists of three prefectures, Ksanthi, Rhodope and Evros. Being a predominantly agricultural and lagging region within the sluggish Greek economy, it is a case of a 'double periphery' that ranks at the low end of the EU scale in terms of per capita income and overall development.[26] The region has an overall low level of education with a high percentage of its inhabitants having only primary-level education (73% in 1991);[27] the percentage of people with only primary education is even higher among the minority.

Across the northern border from the Greek region of Thrace, Bulgaria's south and southeast regions are also home to large and territorially concentrated Turkish and Slav-speaking Muslim communities commonly known as Pomaks. The latter are a Slavophone group who profess Islam and inhabit the highland areas of the Rhodope mountains in the south of Bulgaria. Numbering about 220,000 people, they are primarily a farming rural community occupied in tobacco production and animal husbandry.[28] Further towards the south and the southeast of the country, there is a sizeable population of Turkish Muslims, who make up between 8–10% of Bulgaria's population.[29] They are an

---

[25] Since 1988, Greece is divided into thirteen administrative regions, one of which is East Macedonia and Thrace.

[26] Yannis Ioannides and George Petrakos, 'Regional disparities in Greece: the performance of Crete, Peloponnese and Thessaly', *European Investment Bank Papers*, vol. 5, no. 1, 2000, pp. 32; 36.

[27] *I Anaptixi tis Thrakis – prokliseis kai prooptikes*, Athens: Academy of Athens, 1994, p. 15.

[28] Yulian Konstantinov, 'Strategies for sustaining a vulnerable identity: the case of the Bulgarian Pomaks', Hugh Poulton, and Suha Taji-Farouki (eds.), *Muslim identity and the Balkan State*, New York: NYU Press, 1997, p. 33.

[29] *Rezultati ot Prebrojavaneto na naselenieto – demografski karakteristiki*, vol. 1, Sofia: National Statistical Institute, 1994, p. 194. In the past fifteen years, the size of Bulgaria's Muslim community cannot be estimated with certainty due to profound demographic changes, ongoing emigration and disputes over proper census methods and categories in counting minorities. The 1992 census recorded 800,052 Turkish Muslims (or 9.43% of the

agricultural community with the lowest levels of urbanisation in the country and the highest levels of population concentrated in rural areas. Their highest concentration is in the southeast province of Kircali and the Rhodope mountains in the South Central Region, a mountainous zone that is geographically proximate to Turkey and borders with the Greek region of Thrace to the south.

In the course of the twentieth century, relations between Muslims and the state in Bulgaria and Greece developed in a historical context defined by a triadic pattern of conflict between a host state, an internal minority and an external homeland.[30] During the inter-war period, the nationalist ideas of Kemalist Turkey began to diffuse among the Muslims of Greece and Bulgaria, who until then predominantly made up a religious community. This brought the traditional Muslim religious leaders in these areas into conflict with the secular ideas propagated by adherents of Kemalism.[31] The post-World War II period witnessed the progressive consolidation of an ethnic Turkish consciousness over religious consciousness among Muslims in both countries (with the exception of Slav-speaking Pomaks in Bulgaria). A combination of factors pertaining as much to domestic state policies and structures as to relations with neighbouring Turkey, contributed to their nationalisation.[32] From the 1970s onwards, Bulgaria's Zhivkov regime and Greek governments intensified the politics of nationalism and adopted coercive and discriminatory measures against Muslims. In the former case, the resort to nationalism was an internal policy shift directed against minorities, while in the latter case, it was closely linked to the deterioration of Greek–Turkish relations following the Turkish invasion of Cyprus.

The highly centralised state structures and regional development policies acted as a central mechanism through which nationalism, its discourse, ideology and practices were bolstered and diffused in Greece and Bulgaria. After its failure in the inter-war period, the project of

country's population), which, however, also included a number of Roma and Pomaks (Muslims speaking a Bulgarian dialect) who also identified themselves as Turks. See Mihail Ivanov and Ilona Tomova (1994) and Antonina Zhelyaskova 1999, p. 172.

[30] Roger Brubaker, *Nationalism reframed – nationhood and the national question in the new Europe*, Cambridge: University Press, 1996.

[31] On the Greek case, see Lena Divani, *Ellada kai Mionotites*, Athens: Nefeli, 1995; on the Bulgarian case, see Mihail Ivanov and Ibrahim Yalamouv, 'Turskata obshtnost vuf Bulgaria I neinja perioditchen petchat 1878–1997', *Bulgarsko Mediaznanje*, Sofia: Balkanmedia, 1998.

[32] Dia Anagnostou, 'Collective rights and state security in the new Europe', in Konstantinos Arvanitopoulos (ed.), *Security dilemmas in Eurasia*, Athens: Nireefs Press, 1999.

state-led modernisation, nationalisation and political–administrative centralisation in the Balkans did not resume until the 1940s, with the advent of communist regimes. With the exception of the former Yugoslavia, these regimes saw the strongest centralisation of state authority in the form of democratic centralism and the one-party system.[33] From the 1960s onwards, Bulgaria's communist leaders appealed to the need to defend national unity from internal and external foes in order to reassert and vindicate the concentration of political–economic power in the party-state, to forestall reforms, and to pre-empt dissidents from asserting national sovereignty vis-à-vis the Soviet Union.[34] The fusion of nationalism with state centralism was most pronounced in the minority-inhabited regions where administrative structures and practices, the distribution of resources and economic development strategies, were pervaded by the logic of national unification driven by the overarching imperative to defend state integrity. It found its most coercive expression in the assimilation campaigns of the mid- and late 1960s, and in that of 1984–5, which compelled hundreds of thousands of Muslims to give up their names and take on Christian ones.

Under the centrally planned system, economic development policy, combined with a series of cultural measures characteristic of its early period in power, inadvertently reinforced the formation of a Turkish minority with a distinct consciousness, as well as regional economic and territorial characteristics. Besides undergoing compulsory collectivisation of agriculture, rural areas inhabited by Muslims became a target of special development measures that aimed to maintain a stable agricultural population at a time of rapid industrialisation. Such special development policies bequeathed a distinctive production structure to the minority-populated provinces which intricately tied ethnic differences to regional economic disparities and sustained the rural and peripheral character of Muslims.[35] Ethnic Bulgarians moved in large numbers to the central municipalities and towns where industry and manufacturing, as well as the bulk of infrastructure and administrative resources, were concentrated.[36] Turkish and Slav Muslims, on the other hand, remained in peripheral and less-developed municipalities, which

---

[33] Daniele Caramani, 'State administration and regional construction in Central Europe', in M. Keating and J. Hughes (eds.), *The regional challenge in Central and Eastern Europe*, Brussels: PIE–Peter Lang, 2003, p. 48.

[34] R. J. Crampton, *A concise history of Bulgaria*, Cambridge: Cambridge University Press, 1997, p. 198.

[35] Ali Eminov, *Turkish and other Muslim minorities in Bulgaria*, London: Hurst & Company, 1997, p. 132.

[36] *Informatsia za sustojianieto na obshtina Kircali prez 1993*. Report obtained from the Municipality of Khurdzali, 1993.

depended on the large enterprises at the regional centre for employment, production and resources;[37] they also remained in villages and small towns, where they were overwhelmingly employed in the agricultural sector.[38]

Despite the country's distinct capitalist system, post-war Greek governments, similarly to those in Bulgaria, utilised centralised state structures and regional policies to pursue national imperatives and specific political objectives in minority-inhabited areas. The slow process of unification of different areas and a sense of national insecurity led to the formation of a highly centralised state. Since its foundation in the nineteenth century, this centralist predilection (inspired by the French Napoleonic model), was explicitly geared towards modernisation, national homogenisation and the achievement of social–political unification.[39] Centralisation found its expression in the country's long-lived administrative division into fifty-two prefectures. After World War II, they prevailed as the main public agencies of development policies, directly subordinate to the respective central ministries, and minimally connected to the local social–cultural milieu.[40]

Greek regional economic policies in the post-World War II period and the workings of local and prefecture institutions in Thrace became specifically distorted by nationalist priorities linked to the presence of the minority. Lacking explicit development priorities, the government distributed central transfers in Thrace mainly based on party interests and clientelism; accordingly, rights and benefits fell to those deemed politically loyal.[41] Local Christians and investors with political leverage were granted the bulk of resources and state grants on the basis of their nationalist credentials (*ethnikofrones*), with little if any consideration of development needs and criteria. Furthermore, a series of informal but widespread administrative measures that had the consent of the prefect, local administration and banks, systematically prevented most Muslims from acquiring property or performing even routine matters

---

[37] Robert Begg and John Pickles, 'Institutions, social networks and ethnicity in the cultures of transition', in John Pickles and Adrian Smith (eds.), *Theorizing transition – the political economy of post-communist transformation*, London: Routledge, 1998, pp. 138.

[38] See *Demografski i sotsialno-ekonomitcheski harakteristiki – rusenska oblast*, Sofia: National Statistics Institute, 1994. See also Kristu Petkov and Georgi Fotev (eds.), *Etnitcheskja konflict vuf Bulgaria 1989*, Sofia: Bulgarian Academy of Sciences, Institute of Sociology, 1990, p. 254.

[39] Nikolaos Chlepas, *I topiki dioikisi stin ellada*, Athens: Sakoulas, 1999, pp. 90, 105.

[40] Chlepas, *I topiki dioikisi stin ellada*, p. 128.

[41] Susannah Verney and Fouli Papageorgiou, 'Prefecture councils in Greece: decentralization in the EC', *Regional Politics & Policy*, vol. 2, nos. 1&2, Spring/Summer 1992, p. 111.

such as receiving bank loans or driving licences, finding employment, etc.[42] With the deterioration of Greek–Turkish relations in the 1960s, an overarching ideological imperative of national unity served to justify the reproduction of highly centralised structures and the skewed distribution of resources in Thrace. Depriving Muslims of rights and resources and exclusively privileging Christians were deemed imperative in order to defend the region and country against the 'Turkish threat'.

In systematically denying basic social and economic rights to the minority, state policy put an absolute block on the development of Muslim-inhabited areas; it sustained the region's dependence on agriculture and distorted its economy as a whole. The Muslim-inhabited prefectures of Rhodope and Ksanthi are characterised by glaring disparities between a minority-inhabited mountainous and undeveloped zone in the north, and a southern predominantly Christian zone, which is fertile and more prosperous. Between the two, there is an intermediate belt with mixed population.[43] Up until 1996, the northern mountainous areas entirely populated by the minority were designated as 'restricted zones', where travel by outsiders required special clearance and a permit from the police. The majority of Muslims work in agriculture and have a long tradition in the growing of labour-intensive varieties of tobacco, making up over 90% of its producers in the region.[44] They are active in 'their own' segregated section of the local market occupied by minority suppliers (tradesmen, producers, etc.) and customers, and they largely operate within the confines of their community.[45] The fact that they have tended to export most of their savings abroad (especially to Turkey), also reinforced their socio-economic segregation along ethnic–religious lines; it should be noted though that until the early 1990s, restrictive measures prevented them from investing in the region where they lived.

Clearly then, centralised state structures after World War II were for the most part pervaded by national–political imperatives and foreign policy as opposed to developmental priorities. Combined with

---

[42] Aristeidis Giannopoulos and Dimitris Psaras, 'To "Elliniko 1955"', *Scholiastis*, vol. 85, no.3, 1990, pp. 18–21.

[43] With respect to land ownership, even though Muslims make up about 50% of Ksanthi's population they own 23% of the arable land and Christians own 71% of it. In Rhodope, Muslims make up 65% of the province's population and own 53.5% of the arable land, while 46.5% belongs to Christians. See I *anaptixi tis anatolikis Makedonias kai Thrakis*, p. 48.

[44] I *anaptixi tis anatolikis Makedonias kai Thrakis*, vol. 1, Athens: Commercial Bank of Greece, 1986, p. 238.

[45] See I *anaptixi tis Thrakis*, 1995, p. 18 and p. 49.

discriminatory policies and practices that privileged the national majority, they contributed to the socio-economic marginalisation of Muslims, as well as to their territorial concentration in less developed rural areas. Discriminatory and coercive measures created a fertile ground for the political radicalisation of Muslims who in the late 1980s mobilised to demand restitution of their rights and official recognition of their ethnic Turkish identity. In Bulgaria, such mobilisation was instrumental in precipitating the disintegration of the communist regime in 1989. The democratic transition made possible the restitution of political and cultural rights of minorities. In the Greek case, the radicalisation of Thrace's Muslims that erupted in 1989–90 reached its apex with the election of two independent minority representatives in the Greek Parliament who rallied the support of the minority on the basis of Turkish nationalism and solidarity with 'motherland' Turkey across the border. Fifteen years after Greece's 1974 transition to democracy, their politicisation coincided with the intensification of EU integration processes, following nearly a decade of government ambivalence regarding membership in the EU.

In the 1990s, political–institutional and economic changes taking place within the frame of European integration, post-communist transition to democracy and the market have challenged nationalist-driven regional structures and policies. In different ways, governments in the two countries under study have instituted measures to redress regional disparities and respond to minority problems and grievances. EU membership and the implementation of structural funds enabled the Greek government to redress them by embedding the minority issue in an economic development frame. This both reflected and in turn reinforced a reorientation in the priorities of regional policy and the workings of local government in border areas. The next section of this chapter describes the EU-related regional changes and discusses their effects for the politics and identity of Turkish Muslims. Post-communist democratisation, on the other hand, paved the way for ethnic-based representation at the national and local level through the creation of a minority party. Rallying the support of Turkish Muslims and a sizeable segment of Slav-speaking Muslims, the Movement for Rights and Freedom (MRF) has established itself as the third largest party in national parliament and local government. Since 1999, in the context of Bulgaria's association with the EU, the consolidation of its power in minority-inhabited areas appears to set the frame for ethnic communal politics and demands on a territorial basis. The third part of this chapter describes and analyses the effects of market restructuring and EU enlargement on minority politics in Bulgaria.

Regional development, EU structural funds and the Muslims of Thrace

In the late 1980s, Greece's deteriorating economic performance after nearly a decade of membership raised concerns among its EC partners about the country's ability to achieve convergence and market integration.[46] Such concerns led to the adoption of stabilisation measures under EC supervision, but also to the overhaul of its structural policy in 1988–9 and the doubling of structural funds, with more allocated for regional schemes.[47] Increasing amounts of structural funds were transferred to Greece amounting to nearly 3.7% of the country's GDP by the end of the 1990s.[48] Growing domestic concern with the region's underdevelopment coincided with, and was possibly reinforced by, the political radicalisation of the Muslim population in the late 1980s. In an attempt to diffuse the escalating tensions that erupted with the Christian population in 1990 in Thrace, the Greek government abolished the restrictive measures against the minority and inaugurated a new approach based on 'legal equality – equal citizenship' (*isonomia–isopolitia*).[49]

Compelled on the one hand by the EU to pursue economic convergence, and on the other hand by ethnic mobilisation at the subnational level, the Greek government began to pay closer attention to Thrace's underdevelopment. In 1991–2, the adoption of a new development strategy for the region became possible due to consensus across the two main parties, and made explicit references to the position of the minority. The strategy was introduced with the 'Findings of the Interparty Committee for Border Regions' submitted to the Greek Parliament in 1992.[50] In marked departure from the militaristic language frequently employed in the case of Thrace, the 'findings' defined regional development as the 'armour' of defence against the threat of secessionism. They called for an upgrading of the region's economy, reducing inequalities between Christians and Muslims and promoting social and economic integration of the latter. For the first time, the minority was depicted as a resource rather than a threat or burden, and its integration as a precondition for the region's development.

---

[46] While in 1981 Greek GDP per capita was 53% of the EC average, by 1995 it fell to 45% of the EC average (Ioannides and Petrakos 2000, p. 32).

[47] Ilias Plaskovities, 'EC regional policy in Greece', in Panos Kazakos and P. C. Ioakimidis (eds.), *Greece and EC membership evaluated*, New York: St. Martin's Press, 1994.

[48] Ioannides and Petrakos, 'Regional disparities in Greece', p. 51.

[49] Giannopoulos and Psaras, 'Elliniko 1955', p. 21.

[50] 'Findings of the inter-party committee for border regions', Greek Parliament, Athens, 14 February 1992. Appended in *I anaptixi tis anatolikis Makedonias kai Thrakis*.

As a border region of strategic importance in the post-Cold War Balkans, Thrace was allocated increased resources from structural funds making possible intensified development and infrastructure investments.[51] Of the thirteen regional development programmes under the Community Support Frameworks (CSF) for 1989–93, 1994–9, and 2000–6, Eastern Macedonia and Thrace received the third largest funding in Greece (after the two major urban areas of Athens/Attiki and Thessaloniki in Central Macedonia).[52] The significance of structural funds for Greece and Thrace, both in size but also political importance, cannot be underestimated; it is questionable whether in their absence, regional development policy would have been viable at all in the 1990s.[53] It must be noted here that structural funds did not motivate or in any way lead the government to adopt the new approach towards border regions. However, their influx made it possible to put into practice a comprehensive policy of regional development as defined by the Regional Operational Programme (ROP) of the CSF for Thrace, and to anchor the minority issue firmly within it.

Following the reorientation of the Greek government approach to border regions, the implementation of regional programmes was accompanied by a series of reforms of subnational structures that were launched in 1990s.[54] Characterised as groundbreaking, these combined centrally appointed regional administration with a degree of decentralisation at the prefecture level. In particular, they included the strengthening of thirteen regional departments (*dioikitikes perifereies*), which had since 1988 existed only on paper, and the transformation of fifty-two prefectures into units of self-government with locally elected councils and prefects.[55] The establishment and strengthening of administrative regions was directly linked to the implementation of structural funds: these regions were to participate as partners in the

---

[51] *Stratigiko schedio anaptiksis Makedonias & Thrakis*, vols. B & C, Thessaloniki: Union of Industrialists of North Greece, 1994, pp. 98–100.

[52] Chlepas, *I topiki dioikisi stin Ellada*, p. 164.

[53] Eleni Andrikopoulou and Grigoris Kafkalas, 'Greek regional policy and the process of Europeanisation 1961–2000', in Dionyssis G. Dimitrakopoulos and Argyris G. Passas (eds.), *Greece in the European Union*, London: Routledge, 2004, p. 42. Out of the nearly 1 billion euro of total public expenditure for the Regional Development Program of Eastern Macedonia and Thrace for 2000–6, only 25% came from national funds, while 75% came from EU structural funds. See http://europa.eu.int/comm/regional_policy/country/overmap/gr/gr_en.htm

[54] This section draws from Dia Anagnostou, 'Breaking the cycle of nationalism: the EU, regional policy and the minority of Western Thrace', *South European Societies and Politics*, vol. 6, no. 1 (Summer 2001), 99–124.

[55] Law 2218/1994, Idrisi Nomarchiakis Aftodioikisis kai Tropopioisi gia tin Protovathmia Aftodioikisi kai Perifereia, 1994.

implementation along with national and European authorities within the frame of the CSF. The experience of the EU's Integrated Mediterranean Programmes in the second half of the 1980s had pointed to the endemic weaknesses of Greece's centralised structures to plan development projects, and they rendered conspicuous the need for creating competent subnational structures above the first tier of local government.[56]

The prefecture self-government, on the other hand, was largely an offspring of democratic consolidation and of a new generation of political cadre who came of age in Greece's post-1974 system with a mature and growing consciousness concerning local problems. Domestic demands and a political commitment to decentralisation under Socialist rule in the 1980s, however, had not materialised in practice due to strong opposition from party and national interests.[57] By the early 1990s, when cross-party consensus on EU integration had matured, both regional administration and prefecture self-government were launched with a single reform package. They were assigned a central role in local–regional development largely designed, financed and implemented within the frame of the EU structural policy.

As a result of subnational reforms, the role and functions of regional administration and local government began to transform in response to the pressures and opportunities generated by the implementation of development programmes.[58] This development carried important implications for local and minority politics. In the first place, while not bringing any radical transfer of power from the centre to the periphery, such pressures and opportunities have nonetheless strengthened the role of subnational institutions and triggered greater local mobilisation. The professed emphasis on decentralisation and local development that accompanied the regional reforms since the late 1980s was arguably more rhetorical than actual, symptomatic of the Community 'paradigm' of deregulation. It is seen to have been driven by the need to reduce state spending, in practice implying that local authorities and regions are left to survive on and compete for their own resources.[59] In any case, in a

---

[56] Fouli Papageorgiou and Susannah Verney, 'Regional planning and the integrated Mediterranean programmes in Greece', *Regional Politics & Policy*, vol. 2, nos. 1 & 2 (Spring/Summer 1992), 139–62.

[57] Chlepas, *I topiki dioikisi stin Ellada*, p. 343; Paraskevi Christofilopoulou, 'I nomarchiaki aftodioikisi sto Elliniko politiko-dioikitiko systima', in K. Spanou, A. Rigos and M. Spourdalakis (eds.), *Nomarchiaki aftodioikis – prosdokies kai prooptikes*, Athens: Sakoulas, 1997, p. 56.

[58] P. C. Ioakimidis, 'EU cohesion policy in Greece: the tension between bureaucratic centralism and regionalism', in Liesbet Hooghe (ed.), *Cohesion policy and European integration*, Oxford: University Press 1996, p. 351.

[59] Andrikopoulou and Kafkalas, 'Greek regional policy', p. 40.

highly centralised state like Greece with weak or non-existent traditions of self-government, the reforms of the 1990s stimulated mobilisation of the local population around development goals, despite significant continuity with the preceding centralised structures. Progressively there has been a widening of participation of local actors in regional policy in certain areas and regions in the 1990s, even if mainly symbolic and formalistic rather than substantive.[60]

The expansion of local mobilisation has had profound, albeit contradictory, implications for the political participation of minorities like Muslims, who had remained disenfranchised after the 1974 democratic transition. The transformation of the Prefecture Council into a directly elected institution introduced strong pressures to show responsiveness to local problems dividing the two communities. Neither community could any longer be excluded from development plans that operated on the basis of the region's economy as a whole. With an interest in attracting the Muslim vote, the prefects and the Prefecture Council began to make efforts to tackle the glaring disparities between the northern Muslim and the southern Christian areas. In this way, prefecture local government opened space for the representation and participation of the minority in decisions about resource distribution and regional development. The potential for expanded minority participation, however, provoked reactions both among Greek and Turkish nationalist constituencies in Thrace, who until the early 1990s dominated local politics. The former claimed that it would endanger national interests and strengthen Turkish nationalism in Ksanthi and Rhodope where a Muslim prefect could be elected.[61] To pre-empt this possibility, the law on prefecture local government was modified in the cases of Ksanthi and Rhodope, where a special provision of so-called 'enlarged prefectures' (Law 2218/94, Article 40) in practice consolidated two predominantly Christian areas. Meanwhile, the hard core of Turkish nationalists within the minority equally strongly opposed the reforms and greater participation in the latter, dismissing them as strategy on the part of Greek authorities to co-opt, assimilate and 'Hellenise' the minority.

Notwithstanding their limitations, the institutional and regional economic changes within the frame of EU structural funds implementation reinforced a departure from traditional national politics in border and ethnically divided regions like Thrace. As was described in the previous

---

[60] Ioannides and Petrakos, 'Regional disparities in Greece', p. 46.
[61] Alexandros Kontos and Georgios Pavlou, 'Epifaniakos, anofelos kai ethnika epikindinos', Oikonomikos Tachydromos, 7 July, 1994, pp. 35–6.

section, the prefectures' role in development was previously shaped by national imperatives and political decisions. It was overseen by officials of the local Cultural Affairs Office subordinate to the Ministry of Foreign Affairs and materialised through resource distribution to those loyal to the nation. By the end of the 1990s, prefecture and regional politics seemed to revolve around economic development issues, a marked departure from the preceding decades, when the centre of gravity was national unity and ethnic solidarity. Pressures for effective absorption of funds compelled regional and prefecture authorities to operate within the framework of conditions and development priorities set by the EU's structural policy; they also necessitated a distancing of regional policies from traditional nationalist positions and foreign policy interests. Regional and prefecture authorities have sought explicitly to differentiate development decisions and strategies from the networks of local interests cultivated around the principle of solidarity of the Greek nation. It could be argued that in the frame of regional politics that grew around EU development funds, there has been a growing 'domestication' of minority issues. That is, they are increasingly dealt with as matters of citizenship and development, rather than being viewed through the lens of national interest and foreign policy which had exclusively guided state approach towards such issues until then.

Besides being symptomatic of a fundamental change in state policy towards border regions, the regional economic and institutional changes also became carriers of a new political discourse and normative frame that has the European polity as its sphere of reference. Bearing the seal of the EU, which is perceived as a neutral and multicultural external actor, has facilitated the acceptance of reforms and resistance to nationalist pressures, and appeared to breed variable perceptions of 'Europe'. Professing a strong commitment to the rule of law, the EU offered symbolic and ideological resources to which elected individuals among both Christians and Muslims in Thrace profusely appealed, in order to assert the legitimacy of their actions vis-à-vis nationalist pressures. In stark contrast to the recent past, the language the prefecture and regional authorities used was about legal equality, civil rights and cultural diversity, evident in the frequent invocations of 'legal equality – equal citizenship', rather than an appeal to national unity. Already in the mid-1990s, the then Vice-Prefect and General Secretary of Development and Public Investments of Rhodope (who was Christian) rejected the arbitrary prohibitions as a 'thing of the past', stating: 'We can't deprive Muslims of their rights, like previous governments did, since they are Greek citizens. We are in a united Europe and we must solve each problem in order to make citizens law-abiding'.[62] Since then, prefecture and regional officials have incorporated standard references to socio-economic modernisation, equal treatment, and administrative efficiency as basic principles defining the workings of subnational institutions in contemporary Europe. This is a marked departure from the indisputable priority of national unification that these officials had previously been geared to serve.

Minority members increasingly viewed the EU as an external system providing alternative protection and support, which the regional reforms and institutions brought closer. It appeared to ensure the irreversibility of the changes and to prevent Greece from 'turning the clock back to the old system'. Such a perception of the EU alleviated the minorities' long-standing fears of assimilation which participation in Greek state institutions could purportedly foster. Simultaneously implying integration into the structures of European citizenship, such participation seemed to be viewed more as a *defence* against assimilation. It is notable that frequent references to the EU as an alternative normative frame and external frame of protection have more recently seemed to be invoked alongside appeals to the Lausanne Treaty. As a treaty of the inter-war period, the latter has placed minority protection in the bilateral frame of Greek–Turkish relations, rendering minority position and well-being subject to the ebb and flow of inter-state affairs.[63]

For the minority, perceptions of 'Europe' appeared to combine strong guarantees of ethnic–cultural diversity and minority rights together with an unquestionable imperative of societal integration and political engagement. In the local context, this took the form of the need to take initiative and mobilise more actively in contesting regional funds. This integration principle was aptly conveyed by a minority member in local government who stated that 'there is no racism in Europe, as long as you are responsible with your duties towards the state',[64] a statement that marks a wholesale departure from the declarations of defiance against the state ten to fifteen years ago. This is not an abstract notion but one that comes out of a new generation of minority leaders who have emerged from local and prefecture politics in the past decade. They have adopted a more pragmatic and moderate approach, focused on dealing with specific problems through local government structures; the latter

---

[62] Interview, Komotini 29 May 1995.
[63] For a brief description of the provisions of the Lausanne Treaty, see Christos Rozakis, 'The international protection of minorities in Greece', in Kevin Featherstone and Kostas Ifantis (eds.), *Greece in a changing Europe*, Manchester: Manchester University Press, 1996.
[64] Interview, Komotini 24 April 2005.

are increasingly conceived of as effective avenues to represent and redress their community's grievances, in marked contrast to the intransigent stance of Turkish nationalist leaders more than a decade ago.

Ethnicity, regional restructuring and EU enlargement in post-communist Bulgaria

For the most part of the 1990s, regional reforms and the politics of ethnicity in Bulgaria were inseparably linked to the restructuring of the centrally planned political economy towards democracy and the market. In the aftermath of transition, the country retained many of its pre-existing subnational structures, comprising a large number of municipalities (*obshtini*, 262 in total) as the basic unit of local self-government, and nine regions (*oblasti*). The latter comprised structures of centralised administration, which, however, did not possess any resources. The 1991 Local Self-Government and Administration Act gave a wide range of functions to the municipalities such as construction and development, local economy and environment, health, education and social welfare, the power to form an autonomous budget, restitution of their property and the right to engage independently in economic activity.[65] While municipalities became in principle empowered to redress local problems and needs, in practice they were faced with a sharp decline of revenues from central transfers.[66] At the same time, they had limited capacity to exploit the local and regional economy, and thus to independently generate revenues, as the large regional enterprises remained until 1996 largely centrally managed. The post-communist crisis in local government and economy most strongly afflicted the less developed Turkish and Muslim-inhabited areas. The latter were thoroughly dependent on state subsidies and were confronted with mass unemployment due to a steep decline in the agricultural and industrial economy.

In the period until 1996 Bulgaria was labelled 'a largely unreformed ex-communist polity' which continued to be dominated by the successor

---

[65] The Local Self-Government and Administration Act was published in the *Darzhaven Vestnik* [Government Gazette], Issue no. 77/1991. Reproduced in the volume *Administrativno-Teritorialnata Reforma*, National Centre for Territorial Development and Housing Policy, Sofia: ForKom, 1995, pp. 117–44.

[66] In 1989–91, real municipal revenues in the region of Haskovo (where the province of Khurdzali belongs) decreased by 50%. Even though they nominally increased by 240%, the inflation in the same period was 438%. See 'Socioeconomic conditions and perspectives of the municipalities with mixed ethnic and religious population from the region of Haskovo', Sofia: 'Klub Economica 2000', 1992, pp. 28–31.

communist-renamed Socialist party (BSP).[67] In this period, outstanding structural and organisational advantages enabled the BSP to retain its hold over the political system. While acceding to market reform, the reigning Socialists sought to preserve the centralised state and its role in the economy. The 1991 constitution, of which they were architects, recognised local self-government but opposed the existence of 'autonomous territorial formations'.[68] Reforms suspended privatisation and decentralised production and employment decisions to the directors of large regional enterprises, which, however, continued to be managed and financed by the central state, under the supervision of ministerial bureaucrats. In 1990, the government decided to close down the branch workshops in the minority-inhabited rural areas, leading to massive unemployment among ethnic Turks, but to retain and subsidise production in unprofitable plants in central locations, where the majority of employees were ethnic Bulgarians.[69]

In over twenty municipalities and in several hundred communes where Turkish and Slav-speaking Muslims are demographically predominant, local government power throughout the 1990s and until the present has been held by the minority party Movement for Rights and Freedom (MRF).[70] In the period through 1996 in these municipalities, however, unreformed regional economic and administrative structures were thoroughly permeated by the communist legacy of nationalism of the 1980s.[71] The preservation of centralised economic structures both depended upon and in turn reinforced a Socialist government alliance with the ex-communist *nomenklatura*, comprising enterprise directors, party cadre and public-sector personnel, who had retained their dominant positions in the regional economy and local administration. This *nomenklatura* included many among the participants of the coercive name-changing campaign of the 1980s, who had close links with Bulgarian nationalists in the region and viewed the MRF as a separatist force threatening state integrity. They were able to rally widespread local

---

[67] Kyril Drezov, 'Bulgaria: transition comes full circle, 1989–1997', in Geoffrey Pridham and Tom Gallagher (eds.), *Experimenting with democracy*, London: Routledge, 2000, pp. 195–218.

[68] Drezov, 'Bulgaria: transition comes full circle', p. 205.

[69] Begg and Pickles, 'Institutions, social networks and ethnicity', pp. 131–3.

[70] In the 1991 local elections in Bulgaria, MRF representatives won a majority of seats in 28 municipal councils, in addition to having mayors elected in 653 communes (Dogan 1995). In the 1999 local elections, it won 7.4% of the vote and elected mayors in 22 municipalities. See 'Constitutional Watch', *East European Constitutional Review*, 8, no. 4, Fall 1999.

[71] This section significantly draws from Dia Anagnostou, 'Nationalist legacies and European trajectories: Post-communist liberalization and Turkish minority politics in Bulgaria', *Southeast European and Black Sea Studies*, 5, no. 1, January 2005, pp. 87–109.

support for the central Socialist party in exchange for an on-going inflow of state resources and jobs largely reserved for Bulgarians; this was a mutually beneficial arrangement that allowed both to protect inherited privileges and power. This central–local nexus of clientelistic party connections became a bridge of continuity with the past and with a familiar political logic which projected the preservation of centralised administrative and economic structures as imperative for the defence of Bulgarian national unity and territorial integrity.[72]

The continuity of Bulgarian nationalism in conjunction with the centralised regional economic structures embodied in Socialist rule restricted the MRF's ability to represent and respond to the problems of ethnic Turks through local government. It set the stage for sharp tensions between the MRF and the Socialist party over control and distribution of resources and jobs, as well as over minority religious and language rights, all issues which reinforced central–local and inter-communal tensions along ethnic lines. The on-going fusion of nationalism with centralism led the MRF to differentiate its approach to reform from that of Socialists, which was otherwise more in tune with the interests and problems of Muslims and their municipalities. In particular, the MRF was in favour of the BSP socialist model of restructuring in so far as it espoused a central role of the state in social welfare, as well as in assisting specific sectors of the economy. At the same time, the diffusion of nationalism in the centralised structures of the regional economy, which were sanctioned by the BSP until 1996, led minority representatives to oppose state management of the economy. They saw the latter as a powerful constraint to minority political representation, regional development and democracy.[73] Already in the mid-1990s, the MRF voiced strong demands for greater self-government and decentralisation at the sub-state level. Similar demands have been advanced by minority parties across East Central Europe, and had their referent in the centralised legacy of state socialism which they intended to eradicate.[74]

Having common origins in the dissident movement of the late 1980s, the centre-right Union of Democratic Forces (UDF) shared with the MRF a strong opposition to the communist legacy and espoused decentralisation and market-oriented reforms as a means to promote development. Viewing nationalism as a vestige of communism and a

---

[72] Anagnostou, 'Nationalist legacies and European trajectories', p. 99.

[73] Ahmed Dogan, 'Polititsheski analiz na predizbornata I sledizbornata situatsia', *Prava I Svobodi*, no. 13, 31 March 1995.

[74] Antoni Galubov, 'Mestnata politika – mezhdu samoupravlenieto I administratsiata', *Prava I Svobodi*, no. 34, 1 September 1995, p. 2.

façade for the BSP to preserve the centralised state and economic structures of the former regime, UDF liberals joined the MRF in denouncing BSP nationalist politics in the ethnically mixed areas. From early on, the imperative of thoroughly dismantling communist structures was the central drive for the economic reforms pursued by the UDF.[75] As an antidote to state centralism-cum-nationalism, the UDF supported decentralisation and market restructuring, which it viewed through the lens of privatisation aimed at eliminating the role of the central state in the economy.[76] Its approach as such was exemplified in the reform launched during its brief tenure to power in 1991–2, which initiated the dissolution of state-owned farm collectives and the restitution of land to its original owners.[77] By radically eliminating state management and the centralised regional economic structures, in which communism and nationalism had been gestated, the agricultural reform sought to dismantle the communist legacy where it seemed to be strongest – in the countryside.[78]

The 1997 elections marked a turning point as they brought to power a UDF government that accelerated market restructuring and enterprise privatisation and signed Bulgaria's Accession Partnership with the EU in 1999. In the second half of the 1990s, the process of restructuring the inherited centralised economic structures, however, formed the locus of a sharp conflict between the MRF and the UDF. According to the MRF leader Dogan, this conflict was even more intractable than the preceding one with the socialists.[79] Its origins lay in the 1991–2 agricultural reform that had led the MRF to withdraw its support from the UDF government of Filip Dimitrov in protest of it.[80] While the overall effects of the reform varied regionally, the dissolution of the farm collectives had thoroughly disrupted production. Given the legacy of state socialism, it led to much higher unemployment among ethnic Turks in comparison to Bulgarians.[81] While initially appearing to be about the nature and pace of market reform, in the course of the 1990s the MRF dispute with the liberal UDF grew into a fundamental conflict about the regional

[75] Drezov, 'Bulgaria: transition comes full circle', p. 416.
[76] John Bell, 'Democratization and political participation in 'post-communist' Bulgaria', in Karen Dawisha and Bruce Parrott (eds.), *Politics, power, and the struggle for democracy in South-East Europe*, Cambridge: Cambridge University Press, 1997, pp. 374, 378.
[77] Maya Keliyan, 'The transformation of agriculture', in Jacques Coenen-Huther, (ed.), *Bulgaria at the crossroads*, New York: Nova Science Publishers, Inc., 1996, pp. 237–8.
[78] Gerald Creed, *Domesticating revolution*, University Park, PA: Pennsylvania State University Press, 1998, p. 237.
[79] Ahmed Dogan, 'Bulgarski model za reshavane na maltsinstveni problemi e najvazhnoto postizhenje na prehoda', *Tolerantnost*, 1999a, no. 25.
[80] Bell, 'Democratization and political participation', p. 369.
[81] Begg and Pickles, 'Institutions, social networks and ethnicity', p. 135.

dimension of economic reform, with important potential implications for the territorial structures of the central state.

The liberals' approach to economic decentralisation, as epitomised in the agricultural reform, was premised on a uniform nationwide strategy seeking fast privatisation of enterprises and state withdrawal from the economy. Development would be driven by private entrepreneurial activity and local government units, which would independently generate resources for investment. Such an approach, however, disregarded the inherited structural disadvantages of the overwhelmingly agricultural minority-inhabited municipalities, which had less developed infrastructure than the average for the country.[82] In its alternative approach to reform, the MRF has advocated a regionally specific strategy, in which the central state would assume an instrumental role in steering and assisting economic development of peripheral municipalities.[83] The UDF dismissed MRF demands for state assistance, considering it a residue of communist mentality unwilling to adjust to market conditions and the discipline of reform. While attributing a role to the central state in assisting local development, the MRF also advocates thorough decentralisation, within the frame of the Bulgarian state but increasingly in a way that aspires to demarcate regional economic and political units along ethnic-community lines. The 2001 MRF programme emphasises enhanced local government power to decide about and construct development strategies appropriate to local conditions. Such a regional agenda on the part of the MRF is seen as viable due to the anticipated influx of EU funds in the underdeveloped ethnic regions.[84]

From 2000 onwards, the status of associate candidate state made Bulgaria a beneficiary not only of PHARE, but also of additional funds such as the agriculture-specific SAPARD and ISPA, precursors to structural funds once full membership is in place.[85] Within the frame of the Accession Partnership and its regional policy section, the Bulgarian government established six planning regions corresponding to the NUTS

[82] Petar Mitev, 'Relations of compatibility and incompatibility in the everyday life of Christians and Muslims in Bulgaria', in Petar Mitev (ed.), *Relations of compatibility and incompatibility between Christians and Muslims in Bulgaria*, Sofia: International Centre for Minority Studies and Intercultural Relations, 1995, pp. 205–6.

[83] Giulbie Receb, 'Doverieto na kredit ima granitsi', *Prava I Svobodi*, 1, 5 January 1995, p. 3.

[84] *Bulgaria–Evropa: Nestandarten pat na razvitie*, Programme of the MRF Coalition with the Liberal Union, 17 July 2001, http://www.dps.bg.

[85] PHARE stands for *Pologne-Hongrie: aide à la reconstruction économique*. As its name indicates, it was originally directed to Poland and Hungary but was subsequently extended to the other ex-communist countries as the main form of EU assistance to the latter. The full names of the other two pre-accession funds are Special Accession Programme for Agricultural and Rural Development (SAPARD) and the Instrument for Structural Policies for pre-Accession (ISPA).

II level of the EU[86] and revived the twenty-eight pre-1989 provinces (previously *okruzi*, now *oblasti*). Between local and national government structures, these institutions form components of state administration run by centrally appointed governors and by representatives of the central ministries. The latter are the main actors in a nationally coordinated regional policy to implement pre-accession funds. Within the frame of the Regional Development Act,[87] the Regional Development Council at the Council of Ministers, an inter-ministerial body, coordinates and oversees the National Plan for Regional Development for the period 2000–6.[88] Characteristic of most Central and Eastern European countries that have recently joined the EU or are associate members,[89] such a centrally managed structure appears to resonate closely with the liberals' nationally centred approach to regional economic development described above. Since 2001 (and at the time of writing), the MRF has been a junior partner in the coalition government of the National Movement of Simeon II (NMSV), holding the Ministry of Agriculture, a sector crucial for the minority but also for EU policy. From this position of national power, the MRF leadership has put forth its own development and investment strategy within the context of implementing EU pre-accession funds in the ethnically mixed regions that it controls, which it placed on top of the party's agenda.[90]

Between the liberals' view of nationally centred development strategy and the socialists' approach along the lines of the traditional nation-state, the MRF has consolidated a distinct minority politics that forges a close link between regional territory and the ethnic community. In contrast to the UDF view of the EU as a vehicle of socio-economic modernisation, the MRF alternatively depicts it as the only true guarantor of ethnic identity, which in the European context is no longer considered a disadvantage but a 'strategic advantage'.[91] While the MRF has highlighted the integration of minorities in Bulgarian society, it has over the past few years pronounced as equally, if not more, important the preservation of ethnic–religious identity (Dogan, 'Programna').

[86] Council of Ministers Decree no. 145, 27 July 2001.

[87] Published in *State Gazette*, Issue no. 29, 1999.

[88] Julian Boev, 'Bulgaria: decentralization and modernization of the public administration', in *Mastering decentralization and public administration reforms in central and eastern Europe*, Budapest: Local Government and Public Reform Initiative, 2002, p. 97.

[89] See James Hughes, Gwendolyn Sasse and Claire Gordon, 'Europeanization and regionalization in the EU', p. 169.

[90] See the speech by Ahmet Dogan in the 5th National Conference of the MRF, Sofia, 15–16 February 2003, www.dps.bg

[91] Ahmed Dogan, 'Programna deklaratsia na Dvizhenje za Prava I Svobodi 2000', in http://www.dps.bg

While denouncing aggressive nationalism, Dogan also stated that in the context of European integration, 'we [the Turkish minority] need a moderate nationalism ... to gain legitimacy for our national identity on the basis of liberal values of the European community'.[92] Evident of his ambitions of establishing the movement as a European player, the hitherto undisputed leader admonishes that without the participation of the MRF, Bulgaria 'will not have the requisite internal stability and external weight to open the doors to Europe'.[93] While firmly accepting its territorial integrity, the MRF increasingly talks about Bulgaria in reference to the multi-ethnic state replacing the traditional unitary national state, and it appeals to ethnic Turks to support community-based organisational and political strategies.[94]

Conclusions: EU integration, regional development and the politics of Muslims in Southeast Europe

Regionalisation induced by European-wide processes transforms the historical significance of border areas stemming from their traditional character as citadels of national unity and privileged sites of nation-building. Their historical salience as such is particularly pronounced in Southeast Europe. On the one hand, regionalisation is defined by EU integration and enlargement policies and market integration processes. These act as a catalyst for domestic reform by introducing functional economic imperatives to utilise efficiently administrative resources and structural funds in order to promote development and market integration. Such policies and processes do not mandate specific institutional configurations for subnational structures; the latter are shaped by complex internal forces having to do with pre-existing legacies, democratisation, and domestic party interactions and conflicts.

On the other hand, regionalisation reforms and the related political debates are influenced by bottom-up pressures for recognition of ethnic diversity. Motivated by regional economic constraints, institutional reforms, and the perceived opportunities for structural funds, minorities seek to contest reforms. In some cases, they formulate their own demands for local self-government and decentralisation on the basis of ethnic community.[95] While until now the demands of regional and

---

[92] Ahmed Dogan, 'Triabva ni umeren – natsionalnata idea ne biva da se bazira na mitove a na realnosti I perspektivi', *Prava I Svobodi*, 27 July 1999.

[93] Dogan, 'Programna deklaratsia na Dvizhenje za', *Prava I Svobodi* 2000.

[94] Dogan, 'Triabva ni umeren'.

[95] Bucek, 'Balancing functional and ethnic regionalisation', p. 159; Brusis, 'Regionalisation in the Czech and Slovak Republics', p. 101.

ethnic minorities have had a limited impact on decentralisation reforms in CESE,[96] such a reform process is far from complete. Between influences originating from European-level policies and processes and bottom-level mobilisation asserting regional or ethnic diversity, national governments pursue diverse policies, reforms and accommodation strategies.

Far from mandating specific institutional reforms and policies, EU integration and enlargement have provided economic and normative resources enabling national government to redefine policies towards border minority regions in Southeast Europe. The preceding sections have provided a descriptive overview of regional and post-communist restructuring in minority-inhabited border areas in Greece and Bulgaria, and examined its consequences for (mainly Turkish) Muslim politics and identity. In the context of European integration and enlargement, this essay argues, regional economic constraints and resources promote fundamentally different policy priorities and political discourses that guide central government policy towards Muslim-inhabited border areas. Such priorities and discourses shift the centre of gravity from national unity to regional development and from nation-state building to economic restructuring and institutional modernisation at the regional level. While in the case of Greece regional restructuring becomes a vehicle for integrating minority politics in socio-economic development frames, in Bulgaria it appears to pave the way for increasing politicisation and regional territorial contestation along ethnic lines. Such distinct processes of regional ethnic change stem from diverging legacies of regional political economy in the post-World War II period in Greece and Bulgaria, as well as from different democratisation-cum-European integration trajectories characterising southern and eastern enlargement, respectively.

In a highly schematic fashion, the Greek case could be seen to exemplify the *social–economic development and modernisation* characterising European integration and regional transformation prior to the 1990s, which has largely been shaped by EU cohesion policy. In targeting peripheral regions and seeking to facilitate their integration in the common market, the latter indirectly affected minorities. Combining administrative regionalisation with a degree of decentralisation in prefecture self-government, the subnational reforms of the 1990s have become loci of a more participatory politics around regional development strategies. Reflecting a partial denationalisation of the institutions and politics of Thrace as a border region, such reforms have by no

---

[96] Wolczuk, 'Conclusion: identities, regions and Europe', p. 210.

means been made imperative by the EU, nor have they been directly necessitated by any inherent logic in structural funds implementation. Instead, they have been decisively facilitated and mediated by the gradual emergence of a cross-party consensus existing across national and local levels, pertaining as much to the basic economic orientations as to the normative content of EU integration. Such a consensus matured slowly in the course of a decade after the country's entry into the EU in 1981, in tandem with the diffusion of growing awareness about more participatory politics in the context of the country's democratic consolidation. The early emphasis of the EU structural policy on subsidiarity and partnership and the influx of a large amount of development funds certainly facilitated such consensus and brought the EU closer to local society.

In Bulgaria on the other hand, similarly to several post-communist states of CESE, a number of factors have promoted the *institutionalisation of ethnic-based representation* at the local and national level.[97] While this was initially reinforced by the legacy of communism and the transition to democracy, it has subsequently also been encouraged by a more binding normative frame at the European level emphasising human rights and minority protection after 1989. The creation of minority parties or various kinds of electoral arrangements guaranteeing such representation, combined with the ethnic–territorial legacy of state socialism, paved the way for political contestation and regional mobilisation along ethnic lines. While regional reforms and debates were initially driven by the need to restructure the centrally planned system towards a market economy, by the second half of the 1980s they were increasingly associated with EU conditionality and the pre-accession process which the country entered in 1999. The reforms have been marred by a total lack of consensus across the main parties over the legacy of communism, the priorities of post-communist transformation, and subsequently over the main normative content and economic orientation of EU enlargement. The shift of emphasis of the EU regional policy towards enhancing administrative as well as funds absorption capacity has encouraged centralised institutional designs and regional policy implementation, restricting the involvement of subnational elites in the process.[98]

Whether through mainly economic or normative resources, EU integration and enlargement have not only enhanced the ability of

---

[97] Wlodek Aniol et al., 'Returning to Europe: Central Europe between internationalization and institutionalization', in Peter Katzenstein (ed.), *Tamed power – Germany in Europe*, Ithaca: Cornell University Press, 1997, pp. 195–250.

[98] Hughes, Sasse and Gordon, *Europeanization and regionalization*, p. 162.

governments in Southeast Europe to accommodate Muslim and Turkish minorities, but they have also alleviated fears of assimilation among the latter. Muslim minorities perceive the EU as an external frame that simultaneously encourages social integration while offering robust guarantees for protecting their cultural and religious rights. In Greece, minority politics combines an increasing emphasis on socio-economic integration and individual rights, with a strong assertion of ethnic Turkish identity, without, however, allying it with any territorial demands. In Bulgaria, on the other hand, the MRF draws upon ethnic community support to construct and define a regional-based approach to development as an alternative to the state-centred reform and development strategies that appear to be taking hold. Characteristic of minority politics across Central and Eastern Europe, such a politics develops in opposition as much to the traditional model of nation-state as to a diffused logic of modernisation that pervades and dominates the liberals' approach to democracy, market economic reform and European integration.

While both minority and majority liberals endorse European and market-oriented reforms, they view very differently the relationship between regions, the ethnic community and the central state, attributing a fundamentally divergent content to minority rights and the nature of the EU. The majority's liberalism promotes centrally directed strategies of economic development; it depicts European integration as a vehicle of political–economic modernisation and prioritises the individual. On the other hand, the minority's conception of liberalism advocates decentralised strategies of economic development, while sustaining the central state's social and economic role. It also supports European integration as a multicultural entity and calls on ethnic-community solidarity. The processes of European enlargement in CESE are likely to render more visible the contradiction between the two competing notions of liberalism that reflect fundamentally different visions of political community and ultimately of the EU as it expands eastwards.

By providing an array of resources and incentives to national governments but also credible assurances for cultural protection to minorities, the EU has indirectly helped to contain ethnic crises with the frame of the state and avert broader destabilisation in Southeast Europe. As the Bulgarian and Greek cases show, contemporary minority demands are fundamentally different from historical nationalism; they do not challenge existing state institutions and territorial borders, but seek to reconfigure the latter from within, with reference to European integration. In this regard, the developments in the former Yugoslavia were more the exception rather than the rule in the Balkans. The Bulgarian and Greek cases challenge the oft-encountered view of the latter as being trapped in a historical legacy of exclusive and secessionist ethnic nationalism, in contrast to a liberal and 'benign' civic nationalism purportedly characterising Western and Central Europe.[99] Such views that depict nationalism as an inescapable obstacle to liberalisation and European integration in Southeast Europe misrepresent actual developments in the region.

Bibliography

Administrativno-Teritorialnata Reforma, National Centre for Territorial Development and Housing Policy, Sofia: ForKom, 1995.

Alexandris, Alexis, 'To mionotiko zitima 1954–1987' [The minority issue], *Oi Ellinotourkikes Scheseis 1923–1987* [Greek–Turkish relations 1923–1987], Athens: Gnosi & ELIAMEP, 1988.

Anagnostou, Dia, 'Collective rights and state security in the new Europe: the Lausanne Treaty in western Thrace and the debate about minority protection', in Konstantinos Arvanitopoulos (ed.), *Security dilemmas in Eurasia*, Athens: Nireefs Press, 1999, pp. 115–48.

'Breaking the cycle of nationalism: the EU, regional policy and the minority of western Thrace', *South European Societies and Politics*, vol. 6, no. 1, Summer, 2001, pp. 99–124.

'Nationalist legacies and European trajectories: post-communist liberalization and Turkish minority politics in Bulgaria', *Southeast European and Black Sea Studies*, vol. 5, no. 1, January, 2005a, pp. 87–109.

'National interpretations in Bulgarian writings on the Pomaks from the communist period through the present', *Journal of Southern Europe and the Balkans*, vol. 7, no. 1, April, 2005b, pp. 57–74.

Anderson, Malcolm, *Frontiers – territory and state formation in the modern world*, Cambridge: Polity Press, 1996.

Andrikopoulou, Eleni and Grigoris Kafkalas, 'Greek regional policy and the process of Europeanisation 1961–2000', in Dionyssis G. Dimitrakopoulos and Argyris G. Passas (eds.), *Greece in the European Union*, London: Routledge, 2004, pp. 35–47.

Aniol, Wlodek et al., 'Returning to Europe: Central Europe between internationalization and institutionalization', in Peter Katzenstein (ed.) *Tamed power – Germany in Europe*, Ithaca: Cornell University Press, 1997, pp. 195–250.

Bachtler, John, Ruth Downes and Grzegorz Gorzelak, 'Introduction: challenges of transition for regional development', in John Bachtler, Ruth Downes & Grzegorz Gorzelak (eds.), *Transition, cohesion and regional policy in central and eastern Europe*, Aldershot: Ashgate, 2000.

---

[99] Milada Vachudova and Tim Snyder, 'Are transitions transitory? Two types of political change in eastern Europe Since 1989', *East European Politics and Societies* vol. 11, no. 1, 1997, 1–35.

Batt, Judy, 'Introduction', in Judy Batt and Kataryna Wolczuk (eds.), *Region, state and identity in central and eastern Europe*, London: Frank Cass, 2002, pp. 1–14.

Begg, Robert and John Pickles, 'Institutions, social networks and ethnicity in the cultures of transition', John Pickles and Adrian Smith (eds.), *Theorizing transition – the political economy of post-communist transformation*, London: Routledge, 1998, pp. 115–46.

Bell, John, 'Democratization and political participation in "post-communist" Bulgaria', in Karen Dawisha and Bruce Parrott (eds.), *Politics, power, and the struggle for democracy in south-east Europe*, Cambridge: Cambridge University Press, 1997, pp. 353–402.

Boev, Julian, 'Bulgaria: decentralization and modernization of the public administration', in *Mastering decentralization and public administration reforms in central and eastern Europe*, Budapest: Local government and Public Reform Initiative, 2002, pp. 95–120.

Brubaker, Roger, *Nationalism reframed – nationhood and the national question in the new Europe*, Cambridge: Cambridge University Press, 1996.

Brusis, Martin, 'Regionalisation in the Czech and Slovak Republics: Comparing the influence of the European Union', in Michael Keating and James Hughes (eds.), *The regional challenge in central and eastern Europe. Territorial restructuring and European integration*, Brussels: PIE Peter Lang, 2003.

Bucek, Jan, 'Balancing functional and ethnic regionalisation: lessons from Slovakia', in Michael Keating and James Hughes (eds.), *The regional challenge in central and eastern Europe. Territorial restructuring and European integration*, Brussels: PIE–Peter Lang, 2003.

Bulgaria-Evropa: nestandarten pat na razvitie [Bulgaria-Europe: non-standard path to development], Programme of the MRF Coalition with the Liberal Union, 17 July, 2001, http://www.dps.bg.

Caramani, Daniele, 'State administration and regional construction in central Europe: a comparative-historical perspective', in Michael Keating and James Hughes (eds.), *The regional challenge in central and eastern Europe. Territorial restructuring and European integration*, Brussels: PIE- Peter Lang, 2003.

Chlepas, Nikolaos, *I topiki dioikisi stin Ellada* [The local administration in Greece], Athens: Sakoulas, 1999.

Christofilopoulou, Paraskevi, 'I nomarchiaki aftodioikisi sto Elliniko politiko–dioikitiko systima' [The prefecture self-government in the Greek political-administrative system], in K. Spanou, A. Rigos and M. Spourdalakis (eds.), *Nomarchiaki aftodioikis – prosdokies kai prooptikes* [Prefecture self-government – expectations and prospects], Athens: Sakoulas, 1997, pp. 37–63.

'Constitutional Watch', *East European Constitutional Review*, vol. 8, no. 4 (Fall) 1999.

Coulson, Andrew, 'From democratic centralism to local democracy', in Andrew Coulson (ed.), *Local government in Eastern Europe*, Brookfield, VT: Edward Elgar, 1995, pp. 1–19.

Crampton, R. J., *A concise history of Bulgaria*, Cambridge: Cambridge University Press, 1997.

Creed, Gerald, *Domesticating revolution*, University Park, PA: The Pennsylvania State University Press, 1998.

Demografski I sotsialno–ekonomitcheski harakteristiki – Rusenska oblast [Demographic and socioeconomic aspects – region of Ruse], Sofia: National Statistics Institute, 1994.

Dierevnisi Kritirion Technikis Ypodomis gia ton Prosdiorismo ton Provlimatikon Periochon [Study of the infrastructure criteria for the determination of problematic regions], Ksanthi: Polytechnic School, Demokrition University of Thrace, 1987.

Divani, Lena, *Ellada kai mionotites* [Greece and minorities], Athens: Nefeli, 1995.

Dogan, Ahmed, 'Polititsheski analiz na predizbornata I sledizbornata situatsia', *Prava I Svobodi*, 13, 31 March 1995.

'Bulgarski model za reshavane na maltsinstveni problemi e naj-vazhnoto postizhenje na prehoda', *Tolerantnost*, no. 25, 1999a.

'Triabva ni umeren – natsionalnata idea ne biva da se bazira na mitove a na realnosti I perspektivi' [We must be moderate – the national ideal should not be based on myths but on realistic perspectives], *Prava I Svobodi*, July 27, 1999b.

'Programna deklaratsia na Dvizhenje za Prava I Svobodi' [Party declaration of the MRF], in http://www.dps.bg, 2000.

Speech delivered at the 5th National Conference of the MRF, Sofia, 15–16 February 2003. Available online at: www.dps.bg

Drezov, Kyril, 'Bulgaria: transition comes full circle, 1989–1997', in Geoffrey Pridham and Tom Gallagher (eds.), *Experimenting with democracy*, London: Routledge, 2000.

Eminov, Ali, *Turkish and other Muslim minorities in Bulgaria*, London: Hurst & Company, 1997.

Fowler, Brigid 'Hungary: patterns of political conflict over territorial–administrative reform', in Judy Batt and Kataryna Wolczuk (eds.), *Region, state and identity in central and eastern Europe*, London: Frank Cass, 2002 pp. 15–40.

Galubov, Antoni, 'Mestnata politika – mezhdu samoupravlenieto I administratsiata' [Local politics – between self-government and administration], *Prava I Svobodi*, no. 34, 1 September 1995, p. 2.

Giannopoulos, Aristeidis and Dimitris Psaras, 'To "Elliniko 1955"' [The 'Greek 1955'], *Scholiastis*, vol. 85, no. 3, 1990, pp. 18–21.

Hooghe, Liesbet, 'Reconciling EU-Wide Policy and National Diversity', in Liesbet Hooghe (ed.), *Cohesion policy and European integration*, Oxford: Oxford University Press, 1996, pp. 1–24.

Hughes, James, Gwendolyn Sasse and Claire Gordon, 'EU enlargement, europeanisation and the dynamics of regionalisation in the CEECs', in Michael Keating and James Hughes (eds.), *The regional challenge in central and eastern Europe. Territorial restructuring and European integration*, Brussels: PIE– Peter Lang, 2003.

Europeanization and regionalization in the EU enlargement to central and eastern Europe, New York: Palgrave Macmillan, 2004.

I Anaptixi tis Anatolikis Makedonias kai Thrakis [The Development of Eastern Macedonia & Thrace], vol. 1, Athens: Commercial Bank of Greece, 1986.

I Anaptixi tis Thrakis – Prokliseis kai Prooptikes [Thrace's Development – Challenges and Prospects], Athens: Academy of Athens, 1994.

Informatsia za sustojianieto na obshtina Kircali prez 1993 [Information for the condition of the municipality of Khurdzali], Report obtained from the Municipality of Khurdzali, 1993.

Ioakimidis, P. C., 'EU cohesion policy in Greece: the tension between bureaucratic centralism and regionalism', in Liesbet Hooghe (ed.), *Cohesion policy and European integration*, Oxford: Oxford University Press, 1996, pp. 342–63.

Ioannides, Yannis and George Petrakos, 'Regional disparities in Greece: the performance of Crete, Peloponnese and Thessaly', *European Investment Bank Papers*, vol. 5, no. 1, 2000, pp. 31–60.

Ivanov, Mihail and Ilona Tomova, 'Etnitcheski grupi I mezhdu-etnitcheski otnoshenia vuf Bulgaria' [Ethnic groups and inter-ethnic relations in Bulgaria], in *Aspekti na etnokulturnata situatsia vuf Bulgaria* [Aspects of the ethnocultural situation in Bulgaria], Sofia: ACCESS Association, 1994.

Ivanov, Mihail and Ibrahim Yalamouv, 'Turskata obshtnost vuf Bulgaria I neinja perioditchen petchat 1878–1997' [The Turkish community in Bulgaria and its periodic press 1878–1997], in *Bulgarsko Mediaznanje*, Sofia: Balkanmedia, 1998, pp. 556–601.

Keating, Michael, *The new regionalism in western Europe*, Cheltenham, UK: Edward Elgar, 1998.

'Territorial restructuring and European integration', in Michael Keating and James Hughes (eds.), *The regional challenge in central and eastern Europe. Territorial restructuring and European integration*, Brussels: PIE– Peter Lang.

Keliyan, Maya, 'The transformation of agriculture', in Jacques Coenen-Huther (ed.), *Bulgaria at the crossroads*, New York: Nova Science Publishers, Inc., 1996.

Konstantinov, Yulian, 'Strategies for sustaining a vulnerable identity: the case of the Bulgarian Pomaks', in Poulton, Hugh and Suha Taji-Farouki (eds.), *Muslim identity and the Balkan state*, New York: NYU Press, 1997.

Kontos, Alexandros and Georgios Pavlou, 'Epifaniakos, anofelos kai ethnika epikindinos' [Superficial, useless and nationally perilous], *Oikonomikos Tachydromos*, 7 July, 1994, pp. 35–36.

Lynch, Peter, *Minority nationalism and European integration*, Cardiff: University of Wales Press, 1996.

Mitchell, James, and Michael Cavanagh, 'Context and contingency: constitutional nationalists and Europe', in Michael Keating and John McGarry (eds.), *Minority nationalism and the changing international order*, Oxford: Oxford University Press, 2001, pp. 246–63.

Mitev, Petar, 'Relations of compatibility and incompatibility in the everyday life of Christians and Muslims in Bulgaria', in Petar Mitev (ed.), *Relations of compatibility and incompatibility between Christians and Muslims in Bulgaria*, Sofia: International Centre for Minority Studies and Intercultural Relations, 1995.

Nanetti, Raffaella Y., 'EU cohesion and territorial restructuring in the member states', in Liesbet Hooghe (ed.), *Cohesion policy and European integration*, Oxford: Oxford University Press, 1996, pp. 59–88.

Papageorgiou, Fouli and Susannah Verney, 'Regional planning and the integrated Mediterranean programmes in Greece', *Regional Politics & Policy*, vol. 2, nos. 1&2 (Spring/Summer), 1992, pp. 139–62.

Petkov, Kristu and Georgi Fotev (eds.), *Etnitcheskja konflict vuf*, Bulgaria 1989 [Ethnic conflict in Bulgaria 1989], Sofia: Bulgarian Academy of Sciences, Institute of Sociology, 1990.

Plaskovities, Ilias, 'EC regional policy in Greece', in Panos Kazakos and P. C. Ioakimidis (eds.), *Greece and EC membership evaluated*, New York: St. Martin's Press, 1994.

Porisma Diakomatikis Epitropis gia tis Akritikes Periohes [Findings of the Inter-party Committee for Border Regions], Greek Parliament, Athens, 14 February, 1992.

Receb, Giulbie, 'Doverieto na kredit ima granitsi' [Confidence in credit has its limits], *Prava I Svobodi*, 1, 5 January, 1995.

'Regional policy - Inforegio', European Commission online information on regional policy. Available online at: http://europa.eu.int/comm/ regional_policy/country/overmap/gr/gr_en.htm

Rezultati ot Prebrojavaneto na naselenieto - Demografski Karakteristiki, vol. 1, Sofia: National Statistical Institute, 1994.

Rokkan, Stein and Derek W. Urwin, 'Introduction' and 'Conclusion', in Stein Rokkan and Derek W. Urwin (eds.), *Politics of territorial identity*, London: Sage, 1982, pp. 1–17 and pp. 425–36.

Rozakis, Christos, 'The international protection of minorities in Greece', in Kevin Featherstone and Kostas Ifantis (eds.), *Greece in a changing Europe*, Manchester: Manchester University Press, 1996, pp. 95–116.

Stratigiko schedio anaptiksis Makedonias & Thrakis [Strategic development plan of Macedonia & Thrace.], vols. B & C, Thessaloniki: Union of Industrialists of North Greece, 1994.

Tsoukalis, Loukas, *The new European economy – the politics and economics of integration*, Oxford: Oxford University Press, 1991.

Vachudova, Milada, and Tim Snyder, 'Are transitions transitory? Two types of political change in eastern Europe since 1989', *East European Politics and societies*, vol. 11, no. 1, 1997, pp. 1–35.

Verney, Susannah, 'Central state–local government relations', in Panos Kazakos and P. C. Ioakimidis (eds.), *Greece and EC membership evaluated*, London: Pinter Publishers, 1994, pp. 166–80.

Verney, Susannah and Fouli Papageorgiou, 'Prefecture Councils in Greece: decentralization in the EC', *Regional Politics & Policy*, vol. 2, nos. 1&2 (Spring/Summer), 1992, pp. 109–130.

Wolczuk, Kataryna, 'Conclusion: identities, regions and Europe', Judy Batt and Kataryna Wolczuk (eds.), in *Region, state and identity in central and eastern Europe*, London: Frank Cass, 2002, pp. 203–13.

Zhelyaskova, Antonina, 'Bulgaria's Muslim minorities', in John D. Bell (ed.), *Bulgaria in transition*, Boulder: Westview Press, 1999, pp. 165–87.

9 Breaching the infernal cycle? Turkey, the European Union and religion

Valérie Amiraux

There is something boring about discussing the candidacy of Turkey for membership in the European Union (EU). Reading the vast literature on the topic, it seems the discussion leads either to technical, petty and bureaucratic analysis of reforms, change and prospects for adapting Turkish institutions to European requirements (all with an implicit motto of 'Turkey can do it'), or, on the contrary, it ends up with an accumulation of stereotypes and cultural and essentialist illustrations of how trying to merge Turkey into Europe is nonsense (the subliminal message being 'don't do it!'). In this second category, the core argument is more explicitly related to the identity dimension of the European Union construction. Even if *some* observers have mentioned the centrality of identity politics and religion in this discussion (at least, in their efforts to explain the passionate nature of the positions adopted by the various actors), the particular question of religion remains for the time being implicit rather than explicit.[1] The Pandora's box of the discussion on EU cultural borders and EU religious identity has not yet been properly opened.

United in diversity: this is what Europe supposedly stands for. And indeed, in terms of religion, approximately 15 million Muslims are said to be living in the EU. As recently pointed out by Olivier Roy, the reason

Acknowledgment: I wish to thank Effie Fokas for her patience in editing this text, from its very first draft to the final version.

[1] According to the Independent Commission on Turkey's report entitled 'Turkey in Europe: more than a promise?': 'The prospect of Turkey's EU membership causes considerable discomfort among many Europeans because of its large and predominantly Muslim population, often perceived as the bearers of alien social and cultural traditions.' (2004, p. 26) The Independent Commission on Turkey was established in March 2004. It gathers together a group of distinguished European policymakers wishing to examine the challenges and opportunities presented by Turkey's possible membership of the European Union (see the list of participants on http://www.independentcommissiononturkey.org). The report is available in six languages on http://www.independentcommissiononturkey.org/report.html (last accessed 1 May 2005).

why Europeans are discussing Islam so intensively is directly linked with the fact that Muslims chose to leave the Middle East.[2] However, does this move help Islam to find a legitimate place in Europe? The answer is for the time being still more negative than it is positive, as Islam is quasi-systematically related to political activism, violence and terrorism. And could Turkish accession to the European Union pacify the boiling atmosphere surrounding public discussions on Islam and the European Union?

Turkey was granted candidate status during the Helsinki summit in December 1999, after the Union first chose to decline Turkey's candidacy for full membership.[3] A series of laws has been passed in Turkey following the 1999 decision, in particular in the economic, administrative and judicial sectors. Thus far Turkey is the only state with a predominately Muslim population which has applied to the European Union as a candidate for full membership (if one excepts the Moroccan request in the mid-1980s). To some extent, Turks are already Europeans as they represent the first group of foreigners in Europe, almost 4 million, most of whom are settled in Germany (over 2.5 million). Does Turkey, however, fit into Europe? A perhaps crude and direct way to formulate the central point about the accession of Turkey in the EU would be to ask whether a 99% Muslim population can become a full member of the European Union. On the one hand, Islam is the most obvious element of cultural difference between Turkey and other applicants. On the other hand, this fact has been the least explicitly raised in public discussions in EU contexts, besides of course the limited and somehow provocative public declarations made by prominent politicians.

This chapter is thus an attempt to shed light on a relatively unspoken argument. It is about Islam, and about religion and politics both in Turkey and in the EU. Plenty of questions could be raised within this framework. I will limit myself to what I identify as the most striking ones, and I will try as much as possible to avoid remaining at too abstract a level of analysis, without however falling into the trap of broad historical descriptions. The chapter opens with a consideration of the ties binding politics and religion in Turkey and asks how distant from European norms the experience of Turkey is as far as secularism and pluralism are concerned. It then delves further into this question by assessing the controversies emerging in both contexts, related for

---

[2] Olivier Roy, *La laïcité face à l'islam*, Paris: Stock, 2005.

[3] The first effort by Turkey to be associated with the European Economic Community dates back to 1959. Turkey has been a member of the Council of Europe since 1949. It went on to sign the Ankara Agreement with the EEC in 1963.

example to the Islamic veil. The third part of the chapter examines the role of migration from Turkey to Europe. How has the settlement of Turks in EU countries affected the public discussion in Turkey on religious identity, religious minorities and religious pluralism? Has the presence of Turks in Europe facilitated a better understanding by Europeans of social and political dynamics in Turkey (for instance the rise of political Islam); or, on the contrary, has it brought new stereotypes and negative representations of Turks in general that may today interfere with the negotiations on Turkey's membership? I conclude by questioning more specifically the European conception of secularism, the process of secularisation of European societies and their equivalent in Turkey. Are these 'patterns' of secularism compatible or incompatible with one another?

Turkey and religion: the specific experience of *laïcité*

Few authors have explicitly tackled the issue whether or not Islam is of importance in the discussion on accepting Turkey as a member of the European Union. A recent publication entails an exception by asking whether the fact that the majority of its population is Muslim forms a hindrance to Turkish accession to the European Union.[4] A more precise question emerges on the compatibility between Turkish Islam and European values. The text focuses in particular on the usual series of arguments concerning first the principles and fundamental rights presented by the EU as its core values (including the institutional links between churches and states), and second the supposed specificity of a Turkish Islam. The conclusive answer to the question is negative: 'Neither the historical developments described, nor the characteristics of present-day Turkey and Turkish Islam, could justify the argument that Turkish Islam forms an obstacle to Turkey's accession to the EU.'[5]

When it comes to religion, the discussion on whether Turkey could become an EU member is very often limited to two aspects: the forced secularisation launched by Atatürk in the 1920s as a key factor in opening Turkey to modernity, and the rise of political Islam. The common feature is the following: religion and politics are intimately intertwined in

[4] Netherlands Scientific Council for Government Policy (ed.), *The European Union, Turkey and Islam*, Amsterdam University Press, 2004. This is the English translation of a Dutch report drafted by an independent advisory body to the Dutch government in June 2004. The volume also includes a commissioned study and survey by Erik-Jan Zürcher and Helen van der Linden, 'Searching for the fault line. A survey of the role of Turkish Islam in the accession of Turkey to the European Union in the light of the "clash of civilizations".'

[5] Netherlands Scientific Council for Government Policy, 2004, p. 67.

the history of the nation-building of Turkey. The rise of the Turkish Republic and the reforms carried out by Atatürk belong to the international iconography of authoritarian modernisation, and observers have no doubt that the 'state sponsored modernisation of Turkey can be interpreted as a civilisational conversion, from the Ottoman–Islamic one to the Turkish–Western one'.[6] From that point of view, Turkey's prospective membership of the EU appears as the final stage of a historical process of westernisation that started even in the 1830s with the reforms carried out by the Ottoman administration. Where is the Turkish specificity, then, in terms of the relationship between religion and politics? To make a long story necessarily short and caricaturised, the major aspect lies in the authoritative process that led to the removal of religion from the public sphere, or, better said, the organisation of the control of the religious sphere by the political sphere.[7] To what extent does this specific trajectory impact on the discussion concerning Turkey's relation to European norms? Instead of asking whether there is a distinct Turkish Islam and emphasising the importance of context and local, national narratives to understand the specific zone of settlements of Islam,[8] one should rather concentrate, in the Turkish context, on the following questions: how is Islam translated into institutions, ideas, practices, arts, everyday life and morality? How is religious identity enacted in Turkey and articulated in relation to the secular commitment? Choosing an historical perspective, Yavuz underlines the symbiotic relationship between Islam and Turkish nationalism as an explanation of why the state never properly succeeded in disengaging Islam from debates over the politics of identity.[9]

The role of the Directorate of Religious Affairs, which is attached to the Prime Minister's Office, is central in the political regulation of religion in Turkey. The political sphere's regulation of religion has been

---

[6] Nilüfer Göle, 'Visible women: actresses in the public realm', *New Perspectives Quarterly*, Spring 2004, vol. 21(2), pp. 12–13.

[7] In this respect, Turkish and French *laïcité* differ radically, despite parallel evolutions that were brought to the forefront recently regarding the right to wear an Islamic veil in public schools. One could for instance envisage (but this goes beyond the scope of this article), a comparison between the Islamist/secularist dilemma in Turkey with the strong polarisation of French society in two camps (pro and contra Islamic veil).

[8] According to Hakan Yavuz, 'Although Islam provides a universal set of principles to make life meaningful, these principles are vernacularized and localized in specific narratives.' See Yavuz, 'Is there a Turkish Islam? The emergence of convergence and consensus', *Journal of Muslim Minority Affairs*, vol. 24, no. 2, 2004, p. 215.

[9] See Yavuz, 'Is there a Turkish Islam?', p. 221. Yavuz assumes the existence of a specific way to understand Islamic identity, in particular related to sufi networks, that he designates as the 'liberal and market friendly Islam, dominant in Turkey and Malaysia'. Yavuz, ibid., p. 214.

most visible from 1982 onwards, when the Directorate took the opportunity to control the extraterritorial map of Turkish Islam, in particular to oversee the religious life of Turkish migrants living in Germany.[10] In Turkey, the Directorate regulates a broad range of religious practices, from the training of scholars to the establishment of mosques, to translations of sacred texts and the payment of imams (who are civil servants). Recently, the part played by the Directorate in the Turkish game of political control over religion gained new visibility after it made a recommendation to the imams and preachers to speak more regularly and explicitly about taboo subjects such as honour killings (a crime that is punishable by law) and the need for more gender equality at home but also in the workplace.[11] Sermons represent channels of communication for the government to fight against radicalism and confusion between religion and traditional practices. The Directorate contributes by organising meetings of religious scholars asked to draft the sermons that will be sent out throughout the country, and eventually to the Directorate's mosques abroad. As in other domains, the state-centric culture dominates the religious field. According to Yavuz, the centrality of the state in Turkish Islam explains, in part, the symbiotic relationship between *ulemas* and the state and the strength of a philosophy of cooptation in order to help maintain control.[12]

Notwithstanding the state policy to control religious actors and discourses, today, in 2005, Turkey is ruled by an 'Islamist party'.[13] Turkey has indeed been witnessing the rise of what has been called activism of 'political Islam', as a result of the opening of the political space to a multiparty system in the 1950s. The multiparty system introduced the

---

[10] The Directorate is also known as *DİYANET* for *Diyanet İşleri Başkanlığı*. It is currently under the presidency of Ali Barkadoglu. It is usually designated by the first word (*DİYANET*). We will here use the English term of Directorate. In foreign countries where Turkish citizens have settled, the *DİYANET* has established some offices. In Germany for instance, *DİYANET* is rather known under the acronym of *DİTİB* for *Diyanet İşleri Trk Islam Birliği*. It is a federal umbrella organisation (*Dachverband*) with local representatives. The religious councillor is attached to the Turkish embassy and the 'local' religious attachés are based in the consulates. In Germany, the *DİTİB* is registered as an association under the following name: *Türkisch Islamische Union der Anstalt für Religion e. V.* The current president is Ridvan Çakir.

[11] *Chicago Tribune*, 9 May, 2004.

[12] See Yavuz, 2004; Hakan Yavuz, *Islamic political identity in Turkey*, Oxford: Oxford University Press, 2003; and Levent Tezcan, *Religiöse Strategien der 'machbaren' Gesellschaft. Verwaltete Religion und Islamistische Utopie in der Türkei*, Bielefeld: Transcript, 2003.

[13] If the designation of the AKP as an Islamist party seems to raise no doubt in European minds (except for some scholars familiar with Turkish history and context), it is questioned by the AKP's political activists and leaders: from the outset of the party's establishment, Erdogan and his followers emphasised the notion of conservatism, preferring to be considered as a Muslim equivalent of Christian Democrats.

possibility of politicisation of religious differences and identities: 'Initially, Islamist opposition to the republican project was suppressed; then it was contained, and finally it was integrated into the system.'[14] This emergence of Islamic political parties and associations culminated in the 1990s with the electoral successes of the Welfare Party (*Refah Partisi*, hereafter WP), both locally and nationally. During the 1990s, the nationalist movement had also become a central force in Turkish politics as a 'successful cross fertilization of select elements of the state-sponsored Kemalist nationalist program with grass-roots nationalist and conservative politics',[15] in such a way that helped put the concerns of nationalist *and* Islamist groups at the centre of Turkish politics. The general fear that went throughout Europe when the WP won the local and national elections in 1994 and 1995 was newly reactivated in 2002 when the AKP (*Adalet ve Kalkinma Partisi*, or the Justice and Development Party), came to power after its victory at the parliamentary elections (34.1%). In the aftermath of the elections, both European and Turkish secular elites expressed similar perceptions and reactions of fear of an Islamic threat that would be represented in the Turkish polity by activists, leaders and an electorate identified with an 'Islamist' movement.[16]

The election of a party with a background of 'political Islam' added to the anxiety of European public opinion, their interest in these elections being mostly motivated by the specific nature of the Islamic-rooted winner.[17] Since December 1999, when Turkey was granted the EU candidacy during the Helsinki European Council, all the successive Turkish governments, regardless of political colour, have been slowly but tenaciously activating political reforms, reflecting clearly the 1999 change of perspective. In the wake of the elections, the foreign attention was mostly focusing on the future of Turkey led by an Islamist-oriented

---

[14] Binnaz Toprak, 'A secular democracy: the Turkish model', in Shireen Hunter, Huma Malik (eds.), *Modernization, democracy, and Islam*, Westport: Praeger, 2005, p. 278.

[15] Nergis Canefe and Tanil Bora, 'Intellectual roots of anti-European sentiments in Turkish politics: the case of radical Turkish nationalism', in Ali Çarkoglu and Barry Rubin (eds.), *Turkey and the European Union. Domestic politics, economic integration and international dynamics*, London: Frank Cass, 2003, p. 133.

[16] The national ideology of protecting the state from certain threats (Kurdish movements and Islamist activists being for a long time the two prominent domestic figures of the enemy, mostly redefined as national security threats thanks to the military) is extended today to protecting the society from certain dangers. See Ümit Cizre, *Politics and military in Turkey into the 21st century*, Florence: European University Institute, Working Paper (RSCAS), 2000.

[17] Soli Özel, 'Turkey at the polls. After the tsunami', *Journal of Democracy*, vol. 14, no. 2, pp. 80–94, 2003.

government:[18] would it end up like Iran? Could such leaders be accepted as rulers of an EU member state? Do Turkish political elites share a common pattern of policymaking with EU leaders?

But in the end, compared with other Muslim societies and Middle Eastern regimes, Turkish history is an illustration of the capacity of Islamists to cope with the democratic rules of the game and even to commit to its values. The moderation of the Islamist movements has many explanations, most of which are endemic to the regime (the control by the military, the judiciary and the legal system, and the public commitment to the secular state).[19] Indeed, the AKP too has become a central protagonist of the pro-EU membership camp. The rejection of the label 'Islamist' by Recep Tayyip Erdogan allowed him to run as a 'Muslim Democrat' candidate in the 2002 polls. The reasons for the recent AKP success are manifold but certainly its leaders' ability to disentangle the reference of the party with political Islam, preferring to associate it with a larger and more consensual call for religious values as the centre of the national culture, played a large role in the party's success.[20] The 'Muslim Democrats' reflect the shift from a strictly religiously rooted rhetoric to a simply conservative one. AKP has become today a pro-EU party based on a conservative constituency and aware of its non-homogeneous Islamic political identity.

Yet one of the challenges facing the AKP leadership on the domestic scene consisted in being accepted as state elite: being recognised, on the one hand, as able and legitimate to rule the country, and on the other hand being seen as potentially holding the monopoly over the definition of issues such as secularism and national identity.[21] Conforming to EU norms (and one should also add international norms) has certainly been an incentive for major changes in Turkish politics during the last five years, but niches of resistance still distillate opposition to EU norms and values. Islamists from the Islamist WP and leaders in today's AKP have long been key actors in this opposition. The authenticity of the switch by these same leaders from an anti- to a pro-European position has therefore been more specifically scrutinised: can this radical change be anything but purely opportunistic?

---

[18] The results gave 363 seats for the AKP out of a total number of 550.

[19] See Toprak, 2005; Effie Fokas, 'The Islamist movement and Turkey-EU relations', in Mehmet Ugur and Nergis Canefe (eds.), *Turkey and European integration. Accession prospects and issues*, London: Routledge, 2004, pp. 147–69.

[20] Gilles Dorronsoro, Elise Massicard and Jean-François Pérouse, 'Turquie: changement de gouvernement ou changement de régime?', *Critique Internationale*, no. 18, January 2003, pp. 8–15.

[21] Menderes Cinar, 'The Justice and Development Party in Turkey', available at http://www.networkideas.org/themes/world/jan2003/print/prnt290103_Turkey.htm.

Broadly speaking, one can say that Islamist trends in Turkey changed from hostility towards the European Union to support for the project of accession after a series of developments, including the meeting of the National Security Council on 28 February 1997 (or, the 'February 28th process')[22], the withdrawal of Erbakan from leadership, and the creation of the Virtue Party (VP)[23] and the current AKP. Evoking the party system in Turkey, Taniyici defends the idea of the EU constituting a normative political opportunity structure (an international normative structure) that helped the Islamist leadership to convert into a new image. The WP and its followers ceased to be an ideology-seeking party and shifted 'from an Islamist and state-centred discourse to a democratic, society centred discourse'.[24] For some observers, including Saban Taniyici, the above changes can be explained with reference to the fact that the EU constitutes an international normative structure which may serve – as it did for AKP – as a 'strategic instrument for the party elite'.[25]

It would however be simplistic to limit the 'Islamist' voices inside Turkey to the activists and leaders of the AKP. Journalists, opinion-makers, intellectuals, and writers belonging to the multiple Islamist trends in Turkey adopt a diversity of attitudes, in particular when it comes to Turkey's membership to the EU.[26] For instance the positions can be quite critical: for some, EU membership would damage the Islamic core identity of the country, alienating Turkey from the Islamic world at large and leading the country towards more secularism and less religion in public. In the eyes of many Islamist intellectuals, the EU bill would be too high for Turkish identity, unless the membership remained within a purely cosmetic perspective. Would Turkey lose its soul entering the EU? Placed in an historical perspective, Turkey becoming a full member state of the EU can be conceived as the

---

[22] This date refers to the process whereby the Turkish military gradually limited the power of Erbakan as Prime Minister, particularly on matters to do with religion, in such a strict way as to lead to the gradual collapse of the government. It is in some cases referred to as a 'soft coup' or the 'post-modern coup'.

[23] The Virtue Party (*Fazilet Partisi*) was created in December 1997 after the closing down of the WP. It was banned in June 2001 by decision of the Constitutional Court, and subsequently the Justice and Development Party (*Adalet ve Kalkınma Partisi*) was created by Recep Tayyip Erdoğan, former WP mayor of Istanbul.

[24] Saban Taniyici, 'Transformation of political Islam in Turkey: Islamist Welfare Party's Pro-EU Turn', *Party Politics*, vol. 9, July 2003, p. 476.

[25] Ibid.

[26] For a stimulating review of different Islamist Turkish voices about the EU membership of Turkey, see Burhannettin Duran, 'Islamist redefinition(s) of European and Islamic identities in Turkey', in Mehmet Ugur, Nergis Canefe (ed.), *Turkey and European integration. Accession prospects and issues*, London: Routledge, 2004, pp. 125–146.

conclusion of the long westernisation process that has been carried out by the Republican elites since the 1920s.[27] But there is nevertheless an intellectual and political anti-European tradition in Turkey, in particular amongst Turkish radical nationalists.[28]

The Islamists' perception of the EU is certainly not radically modified, but what seems to have been developing is a representation of the EU as a political space based on common universal values working as common goods (democracy, pluralism, human rights), rather than as a closed Christian club. The 1999 decision certainly helped stimulate the domestic policy reforms that have been actively implemented since late 2001. Therefore 'what appears irrefutable is that an important process of progressive and democratic change is in the making; and that such a change is the most extensive of Turkey's Republican history'.[29] This applies in particular in the sector of human and civil rights.[30] The political leadership's compliance with the Copenhagen criteria demonstrates Turkey's acceptance 'to live up to its commitment to democratic reform as a sine qua non condition of the membership process'.[31] To some observers, the change of tone in the Islamist support for Turkey's EU membership in the 90s, in particular when coming to the Copenhagen criteria, dates back to the 28 February process and the resultant 'internalization of democratic vocabulary while criticizing Kemalism'.[32] The thus explicit and public support for the central values of democracy (secularism, supremacy of law, accountability, protection of fundamental rights and human rights, etc.) made pluralism and citizens' participation central in building the democracy of modern European Turkey. The adhesion of Turkey to the EU had effects on the domestic political positioning of Islamist and Kemalist elites (including political leaders). It appears as a way for Islamist elites to fight with Kemalist elites in their own field, as illustrated with the attempt by the WP leaders to take the case of the party banned in Turkey to the European Court of Human Rights in 1998. But what is at stake is less a fight over the position of religion in the public sphere than a battle for the definition of Turkish identity as a pluralistic or monolithic one: 'The European Union seems to be the major catalyst at the moment

---

[27] Duran, ibid.

[28] Canefe and Bora, 'Intellectual roots of anti-European sentiments', 2003.

[29] Nathalie Tocci, 'Europeanization in Turkey: trigger or anchor to reform?', *South European Society and Politics*, vol. 10, no. 1, March 2005, p. 71.

[30] Such change includes constitutional amendments and harmonization packages that were passed in 2001–3 with important amendments to the Penal Code and the Anti-Terror Law, including the abolition of the death penalty. On that point, see Tocci, 2005.

[31] Özel, 'Turkey at the polls', 2003, p. 85.

[32] Duran, 'Islamist redefinition(s)', 2004, p. 128.

in the acceleration of the process of peaceful coexistence in Turkey.'[33] The nature of this interaction between Turkey's internal reforms and EU accession perspective is a matter worthy of discussion,[34] but it would be exaggerated to limit Turkey's membership prospects to a rational game based on interests and opportunities. It should rather be linked with the domestic perception of social pluralism and diversity, not only focusing on non-Muslim populations, but also looking at the tensions dividing Turkish Muslim citizens.

The denial of pluralism and Muslim claims for equality

The intimate problem in Turkey lies not with Islam or with religion more generally but rather with the public recognition of social pluralism. In the 1980s, the emergence of identity mobilisation (Kurds, Islamists, Alevis) alerted Turkish public authorities to the politicisation of various groups of Turkish citizens, gathering behind various types of flags. These movements opened a high competition on the market of ideas and identities, challenging the central state definition of an exclusive national identity. The difficulties that non-Muslim minorities are facing are also internationally monitored and regularly denounced by NGOs. The 2001 Accession Partnership between the EU and Turkey designated a series of medium term priorities with regard to religious freedom. Various EU harmonisation laws have been passed that encompass amendments improving the situation of non-Muslim religions. For instance the 6th EU Harmonisation Law has introduced changes to construction law and gives the possibility to designate sites for the building of mosques but also churches, synagogues and *cemev* (for Alevis). Though the freedom to perform religious services is guaranteed, there are no rights to administer ecclesiastical foundations, schools, churches, etc. Moreover, according to Human Rights Without Frontiers (hereafter HRWF),[35] 'traditional prejudice towards Non-Muslim minorities is kept alive by the public education system and the state-controlled media'.[36] Exactly as for human

---

[33] Ayhan Kaya and Ferhat Kentel, *Euro Turks. A bridge or a breach between Turkey and the European Union? A comparative study of German-Turks and French-Turks*, Brussels, Centre for European Policy Studies (CEPS), 2005, p. 1.

[34] On this point, see the article by Tocci, 2005.

[35] Human Rights Without Frontiers is an NGO based in Brussels that produces reports and organises the circulation of information related to freedom of religion and beliefs, with special emphasis on country reports. It also organises an observatory on religious, spiritual and philosophical entities, and edits a press review (www.hrwf.net).

[36] HRWF, 22 September 2004 (available at www.hrwf.net). Recently, in a response to EU demands for freedom of religion, the Directorate of Religious Affairs prepared a sermon that made reference to Christian missionaries as the modern embodiment of the Crusaders: *Turkish Daily News*, 24 February 2005.

and civic rights or more importantly democracy promotion, there is a
tendency among religious authorities of non-Muslim minorities – such as
the Christian Orthodox patriarchate in Turkey – to believe that
EU pressure could help secure some fundamental freedom to these
minorities.[37]

Discussing Turkey's membership to the EU means indeed opening
the debate on religious and cultural pluralism and on the strong unitary
thrust deriving from the authoritarian nation-building inherited from
Kemalism. Starting with the exclusive Sunni definition of what is considered to be orthodox national Islam, Alevis are at the core of this
discussion.[38] There are estimated to be between 12 and 20 million living
in Turkey. As illustrated recently in Massicard's study of Alevism, discussing pluralism in the Turkish context means first to launch a discussion inside Muslim populations, where some groups are conceived
as sources of instability and chaos.[39] In its 2004 Regular Report on
Turkey's progress towards accession, the European Commission mentions the Alevi population and underlines: 'Alevis are not officially
recognised as a religious community, they often experience difficulties in
opening places of worship and compulsory religious instruction in
schools fails to acknowledge non-Sunni identities.'[40] Alevis are still not
recognised as a religious minority. What happens to be predominating is
a more and more systematic recourse to the judicial arena, in terms of
mobilisation among individual as well as collective Turkish actors willing to express their interests and get satisfaction of their claims, rather
than having recourse to a civic-rights type of contest. The European
Court of Human Rights (ECHR) is the central site where one can
observe how Turkish citizens consider the opportunity to rely on Europe
rather than on their own nation. This was the case for Kurds in the
1980s, and it is now more systematically becoming the arena in which
Turkish citizens choose to invest when it comes to defending their rights
as Muslims and their claims for equality of treatment as citizens. A
specific feature appears to be common to Muslim activists in Turkey
and EU member states: they prefer to rely on laws to gain access to
equal treatment. Indeed, we can recognise a general tendency to work
on the resolution of political conflictual issues through the use of legal

---

[37] The recurring example to illustrate how the EU can help to resolve the tensions is the
discussion over the potential reopening of the Halki theological seminary in Turkey,
located on the island of Heybeliada (called Halki by the Greeks) that was closed in 1971
as a law was passed limiting activities at post-secondary religious schools in Turkey.

[38] We do not discuss here the peculiar situations of Muslim brotherhoods.

[39] Elise Massicard, *L'autre Turquie*, Paris: PUF (Proche-Orient), 2005.

[40] Regular Report, 2004, p. 44.

provisions in the following developments: the systematised use of legal resources (texts, laws, case law) to gain the attention of a larger public and a voice in the public space, and the identification with one particular case or one figure symbolising a singular experience through the history of one person. These developments can be described as a dialectic process, through which the legal system is relied on to solve difficult social problems.[41]

The headscarf controversies emerged during the 1990s as a common characteristic of certain EU member states and Turkey, almost exclusively involving the education sector (university or public primary and secondary schools). In Turkish society, the historical path is however different from EU countries, even if the public discussions surrounding the controversies somehow end up with the same type of arguments dividing national societies into two camps. The tension between secularists and Islamists is not a new one in the Turkish context and it has been structuring the entire history of the republic. Likewise, the dress code has been central in the definition of norms of citizens' behaviour, for men also but especially for women.[42] The state limitation on dress pursues the project of limiting religion to the private sphere and thus ensures the total control of religion's public expression. For instance, in the Turkish universities students are requested to dress according to the code laid down for civil servants.[43] Furthermore, during the 80th anniversary celebrations of Turkey's emergence as a modern republic, the festivities were overshadowed by discussions over the ban on the Islamic style headscarf in public buildings and state-run schools. As pointed out earlier, the headscarf issue is increasingly played out through the demands for justice carried by individuals to courts and a personal choice to override the main national judicial institutions when there is a possibility to do so.[44] The right to wear a veil in Turkey is not presented as a collective request but rather as an individual choice. Two camps are set in opposition

---

[41] Valérie Amiraux, 'Rights and claims for equality among Muslims in Europe', in NOCRIME (ed. by Jocelyne Cesari and Sean McLoughlin), *European Muslims and the secular state in a comparative perspective*, Aldershot: Ashgate, 2005.

[42] A major study is Nilüfer Göle, *The forbidden modern. Civilization and veiling*, Ann Arbor: Michigan University Press, 1996. See also Elisabeth Özdalga, *The veiling issue: official secularism and popular Islam in modern Turkey*, Ankara: Curzon, 1998.

[43] For an overview of the history of the ban of the headscarf in the universities, see Arat Yesim, 'Group-differentiated rights and the liberal democratic state: rethinking the headscarf controversy in Turkey', *New Perspectives on Turkey*, Fall 2001, 25, 31–46.

[44] Female students preferences to go to *Imam Hatip* schools are for example linked with the opportunity they would have to be free to cover themselves. Rusen Çakir, Irfan Bozan, Balkan Talu, *Imam Hatip high schools: legends and realities*, Istanbul: TESV, June 2004.

over this request, the one claiming for individual freedom of religion, the other defending secularism as an ideal:

The secular state could not allow Islamic dictates to shape the dress code of its university students. Allowing for head covering would allow religion to encroach upon the secular and thus democratic public space of the republic and breach the rights of its secular constituency. One side claimed to experience oppression and the other envisioned a threat to secular democracy.[45]

The restriction of women's choice of dress was reactivated and more widely enforced after the military intervention in February 1997. Until that period, the universities had a case-by-case application of the Law 2547, also known as the Higher Education Act (which concerns veiled women teaching and studying and also touches upon men supporting the veiled women).[46]

As the 2003–4 comeback of a national passionate discussion on the Islamic headscarf in France illustrated, religion is rarely at the centre of the debate. In the French case, the headscarf also adopted other meanings. It spoke for gender equality, for the crisis of national identity, for the failure of integration policies and also for the necessary renewal of a clear definition of the meaning of *laïcité* in the French context.[47] A 2004 Human Rights Watch report stated that in the Turkish case,

many other issues have been intertwined with the religious freedom issue in discussions of headscarves, including: religious fundamentalism and political uses of religious symbols, including the headscarf; oppression of girls and women; a generational clash between girls and their parents; and pluralism versus national integration.[48]

---

[45] Arat, 2001, p. 32.

[46] The Higher Education Act states that: 'Modern dress or appearance shall be compulsory in the rooms and corridors of higher-education institutions, preparatory schools, laboratories, clinics and multidisciplinary clinics. A veil or headscarf covering the neck and hair may be worn out of religious conviction.' Law 2547 was passed in November 1981, when Turkey was still under martial law following the 1980 coup. It was later reinforced at many occasions. Different judgements of the Constitutional Court amended it. In April 1991 (published in July 1991), it for instance stated: 'In higher-education, it is contrary to the principle of secularism and equality for the neck and hair to be covered with a veil or headscarf on grounds of religious belief.' Human Rights Watch report on cases illustrating the political pressure on judges for them to rule against the plaintiffs (punitive transfers) (see HRW, 2004, p. 29).

[47] On the recent French controversies, see Nacira Guénif and Eric Macé, *Les féministes et la garçon arabe*, Paris: Aube, 2005.

[48] HRW, Memorandum to the Turkish Government on Human Rights Watch's Concerns with regard to academic freedom in higher education, and access to higher education for women who wear the headscarf, Human Rights Watch, *HRW Briefing Paper*, 29 June 2004, p. 24.

Should Muslim women expect a specific treatment from EU institutions that Turkish rulers have not allowed until now? The Sahin decision has certainly disappointed Turkish women waiting for the European legal resources to solve their conflict with the Turkish State.[49] The European Court of Human Rights rejected the request by Leyla Sahin which was based on the argument that the ban on wearing the Islamic headscarf in higher education institutions constitutes an unjustified interference with her right to freedom of religion. In its final decision, the Court holds that there has been no violation of Article 9 of the European Convention on Human Rights. Moreover, recalling the history of secularism in Turkey and its centrality in Turkish unity and nationalism, and placing the final decision in a larger European perspective, the Court states that in a democratic society the State is entitled to place restrictions on the wearing of the Islamic headscarf if it is incompatible with the pursued aim of protecting the rights and freedoms of others, public order and public safety. In a country like Turkey where the great majority of the population belong to a particular religion, measures taken in universities to prevent certain fundamentalist religious movements from exerting pressure on students who do not practise that religion or on those who belong to another religion may be justified under Article 9§2 of the Convention. In that context, secular universities may regulate manifestation of the rites and symbols of the said religion by imposing restrictions as to the place and manner of such manifestation with the aim of ensuring peaceful coexistence between students of various faiths and thus protecting public order and the belief of others.[50]

Indeed, as has usually been the case until now, when dealing with the Islamic veil the European Court of Human Rights stands for the moment on the side of the states rather that of the individual applicant (see for instance in Karaduman v. Turkey on 3 May 1993 or Dahlab v. Switzerland in 2001). Banning Muslim headscarves in state schools and more generally in public institutions does not violate the freedom of religion. This decision of banning headscarves is even considered to be appropriate when issued to protect the secular nature of the state. Thinking about the modalities of resolution of disputes and conflicts in conditions of extreme plurality, one has to admit that the Turkish State and the European Court's reading of the meaning of secularism and religious freedom converge, giving priority to the indivisibility and the unity of the nation. But the mobilisation of ECHR authority in the

---

[49] Case of Leyla Sahin v. Turkey, Judgement on 29 June 2004 (appl. No. 44774/98).
[50] Author's summary of the decision; the complete text of the decision can be found on the European Court of Human Rights Portal.

Sahin case also demonstrates the Europeanisation of the juridical arena when it comes to the protection of individual fundamental rights and freedoms. The cases brought to the ECHR on religious issues mostly stem from Turkish citizens living in Turkey. Turkish migrants settled in EU members states are for the moment absent from this scene. This does not mean however that Turks in Europe have been abandoning all forms of involvement in Turkish politics. They are even becoming increasingly involved in the process of reciprocal interaction between national identity and European integration.

Turks in Europe: facilitators, mediators, obstacles?

Turks living in Europe constitute a group characterised by great diversity (linguistic, ethnic, religious to quote but a few variables). They cannot any longer be reduced to the 'guest-worker' stereotypes or be considered as a temporary presence in the EU states where they reside. Their upward mobility has taken place in all the countries of settlement, and wherever they are allowed to, they have attained national citizenship there. For example, as expected, in Germany the number of applications for naturalisation has increased following the coming into force in January 2000 of the new law which relaxes restrictions on naturalisation.[51] In 2005, approximately 700,000 Turks living in Germany have a German passport. As stated in an innovative study in 2005, Turks living in Europe simultaneously provide strong support for, but also represent, an impediment to Turkey's EU membership (Kaya and Kentel, Euro Turks). If Turkey could enter the EU, it could only do so on the basis of a commitment to secular values. This position is very similar to that in the scholarly literature which looks at the settlement of Muslim minorities in Europe with a normative blueprint, stressing that

the inherently liberal and democratic public spheres of Western European societies provide grounds for drastic changes in Muslim thought and social practice and favour a version of Islam with a specific European normative base . . . This category ultimately de-legitimises any model of Islam that deviates from an enlightened European system of values, in harmony with 'secular constitutions'.[52]

---

[51] To sum up, the major change concerns the possibility for children with foreign parents who were born in Germany to acquire German citizenship. Another provision in this law now makes double citizenship possible for children born in Germany until they turn 23 years of age. They will then have to choose one citizenship.

[52] Shirin Amir-Moazami and Armando Salvatore, 'Gender, generation, and the reform of tradition: from Muslim majority society to Western Europe', in Stefano Allievi and Jorgen Nielsen (eds.), *Muslim networks and transnational communities in and across Europe*, Leiden: Brill, 2003, p. 52.

This reading of Islam in Europe should be connected with another, more inventive reading that 'emphasises the plural and changing character of Muslim forms of organisation and social life and identifies privatised components of Islam through its encounter with secularised Western societies'.[53] The debate going on throughout Europe on the necessity to find a unique partner representing Muslims in every single national state (what has been generally called the institutionalisation process) does in a way fit with the Turkish institutional system of having a single Sunni orthodoxy authority (the Directorate for Religious Affairs) in charge of defining and managing Islam, both in terms of worship and as a cultural dimension of national identity.

It is therefore crucial to consider both spaces and territories, Europe and Turkey, in parallel, as Turkish migration helped very much the intensification of the circulation of ideas, goods, values and somehow persons between territories. The interaction between the Turkish political scene and European migration spaces was particularly intense during the 1970s and 1980s. During that period, transnational activism helped repressed mobilisations (of political Islam but also Kurdish movements) to grasp the opportunity of being de-territorialised as a means to reinvest in the national territory of origin. The de-territorialisation process gave reality to the idea that you do not need to live in a specific territory to be an active citizen of it. Boundaries became more and more blurred between Turkey and EU member states where Turks have been settling since the first migration waves: living in Europe does not close the door to political participation and commitment to the Turkish domestic political scene. Paragons of this transnational activism have without doubt been organisations such as the PKK or the *Milli Görüş* networks.[54] European migration destinations operated as spaces for reorganisation of forbidden mobilisation, and the European Union served as a provider of resources, in particular juridical, but also financial. The transnational mobility of political support and commitment made obvious the end of the exclusive traditional territorial citizenship as the only avenue of participation. As a direct consequence of these transnational dynamics, some issues gained visibility and relevance in Turkey thanks to their inscription on the European agendas. Again, the resolution of the Kurdish–Turkish conflicts is a perfect illustration of that trend. The Europeanisation of the mobilisation and the commitment of

---

[53] Ibid.
[54] Valérie Amiraux, *Acteurs de l'islam entre Allemagne et Turquie*, Paris: l'Harmattan, 2001; Hamit Bozarslan, *La question kurde. Etats et minorités au Moyen-Orient*, Paris: Presses de Sciences-Po, 1997; Martin van Bruinessen, *Kurdish ethno-nationalism versus nation-building states. Collected articles*, Istanbul: Isis Press, 2000.

European citizens to the Kurdish cause incited the Turkish government to respond politically to the requests made from abroad. Another recent event in the migratory space may in the long term affect the public management of the Alevi population: in 2000, a local Alevi association located in Berlin applied for local recognition as a religious community. This initiative was taken three months after a local Islamic organisation (*Islamische Föderation Berlin*) was, for the first time, granted the status of religious community and therefore was entitled to provide children with Islamic instruction in Berlin public schools. By the end of 2004, four other regions (*Länder*) have given local Alevi associations the title of religious community, considering them as distinct from Sunni Muslims.[55]

Does Islam contribute to a distinct identity articulation as far as Turks living in Europe are concerned?[56] In terms of practice and institutional links, a majority of Turks living in Germany (nowadays called German Turks rather than *Gastarbeiter* for guest workers) are not affiliated with any ethnic or religious association (61%).[57] The current trend appears to be more toward commitment to political parties rather than to religious organisations, differing from what used to be the case for instance in the 1970s or 1980s.[58] While most Turks are not affiliated with a religious association, for those individuals who are committed in associative networks and activities, religious associations remain the most favoured ones among German Turks (45%).[59] 21% of German Turks and 11% of Turks living in France regard the EU as a Christian club.[60] The differences from one country of residence to the other become more evident when interviewees are asked to identify what is the greatest problem in Turkey. Referring to the 'pressure on religiosity in the name of laicism', 12% of German Turks placed this problem in third position while only 7% of French Turks placed it in fifth position.[61] Another interesting perspective is given by the request to draw a comparison

---

[55] Krisztina Kehl-Bodrogi, 'Alevis in Germany. On the way to public recognition?', *ISIM Newsletter*, no. 8, 2001, p. 9 (available at http://www.isim.nl/files/newsl_8.pdf); see also Massicard, *L'autre Turquie*, 2005, pp. 293–9.

[56] Talip Küçükcan, *Politics of ethnicity, identity and religion. Turkish Muslims in Britain*, Aldershot: Ashgate, 1999.

[57] Kaya and Kentel, *Euro Turks*, p. 38.

[58] Kaya and Kentel identify various generational types of discourse. They argue in the 1960s and 70s, the first generation was more inclined to produce a discourse focused on economic problems; in the 80s, all issues were political and related to the home context. In the 90s, the young generations felt more concerned by 'culture specific discourse' (Kaya and Kentel, *Euro Turks*. p. 57): dealing with intercultural dialogue, symbolic and cultural capital, diversity, tolerance and multiculturalism.

[59] Ibid: 40–1.

[60] Ibid: 50.

[61] Ibid: 34.

between the country they live in and Turkey concerning issues such as democracy and human rights, equal treatment for all, and moral social values. When it comes to respecting cultures and religions German Turks consider Germany (48.5%) better than Turkey (25.6%) while Turks living in France consider France and Turkey as equal (around 34%). German Turks seem in general to have stronger religious affiliations: 6% of Turks living in France say they are atheist compared to less than 1% of German Turks. Apparently then, the context in which immigrants have settled is an extremely important factor in their self-identification as secular or religious. On the basis of the figures presented above, one can distinguish between three groups among Turks living in Germany and France: the bridging persons (linking the contexts of country of origin and of destination), the breaching ones (religious extremists), and the assimilated ones. As usual in elaborating categories and ideal types, the borders should not be seen as hermetic and one should simply underline the existence of floating trajectories that exhibit a bit of each of the three profiles. When it comes to religious feelings and processes of identification, it seems that the context of living is slowly but efficiently organising the distance with the political culture of the country of origin. In the perspective of the adhesion of Turkey to the EU, this tendency could indicate the emergence of a de-institutionalisation of the tie binding individuals to their community of belief that could, as a pure theoretical hypothesis, encourage the de-politicisation of religion in Turkey.

Concluding remarks: a loose relation to institutional religion? Cross perspectives from Europe and Turkey

Based on the Annual Progress Reports, the European Commission decided in December 2004 that accession negotiations with Turkey would finally be opened. This prospect has given way to a great deal of emotion, fears and passion entering the political sphere.[62] It raises, explicitly now, what has thus far been almost exclusively dealt with as an implicit agenda of the European Union constitution: identity and culture. Indeed there have been very few occasions to discuss the cultural common patrimony of Europe. The agreement on values and fundamental rights apparently constitutes the universalistic agreement beyond which one should not discuss[63] – 'If we do agree on so many basic and

---

[62] The fears related to Turkey's EU membership are numerous and include religious but also demographic ones. Gabriel Martinez-Gros and Lucette Valensi, *L'islam en dissidence. Genèse d'un affrontement*, Paris: Seuil, 2004, p. 26.

[63] As expressed in the Preamble of the Treaty for a Constitution of Europe recently rejected by referendum in the Netherlands and in France: 'drawing inspiration from the

fundamental things, why should it not be enough?' 'Is it not sufficient to build trust in European institutions? Do we need more?' Actually, the only real discussion addressing the culture and identity question arose within the context of debates over the Preamble to the Constitutional Treaty of the EU. The heart of the tense debate laid in the strong opposition of some countries, in particular France, to the mention of 'religious values' as grounds for the European project.[64]

It would be artificial to seek to draw conclusions about contemporary Turkish citizens from the historic centrality of Islam in terms of political behaviour, exactly as it would be exaggerated to state that Europeans act as they do because of their Christian background. We cannot trace here any logical and causal link between religious belief and social acts.[65] Some trends can, however, be identified both in EU member states and in Turkey as far as the relation between individuals and their beliefs are concerned. Perhaps it would be adequate to speak about a 'common religious moment' of Europe at large, and the significant role of prosperity in providing more opportunity to pick and choose in defining one's personal identity.[66] Europe faces a double process of decreasing influence of institutional religions and individualisation of belief. Notwithstanding the circulation and exchange movements, religious cultures remain highly distinct and distant from one another. The number of Europeans declaring themselves to believe in God is decreasing. The imposition of meanings by strong institutions is losing significance. Moreover, there is 'a patrimonial tie to a memory that has been commonly shared for a long time, not committing anybody to a collective belief but still being the rationale – even with the distance of time – behind identity collective reflexes'.[67] Do Turks in Turkey follow similar paths to Europeans when it

---

cultural, religious and humanist inheritance of Europe, from which have developed the universal values of the inviolable and inalienable rights of the human person, freedom, democracy, equality and the rule of law'.

[64] 'The origins of the current problems in Turkey–EU relations are, to a certain extent, due to the inward-oriented nature of the EU.' Ziya Önis, 'Domestic politics, international norms and challenges to the state: Turkey–EU relations in the post-Helsinki era', in Ali Çarkoglu, Barry Rubin (eds.), *Turkey and the European Union. Domestic politics, economic integration and international dynamics*, London: Frank Cass 2003, p. 28.

[65] Roy, *La laïcité face à l'islam*.

[66] Danièle Hervieu-Léger, 'Les tendances du religieux en Europe', in Commissariat Général du Plan, Institut Universitaire Européen de Florence, Chaire Jean Monnet d'études européennes, *Croyances religieuses, morales et éthiques dans le processus de construction européenne*, Paris, May 2002, pp. 9–22. See also Yavuz, 'Is the a Turkish Islam'.

[67] 'Un rapport patrimonial à une mémoire partagée de loin, qui n'engage plus un croire commun, mais qui commande encore – comme à distance – des réflexes collectifs identitaires.' Hervieu-Léger, *Croyances religieuses*, Paris, May 2002, p. 12.

comes to religious believing and belonging? Europeans do go to places of worship less and less often, religious belonging is increasingly defined in individual terms, and the generational gap is growing when it comes to religion and religious education. In a study they conducted on religion, society and politics in Turkey in 2000,[68] Ali Carkoglu and Binnaz Toprak examined the role of Islam in public life and more specifically the degree to which the modernisation project of the republic has been internalised by Turkish society. The tension is articulated around the incentive to limit religious life exclusively to the private sphere and the political wish to keep control over Islamic institutions by bringing them under state control. Turkish people do not feel particularly religious but define themselves as believers (86%), even though they fulfil some obligations (46% pray five times a day, 84% regularly participate in Friday prayers). They do not support the idea that religion should play a role in public life, and most support the project of a secular republic in which the state should not interfere with religious life. The majority of the population studied identifies itself as Turkish (in terms of nationality) rather than as Muslims (in terms of religiosity). The study reveals that there is no secular versus Islamist dimension at the level of personal life, but it exists at the political level. Tolerance for religious difference remains abstract and is not supported at an individual level. Finally, a majority of women cover themselves; only 27.3% of the sample say they do not cover their heads. The general conclusion that can be drawn from this study does not reflect the common idea of a Turkish society being strongly divided between those who defend secularism as a religion, and those who support subversive political projects based on religious Islamic references. Moreover, Carkoglu and Toprak's study does not illustrate a polarisation leading to radical intolerance of one another's lifestyles. Rather, it provides us with the picture of a relatively religiously pacified society, rendering evident the discrepancy between what Turkey represents in the EU member state public opinions, and the process of secularisation that affects Turkish society, not only in terms of distance towards the institution representing worship, but also in terms of the end of the centrality of religion in a person's daily life. In that respect, examining Turkey in religious terms is not useful for understanding the specificity of Muslim societies, but rather serves as an illustration of a broader process of secularisation of democratic contexts, similar to that which occurs in European contexts as well.

---

[68] Ali Carkoglu and Binnaz Toprak, *Türkiye'de Din Toplum ve Siyaset*, Istanbul, Turkish Economic and Social Studies Foundation (TESEV), 2000. See the English summary of the report, p. 4 (available at http://www.tesev.org.tr/eng/project/TESEV_search.pdf).

Moreover, just as Muslims living in Europe are rarely considered independently from the international context, one should not ignore the significance that Turkey's EU membership would have for other Muslim societies. Indeed, as pointed out by Zürcher and van der Linden in their survey, it could constitute a hopeful sign that the EU does not support the 'clash of civilizations' perspective.[69] But Turkey's potential EU membership also entails a challenge to conceptions of the definition of Europe – beyond, that is, the question of religion: for instance, on what basis would other Mediterranean countries such as Morocco, Tunisia and Israel be excluded, if the geographical definition of Europe is flexible enough to include Turkey?[70] According to Bozarslan, the most frightening perspective about Turkey entering the EU regards the long term effect on the political definition of the EU. Rather than looking at religion as the reason behind the slow process of the EU's acceptance of Turkey, then, one should consider delays related to the way Turkish governments have conditioned the Brussels-mandated reforms in order to protect 'Turkishness'. Currently, Turkey seems indeed still to belong very much to an authoritative tradition of governance; and it faces the challenge to demonstrate its ability to fit in with the contemporary criteria of democracy, as defined by EU member states, before the enlargement's first wave.

It is difficult to argue that there is an incompatibility between Islam and democracy when it comes to Turkey, where free elections do regularly take place, and where a pluralist party system allowed an Islamist-oriented party to come to power. Nor can Turkey be criticised, as is usually the case for Muslim countries, for the absence of distinction between religion and politics, though they are connected through the control of the former by the latter. In the same way, it is difficult to think of the EU as a place where Islam is considered to be a danger as being a Muslim and practising for decades have seemed to be easier for most Muslim immigrants than it was in their home countries, even if since 11 September 2001 Islam has been more and more systematically defined as a security problem. It seems that the discussion on religion should in the first instance take into consideration the great variety of models of relations binding or separating churches and states, and politics and religion in the EU. For instance, the French principle of *laïcité* (strict separation of church and state) cannot be equated with the Turkish secular system (the

---

[69] Netherlands Scientific Council for Government Policy, 2004, p. 74.
[70] Hamit Bozarslan, 'De la Turquie, du sable et de l'empire', in Korine Amacher and Nicolas Levrat (ed.), *Jusqu'où ira l'Europe?*, Genève: Institut européen, 2005, pp. 109–18.

state controls religious education, regulates the opening of mosques, employs religious authorities as civil servants). Seen from Turkey, the prospect of the accession to the EU, its conditions and incentives, have certainly worked as factors driving stability in domestic politics, even helping the pacification of, or at least the possibility amongst opponents to negotiate over extremely controversial and bloody issues such as the Kurdish question.

The discussion on European identity has been conducted in parallel with the construction of EU political institutions, with the climax of the debate arising during the drafting of the Charter of Fundamental Rights in 2000. European identity as a Christian concept developed historically largely in relation to the Ottoman Muslim 'other'. However, the contemporary question of the religious identity of Europe is not exclusively borne out by the presence of Muslims. The EU did not need Turkey to enter into controversies and never-ending discussions over the legitimacy of inscribing the 'common religious values' as central part of the European patrimony.[71] Being European is first a cultural claim. It is articulated with shared values, shared history and memory that work as a basis for economic, political and security agreements and alliances.[72] When discussing the prospect of Turkey as a member of the EU, Islam intervenes indeed in cultural terms rather than in terms of religion or worship.[73] Theology and religious concepts are absent from most of the discussions, when not limited to provocative positioning of leading intellectuals (one thinks of Oriana Fallaci in the Italian context, or Michel Houellebecq in the French one) or politicians (Valéry Giscard d'Estaing to mention just one). Culture should be considered as 'fixed in relation to the structures of polity and world order within which they currently express

---

[71] At the end, Article I-52 of the Treaty establishing a Constitution for Europe, regarding the status of churches and non-confessional organisations, says the following:

1. The Union respects and does not prejudice the status under national law of churches and religious associations or communities in the Member states.
2. The Union equally respects the status under national law of philosophical and non-confessional organisations.
3. Recognising their identity and their specific contributions, the Union shall maintain an open, transparent and regular dialogue with these churches and organisations.

[72] William Wallace, 'Where does Europe end? Dilemmas on inclusion and exclusion', in Jan Zielonka (ed.), *Europe unbound. Enlarging and reshaping the boundaries of the European Union*, Aldershot: Ashgate, 2002, p. 78.

[73] This also corresponds to the positions Catholic authorities have on justifying the reference to religion in the EU construction process. The newly elected Pope, Josef Ratzinger in an interview he gave in August 2004 to a French weekly magazine (*Le Figaro Magazine*), declared Christian faith had something to tell Europe, 'not conceived as a geographical territory but as a cultural continent'.

themselves'.[74] The main gap over Turkey's prospective membership seems to exist between the experts and technicians of the process, who know from inside the recent evolution of Turkey as a liberal democracy, and the European citizens who still continue to consider the opening of the EU towards the Southeast region as a sign of cultural betrayal, and a future source of weakening of European democracy. In this gap, all sorts of imaginaries compete, from the representations of the Ottoman Empire to the stereotypes anchored in public opinions that associate Islam and Muslims with terrorism and barbarism. The establishment of a concrete religious pluralism enacted by the different EU member states seems more than ever to be the key to a de facto secularised political culture that would enable the coexistence of different beliefs and various profiles of believers.

Bibliography

Amir-Moazami, Shirin and Armando Salvatore, 'Gender, generation, and the reform of tradition: from Muslim majority society to Western Europe', in Stefano Allievi and Jorgen Nielsen (eds.), *Muslim networks and transnational communities in and across Europe*, Leiden: Brill, 2003, pp. 52–77.

Amiraux, Valérie, *Acteurs de l'islam entre Allemagne et Turquie*, Paris: l'Harmattan, 2001.

'Rights and claims for equality among Muslims in Europe', in NOCRIME Jocelyne Cesari and Sean McLoughlin (eds.), *European Muslims and the secular state in a comparative perspective*, 2005.

Arat, Yesim, 'Group-differentiated rights and the liberal democratic state: rethinking the headscarf controversy in Turkey', *New Perspectives on Turkey*, 25, Fall 2001, pp. 31–46.

Arikan, Harun, *Turkey and the EU. An awkward candidate for EU membership?*, Aldershot: Ashgate, 2003.

Bozarslan, Hamit, *La question kurde. Etats et minorités au Moyen-Orient*, Paris: Presses de Sciences-Po, 1997.

'De la Turquie, du sable et de l'empire', in Korine Amacher and Nicolas Levrat (eds.), *Jusqu'où ira l'Europe?*, Genève: Institut européen, 2005, pp. 109–18.

Bruinessen, Martin van, *Kurdish ethno-nationalism versus nation-building states. Collected articles*, Istanbul: Isis Press, 2000.

Çakir, Rusen, Bozan Irfan and Talu Balkan, *Imam hatip high schools: legends and realities*, Istanbul: TESEV, June 2004.

Canefe, Nergis, and Tanil Bora, 'Intellectual roots of anti-European sentiments in Turkish politics: the case of radical Turkish nationalism', in Ali Çarkoglu and

---

[74] Sami Zemni and Christopher Parker, 'Islam, the European Union, and the challenge of multiculturalism', in Shireen Hunter (ed.), *Islam, Europe's second religion. The new social, cultural, and political landscape*, Westport: Praeger, 2002, p. 236.

Barry Rubin (eds.), *Turkey and the European Union. Domestic politics, economic integration and international dynamics*, London: Frank Cass, 2003, pp. 127–48.

Carkoglu, Ali and Binnaz Toprak, *Türkiye'de Din Toplum ve Siyaset*, Istanbul: Turkish Economic and Social Studies Foundation (TESEV), 2000: (for an English language summary, see: http://www.tesev.org.tr/eng/project/ TESEV_search.pdf).

Cinar Menderes, '*The Justice and Development Party in Turkey*', available at http:// www.networkideas.org/themes/world/jan2003/print/prnt290103_Turkey.htm

Cizre, Sakallioğlu Ümit, 'Rethinking the connections between Turkey's "Western" identity versus Islam', *Critique*, no. 12, Spring 1998, pp. 3–18. Politics and military in Turkey into the 21st century, Florence, European University Institute, Working Paper (RSCAS), 2000.

Dorronsoro Gilles, Elise Massicard and Jean-François Pérouse, 'Turquie: changement de gouvernement ou changement de régime?', *Critique internationale*, no. 18, January 2003, pp. 8–15.

Duran, Burhannettin, 'Islamist redefinition(s) of European and Islamic identities in Turkey', in Ugur Mehmet and Nergis Canefe (eds.), *Turkey and European integration. Accession prospects and issues*, London: Routledge, 2004, pp. 125–46.

Fokas, Effie, 'The Islamist movement and Turkey–EU relations', in Ugur Mehmet and Nergis Canefe (eds.), *Turkey and European integration. Accession prospects and issues*, London: Routledge, 2004, pp. 147–69.

Guénif, Nacira, and Eric Macé, *Les féministes et le garçon arabe*, La Tour-d'Aigues: Aube, 2005.

Göle, Nilüfer, *The forbidden modern. Civilization and veiling*, Ann Arbor: Michigan University Press, 1996.
'Visible women: actresses in the public realm', *New Perspectives Quarterly*, Spring 2004, pp. 12–13.

Hervieu-Léger, Danièle, 'Les tendances du religieux en Europe', in Commissariat Général du Plan, Institut Universitaire Européen de Florence, Chaire Jean Monnet d'études européennes, *Croyances religieuses, morales et éthiques dans le processus de construction européenne*, Paris, May 2002, pp. 9–22.

HRW, *Memorandum to the Turkish government on Human Right's Watch's concerns with regard to academic freedom in higher education, and access to higher education for women who wear the headscarf*, Human Rights Watch, HRW Briefing Paper, June 29 2004 (available at http://www.hrw.org).

Kaya, Ayhan and Ferhat Kentel, *Euro Turks. A bridge or a breach between Turkey and the European Union? A comparative study of German-Turks and French-Turks*, Brussels, Centre for European Policy Studies (CEPS), 2005.

Kehl-Bodrogi, Krisztina, 'Alevis in Germany. On the way to public recognition?', *ISIM Newsletter*, no. 8, 2001, p. 9 (available at http://www. isim.nl/files/newsl_8.pdf).

Küçükcan, Talip, *Politics of ethnicity, identity and religion. Turkish Muslims in Britain*, Aldershot: Ashgate, 1999.

Martinez-Gros, Gabriel, and Lucette Valensi, *L'islam en dissidence. Genèse d'un affrontement*, Paris: Seuil, 2004.

Massicard, Elise, *L'autre Turquie*, Paris: PUF (Proche-Orient), 2005.

Netherlands Scientific Council for Government Policy (ed.), *The European Union, Turkey and Islam*, Amsterdam: Amsterdam University Press, 2004.

Önis, Ziya, 'Domestic politics, international norms and challenges to the state: Turkey–EU relations in the post-Helsinki era', in Ali Çarkoglu and Barry Rubin (eds.), *Turkey and the European Union. Domestic politics, economic integration and international dynamics*, London: Frank Cass, 2003, pp. 9–34.

Özdalga, Elisabeth, *The veiling issue: official secularism and popular Islam in modern Turkey*, Ankara: Curzon, 1998.

Özel, Soli, 'Turkey at the polls. After the tsunami', *Journal of Democracy*, vol. 14, no. 2, 2003, pp. 80–94.

Roy, Olivier, *La laïcité face à l'islam*, Paris: Stock, 2005.

Taniyici, Saban, 'Transformation of political Islam in Turkey: Islamist Welfare Party's pro-EU turn', *Party Politics*, 9, July 2003, pp. 463–83.

Tezcan, Levent, *Religiöse strategien der 'machbaren' Gesellschaft. verwaltete Religion und Islamistische utopie in der Türkei*, Bielefeld, Transcript, 2003.

Tocci, Nathalie, 'Europeanization in Turkey: trigger or anchor to Reform?', *South European Society and Politics*, vol. 10, no. 1, March 2005, pp. 71–81.

Toprak, Binnaz, 'A secular democracy: the Turkish model', in Shireen Hunter and Huma Malik (eds.), *Modernization, democracy, and Islam*, Westport: Praeger, 2005, pp. 276–92.

'Turkey in Europe: more than a promise?', Report by the Independent Commission on Turkey, available online at http://www.independentcommissiononturkey. org/report.html

Ugur, Mehmet, *The European Union and Turkey: an anchor/credibility dilemma*, Aldershot: Ashgate, 1999.

Wagner, Peter, 'The political form of Europe, Europe as a political form', *Thesis Eleven*, no. 80, February 2005, pp. 47–73.

Wallace, William, 'Where does Europe end? Dilemmas on inclusion and exclusion', in Jan Zielonka (ed.), *Europe unbound. Enlarging and reshaping the boundaries of the European Union*, Aldershot: Ashgate, 2002, pp. 78–94.

Yavuz, Hakan, *Islamic political identity in Turkey*, Oxford: Oxford University Press, 2003.

'Is there a Turkish Islam? The emergence of convergence and consensus', *Journal of Muslim Minority Affairs*, vol. 24, no. 2, 2004, pp. 213–32.

Zemni, Sami, and Christopher Parker, 'Islam, the European Union, and the challenge of multiculturalism', in Shireen Hunter (ed.), *Islam, Europe's second religion. The new social, cultural, and political landscape*, Westport: Praeger, 2002, pp. 231–44.

Zürcher, Erik-Jan, and Helen van der Linden, 'Searching for the fault line. A survey of the role of Turkish Islam in the accession of Turkey to the European Union in the light of the "clash of civilization"', in Netherlands Scientific Council for Government Policy, *The European Union, Turkey and Islam*, Amsterdam University Press, 2004.

10   Afterword

Aziz Al-Azmeh

One matter that emerges most clearly from the studies gathered in this book is the complexity of the issues discussed. It is manifest that any attempt to look at Muslims in Europe as a homogeneous mass is illusory, quite apart from being inadequate, both empirically and cognitively. Bosnian Muslims live under conditions and in ways which are both internally differentiated and complex. Algerians in Aulney-sur-Bois, Kashmiris in Bradford, Kurds in Oslo or Turks in Kreuzberg all live in similarly diverse conditions.

Yet we are being told repeatedly Muslims, European or otherwise, are above all Muslims, and that by this token alone they are distinctive and must be treated as such. In recent years, this oversimplified opinion has gained momentum, overcoming common sense, to the extent that some sections of the public regard all Muslims with various degrees of xenophobia, often with a mild, implicitly tribal sentiment of communal intimacy. This xenophobia is reflected in much of what is said about European heritage by politicians (not only conservative ones), sections of the press, and certain prelates. It is shared, and expressed in different tonalities, with deliberate alarmism, overtly malignant as well as see-mingly benign, as in the case of nativist political parties, certain sections of the press (most notably in Italy) or notorious publicists such as Oriana Fallacci.

Other sections of public opinion prefer a more measured scale of tonality, emphasising the need for an inclusive Europe conducive to social harmony. The shades of opinion here range between an attitude of res-ignation to a situation of religious multiplicity as seemingly incongruent as it is unavoidable, requiring sensitivity and deftness, to, at the other end of the scale, an attitude of impassioned xenophilia energised by a notion of multiculturalism boundlessly utopian in mood, extending to human heterogeneity within Europe, with the same kind of caring regard as that extended to trees, whales and other endangered species.

The curious fact is that the positions just outlined, antagonistic as they are in the daily realities of political, ideological and social life in

Europe, are joined at once by a perception of European realities that is in varying measures contra-factual, and by an underlying ideological assumption of culturalist differentialism. It is curious that the presumably Republicanist French President Jacques Chirac, for instance, declared that Turkey required a 'cultural revolution' to qualify properly for entry into the European Union, thus discounting a century and a half of almost continuous 'cultural revolution' in a country at least as resolutely secular as France. Turkey, on this particular score would seem eminently more qualified for entry into the European club than Poland, for instance, if one considered discourses on nationality along with rates of religious observance. Clearly, symbolic strangeness, in terms of language, religion and culture, takes precedence over the consideration of social and historical reality.

There is clearly in Europe today a view of European Muslims, and of Muslims in general, that takes them for a cliché irrespective of the realities of the lives of Muslims everywhere: the cliché of a homogeneous collectivity innocent of modernity, cantankerously or morosely obsessed with prayer, fasting, veiling, medieval social and penal arrangements, unreconstructed and unreconstructable, whose presence in Europe is in certain determinate ways accidental, or indeed extra-territorial. This is a view that has gathered force considerably as European economies and societies have become globalised, with the attendant socio-economic differentiations and stresses, most often associated with ethnic differentiation. This cliché gathered force as the European imagine bereft of an idea or of an ideological centre, except by default and in response to the Islamist example, spawned nativist right-wing movements. These transposed, sublimated and sanitised what, until the end of the Second World War, was a notion of race and of racial purity and exclusivity, into a notion of culture, now that the previous internal enemy – the Jew – could no longer legitimately be conceived as such. In very significant ways, it seems that post-1989 Europe, and more especially the European Union after its expansion in 2004, is reconnecting with its pre-1939 history, rejecting the deliberate civilising policies, Keynesian and otherwise, to which it had been subjected after the Second World War.

Yet what is in fact known – a knowledge increasingly less apparent and less disseminated, but clearly brought out in the chapters in this book – is that only a minority of Muslims in Europe and beyond hold to the morose or enthusiastic obsessions attributed to them, and that attachment to such obsessions, where evident, is of recent vintage. This attachment derives simultaneously from the internalisation of European attitudes with the almost deliberate manufacture of otherness, determinedly cultivated by Muslim organisations and by state-sponsored multiculturalist vested interests, as stigmata of differentiation, in what amounts to an almost deliberate manufacture of enclaves of alienation. This is enforced by structural marginalisation, and by the unravelling of European state control over processes of social engineering and the deregulation of both economy and of culture. This is happening at a time when European integration is devolving to integration at the level of the supranational and supraterritorial market, and also devolving social policies to the level of local and ethnic (and by extension religious) mobilisation, often termed 'empowerment'.

These trends towards social involution derive from the rise of Islamist political forces in the countries of origin of European Muslims, which are themselves a function of the recession of modernist social, cultural and national aspirations under conditions of global neo-liberalism and conditions of national disempowerment attendant upon neo-imperial pressure – the Arab World is the most pertinent case in point. One result of this development, born in the 1970s and gathering force ever since, is the emergence of areas of spatial, social and cultural marginality at a time of extremely intense internal socio-economic differentiation and of immigration from the countryside, producing not so much urbanism, except in a purely spatial sense, but rather the ruralisation of many urban communities. This is a situation, not unlike that of immigration to European cities, conducive to various forms of social involution, the invention, regeneration and reaffirmation of archaic social forms, but also and correlatively to socio-economic disaggregation and to various manifestations of anomie, which is fertile ground for the formation of subcultures and of sects. In view of the anomie and systemic alienation which accompany structural marginalisation, it is unsurprising that some young European Muslims move between drugs and God, as was the case with some of the bombers in Madrid and London, and was also the case with bombers Algeria and elsewhere.

Seemingly inhospitable countries of origin, and a similar form of inhospitality in Europe, join together these subcultural and sectarian milieus in a transnational world of hyper-reality, common to Europe and the Arab World, which reproduces itself through a variety of agencies, not least the international Islamic and Islamist charitable, educational and devotional infrastructures (assiduously constructed in the 1970s, 1980s and 1990s, and brought into full play by the momentous Rushdie affair). These are mediated through family and other social byways, frequently dense rural communities which become reconstructed in Europe, such as the Mirpuri Pakistanis in the United Kingdom who might feel equally alien in any city, be it Karachi or Bradford. This sense of alienation is reinforced by European policies, especially in Protestant countries with denominationalist conceptions of diversity, which favour 'separate development', and marry notions of particularity with mechanisms of socio-economic exclusion conducive to the formation of an underclass distinctive in appearance.

Thus emerges a spectacle of impressive theatricality, with exhibitionistic and sometimes self-parodic manifestations of Muslim religiosity. This image is much sought after by the media and by sections of 'civil society', but the image of Muslims held by society at large and propagated by the media sometimes degenerates into something much more sinister, associated with acts of nihilistic terror such as the 2005 bombings in London and Madrid, and similar acts of terrorism, on a smaller scale, such as the bombings in Holland and elsewhere. In the public eye, these are conjugated with incidences of 'honour murders' in Sweden, Germany and other countries – incidents which are linked to quite distinct social conditions: the attempted reinforcement of rural (especially Kurdish) systems of patriarchal social control under conditions of social deracination. Although similar acts of terror have also been perpetrated, in structurally similar settings, in Algeria, Egypt, Syria, Morocco and Saudi Arabia, this is not normally mentioned in connection with events that occur in Europe.

The most grievous error of judgement in my view, and the most blatant form of misconception of non-Muslim Europeans at large, is to regard these subcultural and sectarian acts as if they were central to what a Muslim in Europe is, or must inevitably become. Even from a more benign perspective, these acts appear extreme, although not unrepresentative and not inauthentic manifestations of Islamism. This takes us back to the issues of counter-factuality and differentialism. Along with much accumulated scholarship on Islam in Europe, the chapters in this book warn, almost but not quite uniformly, against exaggerating the role of religion in the lives of Muslims, against culturalism, against taking culture as a kind of genetic code governing the lives of Muslims, reducing culture to religion, and reducing religion to a Book. They also warn against the essentialisation of both dominant and minority cultures in Europe, where everyone assumes that all Muslims are the same, born with the same set of innate characteristics. The chapters in this book show, among other things, how Turks in Europe are more likely to join political than religious associations, that the attitudes of Turks to religious belief are more sceptical in France than in Germany, that there is no logical or social link between religious belief and social acts, a fact that applies to Europeans overall without reference to the religions into which they were born. In short, and bearing in mind their diversity in terms of their countries of origin, education and a variety of other variables, European Muslims might be Muslims in terms of birth; but referring to them simply as 'Muslims' is meaningless, and must be seen as irrelevant to their status as citizens. Not all European 'Muslims' make exorbitant demands for a particularity, or for legal extraterritoriality, which is increasingly construed along Wahhabist lines.

However, there is a general feeling among non-Muslim Europeans that all Muslims are generically 'different' from them: a perception underlined by the sometimes exorbitant special pleading to which Muslim organisations are given. Because Muslims are perceived to be generically different, as a community they often get the blame for social disturbances and unrest. Take, for instance, the serious social disorders in France between the end of October and early November 2005. These repeated on a larger scale similar disorders in Bradford and elsewhere in Britain, and involved a very definite rebellious explosion of the socially marginalised as a result of previous socio-economic policies, which must be understood as socio-economic rather than religious or 'cultural'. Despite the fact that the perpetrators of these riots in France were decidedly multicultural and multiethnic, the French Minister of the Interior, the ethnically Hungarian Nicolas Sarkozy, immediately and almost with a Pavlovian predictability met with mosque leaders rather than consulting a broader constituency. It was as if in this particular instance the much feared and very exotic phenomenon of Islamism should now be used as a means of social control. Yet these so-called 'Muslim riots', acts of large-scale nihilistic vandalism, took place to the rhythms of rap and heavy metal, not of Koranic cantillation, and the evidence indicates the absence of any 'Muslim' component such as the second and third generation Frenchmen of sub-Saharan African and North African origin who are still today referred to as 'immigrants'.

Similarly, consider the controversy over the Danish cartoons of *Jyllands-Posten*. Some of these were simply tasteless and witless, others, demonising and reminiscent of the long tradition of satirising Jews, were the result of a specific confluence: between the xenophobic mood in Denmark deliberately cultivated by nativist and populist political forces to whom parts of the ruling party (including the Prime Minister) pander in the context of electoral and inner-party calculations, and local imams, some clearly duplicitous and mendacious, seeking to enhance their own authority by claiming to speak for the majority of Danish 'Muslims' (not an especially devout lot) and indeed for Muslims everywhere. The latter were aided and abetted by Muslim clerics elsewhere, and the situation was politically exploited by a number of countries in the Middle East and beyond. The overall assumption is that 'Muslims' are a hypersensitive lot, and that on this score alone, their 'culture', inimical to freedom of expression, stops them from being fully integrated into mainstream Europe and does not take account of their special pleading beyond the general requirements of European citizenship. Overall, the politics of the affair are ejected from the realm of discussion, and both Europeans and those who presume to 'represent' Muslims seem determined to straightjacket 'Muslims' by lumping together a militant or self-interested minority with the vast majority of European Muslims, whose rates of religious observance (Britain excepted due to the influence of conditions prevailing in Pakistan), and very likely of religious sentiment, are generally in keeping with the national levels of the countries in which they live. This small minority of 'Muslims', have invented traditions of dress and social conventions, exhumed from ancient books only scantily comprehended, which were largely unknown in their countries of origin and long-forgotten. Many Europeans insist, counter-factually, that all Muslims are Muslims in the sense carried by the stereotypes of strangeness deliberately fostered by this small minority. The Rushdie affair promoted this stereotype of the Muslim in the public eye; the Danish cartoon affair acted as, and was perceived as, a confirmation. In the public eye, this corresponded to a move from a largely indifferent incomprehension, with a passage through nihilistic terrorism, to a decidedly perturbed, hostile, and increasingly granitic misapprehension.

These are just two cases which highlight the way in which Europeans of Muslim origin are not only misconceived as somehow identifiably, homogeneously and as a consequence controllably or uncontrollably Muslim (a misconception in which some 'Muslim leaders' in Europe are fully and quite often cravenly complicit, as are some European multiculturalists). It is almost as if virtually any European of Muslim origin is being compelled to regard himself or herself as such, to react and speak as such, and ultimately to dress and arrange his or her personal appearance and behaviour in bizarre ways, frequently *contre-coeur*. This is so not least because many Europeans of Muslim origin feel constrained to make a virtue out of such differentialism, and to celebrate appearing in the eyes of the 'host society' at large as congenitally incapable of advancement in the direction of becoming Europeans. Europe, meanwhile, is here understood not so much as reality, but as a territory or a cartographic notion, defined with some imprecision, but in principle marked by an historical development (which the European Muslims' countries of origin shared, unevenly but decidedly) tending towards the privatisation of religion in terms of common citizenship blind to origins, private orientations and eccentricities. Instead of receiving a discourse of citizenship, Muslims have to prime themselves for a dialogue of 'civilisations' *à la* Blair and Zapatero. This dialogue concentrates on the mystification and sublimation of 'civilisation', to the neglect of more urgent socio-economic and cultural affairs. Because of this neglect, economic affairs move to the hidden hand of the market, and the serious matter of European strategic relations with areas of Muslim majority across the Mediterranean is left to the United States.

The outcome of this dialogue is of course the gentrification of stigma, and the rewards, social and otherwise, are in certain countries tangible, if confined. The rice pays Europe to have is quite clearly to long manage social disaggregation under the banner of 'culture'. This will result from deregulation in a manner that is far more incendiary than if they were regarded as social disaggregations, inequities and inequalities pure and simple, because they are conjugated with race and social geography, and sublimated as religion, culture, and even civilisation (it is often forgotten that Muslim civilisation no longer exists, and is but a bookish memory, like the Roman or the Greek). Clearly, Europe must look forward to turbulent times. But for these to become in some way banalised after the manner in which history causes matters to be banalised, for the idea of Europe to be transposed from the mode of Romance, the romance of heritage and particularity, to conform to the humble prosaic nature of her real present, these disaggregations and their management must be conducted without special pleading for Muslims, *pro* or *contra*, both equally romances, the one mirroring the other. Europe needs to awaken to her own uneven historical itinerary of secularism, to the generation of citizenship and to a social politics beyond 'communicative action', towards an exploration of the differences in culture and customs between all its Muslim and non-Muslim citizens. Tolerance and mutual exploration could lead, as it already has in many parts of Europe and elsewhere, to delightful new culinary experiences, and the sharing of many other cultural treasures, giving new pleasures to the senses and fresh inspiration to the collective intellect. Yet many Europeans seem less than convinced of this: while France quite rightly banned the wearing of distinctive religious symbols in schools in terms of a policy of integration in terms of citizenship, some German states still believe in the primacy of *Leitkultur* over the culture of citizenship, and ban veils but not crosses and kippas (though how the latter might be considered to be part of German *Leitkultur* is a matter that entirely escapes me). In Baden-Württemberg, Holland, and increasingly so elsewhere, Muslim applicants for citizenship are required to sit special tests, answering questions which are both discriminatory and clichéd. The Baden-Württemberg tests include questions on topics such as homosexuality and Israeli politics which could not be answered correctly by many members of the autochthonous population, including many staunch Christians and politicians.

Religious differences in the context of citizenship should become a matter for individual conscience and devotional practice, not a primitivist marker of communities. European politics needs to rise above religion, to ensure that all communities in Europe are served according to the specific social and economic needs of each community, whatever that community's religious label. Religion should not be used as a political tool to enable one narrow group of people to create an idealised society by subjecting them to laws which others in society at large are not subject to. As for 'Euro-Islam', it is a particularly inept notion, to which I must aver I was party a decade ago: it implies a certain pan-European ultramontanism without a discernible and distinct form – which is opposed to the hyper-real centre of European and international Islamism. That the Muslim cult, and the religious representations that European Muslims will have to develop *nolens volens*, will come to conform to European and by extension universal cognitive, social and political norms is a matter for individual European states of which persons of Muslim origin, including those who regard themselves as Muslims, are citizens. These norms, it should be noted, resulted from an historical itinerary which Christianity had already had to reckon with, and to which, after much resistance, it felt constrained to adapt.

That Islam, at the end of the nineteenth century, adapted similarly to modernity, that Muslim analogues exist of Italian bishops, of Archbishop Christodoulos, or the American Pat Robertson (who still think it possible to roll back history that intervened since the eighteenth century), is true, but inconsequential. Religions change with history, and evolve, developing sometimes in tandem with and at other times and for certain textual communities out of synchrony with overall social and historical development, all the while preserving a hard core of irrationalism without which they cannot remain religions. This applies to Islam as it applies to other religions, notwithstanding mystifications about exceptionalism perpetrated alike by many Europeans and by those European and non-European Muslims with a stake in presumptions of Muslim exceptionalism, providentialist or sociologistic. That the desired development might be too late in coming, that it is indeed too late for it, bears some consideration, given the incendiary mix of religion taken for culture, ethnicity and social exclusion.

Index